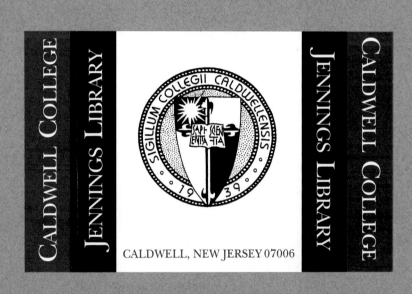

GI JEWS

GI JEWS

✪ ✪ ✪ ✪ ✪ ✪ ✪ ✪

HOW WORLD WAR II
CHANGED A GENERATION

DEBORAH DASH MOORE

The Belknap Press of
Harvard University Press
Cambridge, Massachusetts
London, England

2004

Excerpt from "Reflection by a Mailbox" by Stanley Kunitz is reprinted from *The Collected Poems* by Stanley Kunitz, copyright © 2000 by Stanley Kunitz, used by permission of W. W. Norton & Company, Inc. Excerpt from "To Jewishness" by Kenneth Koch is reprinted from Kenneth Koch, *New Addresses* (Alfred A. Knopf, 2000), by permission of the Kenneth Koch Literary Estate. Excerpt from "Sunday: New Guinea" by Karl Shapiro is reprinted from *V-Letter and Other Poems* by Karl Shapiro (New York: Reynal & Hitchcock, 1944), p. 13, by permission of The Estate of Karl Shapiro. Excerpt from "IFF [Identification Friend or Foe]" by Howard Nemerov is reprinted from Howard Nemerov, *War Stories: Poems about Long Ago and Now* (University of Chicago Press, 1987), reprinted by permission. Excerpt from "The Room" by Anthony Hecht is reprinted from *Collected Earlier Poems* by Anthony Hecht, copyright © 1990 by Anthony E. Hecht, used by permission of Alfred A. Knopf, a division of Random House, Inc., and by permission of the author. Excerpt from "A Song for the Year's End" by Louis Zukovsky is reprinted from *Complete Short Poetry* by Louis Zukovsky, p. 111, copyright © 1991, reprinted with permission of the Johns Hopkins University Press.

Library of Congress Cataloging-in-Publication Data

Moore, Deborah Dash, 1946–
GI Jews : how World War II changed a generation / Deborah Dash Moore
p.   cm.
Includes bibliographical references (p.) and index.
ISBN 0-674-01509-6 (alk. paper)
1. Jews—United States—History—20th century.
2. World War, 1939–1945—Participation, Jewish.
3. Jewish soldiers—United States.
4. World War, 1939–1945—Influence
5. United States—Ethnic relations. I. Title
E184.J5M6639 2004
940.54'1273'08924—dc22   2004047353

For Arthur Aryeh Goren

American Jewish GI,
friend, and teacher

CONTENTS

✪ ✪ ✪

PREFACE
✪ ✪ ✪

Events press upon historians. Amid public celebrations of the fiftieth anniversary of the end of World War II, I began to reflect upon the impact of the war on American Jews who had served in the armed forces. Jewish veterans had been content to let the shadows cast by the Holocaust and the hopeful rays of Israel's birth occupy the center of the Jewish historical stage. Their wartime story did not seem to warrant any more particular attention than that of any other veteran who was integrated into the military. But I suspected that their military service had not only transformed their sense of Jewish identity but also significantly altered the terms of American Jewish life in general. My post–World War II world bore the impression of their years in uniform and its aftermath.

My father, Martin Dash, is a veteran, as are all of his boyhood friends, members of a Brooklyn social and athletic club called the Dragons. I had grown up hearing snippets of wartime tales that often were humorous or self-deprecating. Now I wondered about what it had meant to enter military service as a Jew. Even when one wore the same uniform as one's fellow Americans I assumed that being a Jew mattered, as it mattered in all other aspects of pre–World War II life. Few scholars had looked at Jews in the armed forces. Most historians writing on American Jews during World War II had focused on the home front and examined the pressing question of what American Jews did to rescue European Jews. Yet without the history of the front lines, a critical piece of the American Jewish past was missing. I decided to interview Jewish veterans, read their letters and diaries, and seek their interpretations of their experiences as recorded in their memoirs. The circle widened from my father and the Dragons to include many friends' fathers.

This book follows the journeys of fifteen men into military service until their return to civilian life at the end of the war. I am indebted to all who shared their stories with me, even as I recognize how my interpretation of their accounts, derived from my historical knowledge, differs from their perspective. I chose such an approach because I wanted to evoke both drama and coherence and to suggest meaning for an experience that transformed a generation. Finally, I sought to write the individual into history. The ordinary ordeals of these fifteen men reflect important strands of experience among the more than half a million other Jews who entered the United States armed forces.

The military can be seen as abstract, a huge impersonal institution, or it can be appreciated as a very personal encounter. Under its imposed uniformity lay difference and ambivalence. I discovered that the men's Jewishness often resided there. And I learned that the war intensified the interdependence of the men's American and Jewish identities. Paradoxically, donning an American uniform made Jews both more American and more Jewish. Wartime service changed their attitudes toward themselves as Americans, as Jews, and as men.

My history hews closely to the men's narration of how war was experienced by them. Their story was haunted by antisemitism but not determined by it. Military service inducted these young Jews into an America where differences of religion and ethnicity were more rigid than they are today. Those who were accustomed to a home environment that sustained rich and public Jewish ways of life faced the necessity of internalizing their Jewishness in the service. Yet these individual accommodations occurred at the same time as the military itself was adjusting to the diversity of its recruits by adopting procedures that actually facilitated public Jewish expression. Both experiences helped to alter American Jewish identity.

When Jewish veterans returned home, they realized that important things had changed in their lives, even if the din of events sometimes obscured the meaning of those changes. Collectively they had become agents of a shift in the legitimization of American Jewish identity, one that would deepen the sense that Jews were at home in America. Belief in American exceptionalism was apparently being rewarded; things were different over here. Military policy had made possible the emergence of a civil religion for American democracy, soon to be widely known as the "Judeo-Christian tradition" and alternatively by the threefold handle of "Protestant-Catholic-Jew." Today educated Americans assume that the Judeo-Christian tradition is, in fact, a real tradition, that it has existed for centuries. But it was largely a creation of the American military in World War II, and it gave Jews a measure of freedom to be just that, American Jews.

Returning veterans might well have imagined that, having known the worst, they could get on with their lives in a more normal world. The war against the Axis was over. Though they could not have foreseen the world that emerged after World War II, Jewish veterans could feel that in doing their part for America they had knocked down (if not out) stereotypes about Jewish men as conniving, unpatriotic cowards. They had absorbed all that the military experience had dealt them. But a confluence of postwar events would obscure the impact of their experiences, the importance of their stories. I recount their history here to clarify how their everyday resolve in a time of crisis helped to recast the foundations of American Jewish life.

THE MEN
✪ ✪ ✪

MARTIN DASH, raised in Brooklyn, Yale graduate, member of the Dragons, married to Irene, served as an officer in the Naval Reserves on the destroyer *USS McCormick* in the Atlantic.

HAROLD FREEMAN, raised in Brooklyn, three years of college, antifascist, married to Bea, served as a rifleman in the 83rd Infantry Division in the European Theater.

VICTOR GELLER, born in the Bronx, Yeshiva-educated, second-generation Orthodox Jew of Hungarian parents, entered the military as a teenager, served as a rifleman in the 346th Infantry Regiment in the European Theater.

ARTHUR GORENSTEIN, educated in Washington, D.C., high school graduate, socialist Zionist, served in the Army Air Corps, training as a Combat Engineer when the war ended.

JEREMIAH GUTMAN, born in Brooklyn, CCNY graduate, served as a rifleman in the 69th Infantry Division in the European Theater.

RALPH JACKSON, born in Brooklyn, two years of college, member of the Dragons, married to Rita, served as a navigator/bombardier in the 67th Bomb Squadron of the 8th Air Force based in England.

SY KAHN, born in Manhattan, high school graduate, served in the 495th Port Battalion of the Army Transportation Corps in New Guinea.

IRA KOPLOW, born and raised in Sioux Falls, South Dakota, second-generation Jew of Lithuanian parents, two years of college, served in the Battalion Supply Office of the 10th Armored Division in the European Theater.

JEROME MINKOW, born in the Bronx, high school graduate, arrived in Manila as a replacement infantryman as peace was signed with the Japanese.

MERV REINES, raised in Patterson, New Jersey, and the Bronx, attended Penn State, married to Cheryl, served as a supply officer in the Marines in the Pacific Theater.

HOWARD SACHS, born in Brooklyn, educated in Hebraist elementary school, NYU graduate, served as a medic in the 71st Infantry Division in the European Theater.

HAROLD SAPERSTEIN, born and raised in Troy, New York, Cornell graduate, Reform rabbi of a congregation in Lynbrook, Long Island, pacifist and Zionist, married to Marcia with a son, served as a chaplain in the European Theater (Italy, France, Germany).

AKIVA SKIDELL, born and educated in Grodno, Poland, college education in Toronto, emigrated to New York City, socialist Zionist activist, married to Ettie with a daughter, served as a radio operator in reconnaissance company in the 2nd Armored Division in the European Theater.

PAUL STEINFELD, born and educated in the Bronx, graduate of CCNY and Teacher's Institute of Jewish Theological Seminary, Zionist, married to Lillian, served as a rifleman in the 95th Infantry Division in the European Theater.

HERBERT WALTERS, born in Brooklyn, college graduate, a lawyer, served in the 211th Anti-Aircraft Battalion in the Pacific Theater.

GI JEWS

1

WAR AND IDENTITY

For [Jews], solidarity is a created and always liquid condition, reversible as the tide, not a solid-state to be taken for granted.

—MAX KOZLOFF[1]

SEPTEMBER 1, 1939. Harold Saperstein boarded the *Queen Mary* to sail home to Long Island after three months in Europe and Palestine. As excited as he had been to leave in June, he was even more eager to come back to the United States. Saperstein had taken a busman's holiday. The rabbi of a Reform congregation in Lynbrook, he had used his vacation to visit Jewish communities in Poland, Rumania, Egypt, and Palestine and to attend the Twenty-first World Zionist Congress in Geneva on August 16–26. Now he was returning as Europe plunged into fresh conflict. Before dawn that morning, the tanks of the Third Reich had crossed the border into Poland. Writing home from Danzig in July, Saperstein had prophesied that war was inevitable. As soon as he had disembarked from the train there, he had seen Nazi Storm Troopers, the SS, everywhere. The ruins of the magnificent synagogue that the Nazis had recently dismantled profoundly disturbed him.[2] In truth, it didn't take a prophet to predict war. Everyone on the continent knew it was coming.[3] The Hitler-Stalin nonaggression pact of August 23 guaranteed that Germany could invade Poland unopposed by the Soviet Union.[4]

1

As Saperstein stood on the ship's darkened deck, he contemplated an Atlantic newly treacherous. His grim mood reflected the spirit of the voyage. He was less fearful of present danger — the Germans had already torpedoed an ocean liner carrying 1400 passengers — than worried about the future.[5] Only twenty years after the peace treaties of Versailles had ended the Great War, the world was on the brink of another. Saperstein knew that war spelled disaster for Jews. "War means the annihilation of our values and of our existence," he had proclaimed from the pulpit. Now he pondered his pacifist commitment. Reluctantly he admitted, first to himself and then to his congregation, that war in this instance was the "lesser of two evils." It was better for Britain and France to declare war on Germany than to yield "to the triumphal march of Nazi barbarism."[6] But America, he thought, owed it to itself to stay out of the conflict. Yet Saperstein anticipated that war, even one on a distant continent, would spiritually challenge Americans.[7] Although American antisemitism did not come close to rivaling European state-supported varieties, prejudice, hatred, and discrimination found many champions in the United States, and war promised to exacerbate ethnic, religious, and racial conflict.[8]

Saperstein's immersion in Jewish life made him aware that few American Jews shared his outlook. Once he walked down the gangplank onto a Manhattan west-side pier, he entered a world far removed from the violence of Europe and the Middle East. Unlike their European cousins, American Jews enjoyed the luxury of security and could ignore politics if they were so inclined. Sports contests, movies, and popular music competed for their attention. The weekend of September 1 when the Germans invaded Poland, the Giants were facing the Dodgers at the Polo Grounds in a doubleheader while the Yanks were returning to the city with a thirteen-and-a-half-game lead after finishing a successful road trip. *The Wizard of Oz* had recently opened in movie theaters, and Judy Garland was appearing in person on stage at the Capitol Theater for the third week. Other movies, including Gary Cooper in *Beau Geste* and Cary Grant and Carole Lombard in *In Name Only,* competed with Broadway plays such as Robert Sherwood's *Abe Lincoln in Illinois* and the popular trade union musical *Pins and Needles.*[9] Novel events also beckoned. In the spring of 1939 the New York World's Fair had opened for a five-month season to great fanfare. With its Trylon and Perisphere and the exhibits of the latest technologies, the fair promised millions a peek at a peaceful "world of tomorrow." Visitors marveled at the latest "futurama" and savored its American optimism.[10]

Every day that same summer Martin Dash, a teenage Jewish college student, left his parents' house in Flatbush, Brooklyn, and headed to the World's Fair at Flushing Meadow Park. He came not to visit and enjoy the exhibits but to work at his sister's concession. Wearing a ruffled jacket evocative of Spanish dancers, Dash would stand for hours in the shadow of a diminutive El Morro Castle, shaking the maracas in rhythm and trying to entice customers to buy a souvenir from the Cuban Village. Dash needed the money for college. The Depression had eaten away his family's savings, and he was uncertain whether he could afford to continue his junior year at Yale University. Although he read the newspapers and listened to the radio, European affairs did not preoccupy him. Neither of his parents was born abroad; there were no relatives from Europe writing with dire news or seeking to emigrate; and Dash did not consider himself political. When he got together with his neighborhood buddies that summer, a group of friends called "the Dragons," they preferred to talk about sports and movies, parties and girls. Some were going to college; others had found jobs, usually working with their fathers. At the start of the long Labor Day weekend, war was not foremost in their minds.[11]

Growing up in Brooklyn, Dash and the Dragons had matured in a milieu where Jewishness belonged not only to the home and synagogue but also to the streets and playgrounds of his neighborhood. Here ordinary urban behaviors assumed Jewish inflections, even as speech absorbed the city's multiethnic influences. Dash relished Jewish foods and identified them with family. Even if his mother didn't keep a strictly kosher home, she nurtured distinctive tastes.[12] He loved delicatessen food — spicy salamis and pastramis, hot dogs with mustard and sauerkraut, garlic dill pickles — as well as dairy foods, lox and cream cheese on a bagel, pickled herring in sour cream, and gefilte fish with fiery horseradish.[13] Along with familiar food and close family came religious education and language. Dash studied prayerbook Hebrew in the afternoons after the regular public school day ended. His supplementary Jewish education culminated in bar mitzvah at age thirteen. Although rote learning of Hebrew prayers hardly inspired him to continue studying, and his father's antagonism to organized religion sanctioned an attitude of benign neglect, bar mitzvah education set Dash and his buddies apart from their Christian schoolmates. It taught them that Jews were different, a minority in America, even if they were a majority in their neighborhood or public school. Distinctiveness depended as much upon the mundane, close-knit Jewish world of work and leisure, school and friends, as it did upon family, politics, and religion. Jewishness was a way of being and thinking, part of one's public as well as private self, recognized by both Jews and their gentile neighbors.[14]

Jewish parents and teachers encouraged their children to be wary around gentiles. Christians, they explained, held unsavory opinions of Jews and falsely accused them of killing Jesus

United States Army bomber in flight over New York City, ca. 1938. Despite occasional flights by bombers over New York City, the war in Europe seemed both distant and troubling to American Jews, who watched and worried from afar.

Christ.[15] However, Dash believed that America promised opportunities for Jews if they looked in the right places. He knew that
antisemitism might restrict Jews from living in certain neighborhoods, obtaining jobs in large industries, entering prestigious
professions, or studying in elite universities. But excellence, as
his parents assured him, opened doors. Editor-in-chief of his
public high school paper, Dash succeeded in winning admission
to Yale despite its quotas restricting Jewish enrollment.[16] Like
other Jewish parents, his folks taught him and his sister how to
succeed in areas circumscribed by their Jewishness, encouraging their children to enlarge these circumferences by hard work
and achievement.

If the possibility of war in Europe did not particularly preoccupy Dash and the Dragons, politically engaged Jews could
think of little else. Twenty-four-year-old Akiva Skidell had arrived in New York City only two years earlier. He had come
from Toronto to lead a Labor Zionist youth movement, Habonim (the builders), and immediately fell in love with Ettie
Mussin at the Habonim camp at Accord, New York, in the Catskills. Sharing the same aspirations, they married in January
1938, eager to dedicate their lives to each other and to Labor
Zionism. Skidell dreamed of recruiting American Jewish teenagers like the Dragons to his Zionist vision of a socialist Jewish
state in Palestine. He and Ettie planned to participate personally in building it. News of the German invasion of Poland physically threatened his own family. When Skidell had departed
from Grodno, Poland, for Toronto as a teenager, he left behind
many family members, including his widowed father.[17]

Skidell's socialist Zionism heightened his awareness of fascism. In Toronto he had taken part in rallies against Hitler and
his fascist followers who burned books and expelled Jews from
universities. But he hoped that Nazism could be contained and

eventually overthrown through boycotts, sanctions, and diplomacy. Kristallnacht, the Night of Broken Glass on November 9–10, 1938, when Nazi SS and other Germans burned hundreds of German synagogues, looted and smashed Jewish stores, and interned thousands of Jews in concentration camps, had jolted him. He joined other outraged Americans in expressing popular fury at the atrocities.[18]

Skidell knew that he was competing in a vigorous marketplace of political ideas. Zionism was not the only ideology that appealed to young Jews. The popular front, initiated by Communists to unite radical groups under a common banner, enlisted Jewish enthusiasts attracted to its antifascist politics at home and abroad. Many rallied around the Loyalists when the Spanish Civil War began in 1936, and sympathizers even went to fight there in the Abraham Lincoln Brigades.[19] But Skidell focused on his main goal of socialist Zionism and adhered to his antiwar position. For three years as civil war raged in Spain and the left railed against American neutrality, Skidell held fast to his views. He abhorred Stalin, who had come to the aid of the Loyalists, and opposed the popular front's glorification of the Soviet Union.[20]

Despite his neutral stance on Spain, Skidell joined in condemning Japanese militarism. He decried Japan's seizure of Mongolia, its march into China and occupation of Peking, Nanking, and Shanghai. The slaughter of as many as 200,000 civilians in Nanking stunned him and many others who would later see the "Rape of Nanking," as the eight weeks of Japanese mayhem in 1937 came to be called, as the forerunner of European war atrocities.[21] Like Kristallnacht, the "Rape of Nanking" shocked Americans. In the popular-front antifascist spirit, young Jewish women foreswore silk stockings. "If you'll be in style, wear stockings of lisle, don't buy anything Japanese!" they sang to the melody of "Bei Mir Bist du Schoen," the popular Andrews Sisters' hit. "Your brothers and sons, don't give them to guns, don't buy anything Japanese!"[22] Boycott seemed an appropriate, pacifist answer to war in the Pacific. Akiva Skidell agreed with Saperstein's pacifism. In Toronto as a young immigrant student, Skidell had subscribed to the "Oxford Oath," pledging not to fight in any war.[23]

Then came the "knife in the back of the Jews," as Jewish socialists called the Molotov-Ribbentrop Non-Aggression Pact that preceded the German invasion of Poland.[24] The pact disillusioned many young people aligned with the antifascist popular front and its support of Soviet policies. The popular front collapsed, although some American Communists adjusted their politics to fit the Soviet Union's accord with the Axis powers, Germany, Italy, and Japan.[25] Skidell, who had always opposed Communists as being antidemocratic and anti-Jewish, hoped that others would recognize the political immorality of Soviet-sponsored campaigns for peace.[26]

Now on September 2, the day after Hitler's invasion of Poland, Skidell was spending his Saturday night up in the Catskills huddled with friends around the radio.[27] Head buried in his hands, he listened to the depressing news. What would Britain and France do once Hitler had rejected Chamberlain's ultimatum? War or peace? When the news finally came around midnight that France and Britain had declared war on Germany, a tremor ran through the group of young Zionists. A cataclysmic event had occurred. All night they debated their commitment to peace. Should they participate in this "war for survival," as they imagined it?[28]

Irrespective of their views on the events of September 1939, Saperstein, Dash, and Skidell could not anticipate how the war beginning in Europe would sweep them up in its grip. Nor could they realize how their years in military service would change them. Within four years they would all be in the armed forces. Dash would go first, along with the rest of the Dragons, without any pacifist qualms. He knew he would be drafted, so he preferred to enlist. Saperstein and Skidell would follow in 1943, the former volunteering for service as a military chaplain and the latter drafted, like the vast majority of American servicemen. These three joined more than half a million other American Jews in uniform.[29] Immigrant or native-born, Reform Jew or Zionist no longer mattered. Their military experiences would make them proud Americans, deepening their identification with the democratic ideals of the United States and strengthening their opposition to fascism and everything the Axis alliance represented.[30]

There would be other significant changes. Dash and Skidell, respectively in the Navy and the Army, would become fighters, master the technologies of war, learn to take orders, to lead, and to risk their lives to get the job done. As they joined millions of other Americans in that transition, they simultaneously would fulfill a long-standing dream of Jewish radical movements to transform Jews into warriors.[31] Military service, which would teach Dash and Skidell how to fight, also would instruct them in the importance of fighting and of their right to fight. *Yidishe Kemfer* (Jewish Fighter), the name of a Labor Zionist journal that Skidell read, no longer referred only to proud and militant Zionists. The title also applied to Dash and the Dragons, young men who would forge new Jewish identities based on American military norms of virility, cooperation, and initiative. Learning how to handle weapons and defend themselves would become part of their understanding of manhood, an understanding that would accompany them back to civilian life, linking them to other American veterans as well as to activist Jewish movements and the popular image of the American cowboy.

At the same time, as Saperstein would discover, Jews in the service unexpectedly came to appreciate Judaism in a new way in part because the armed forces treated it with respect. As one of the three "fighting faiths of democracy," Judaism assumed an American legitimacy unanticipated at the start of the war.[32] Protestantism, Catholicism, and Judaism were deemed to share common values that made them religions of democracy. Those values included belief in God and in the brotherhood of all men; they mandated respect for individual Jews, Catholics, and Protestants in their differences. But the military not only accepted the idea of a "Judeo-Christian" tradition, it also developed ceremonies that celebrated this tradition. Saperstein would improvise observances with Catholic and Protestant chaplains to construct a common framework for the three historic religions. The pragmatic practice of this new "tradition," despite difficulties, produced rituals of accommodation and experiences of worshipping together that would raise Jewish self-esteem while at the same time transforming Jews' self-understanding.[33]

The war would do more than enshrine the Judeo-Christian tradition as America's faith. To Saperstein's surprise, it would subsequently delegitimize those who claimed that the United States was a Christian country and that only Protestants were Christian. Acceptance of the Judeo-Christian tradition in the armed forces would force Protestants to share the Christian label with Catholics and include Jews as equal partners in America.[34] Saperstein would also note parallel adjustments among Jews, encouraging an ecumenism among Conservative, Orthodox, and Reform chaplains. All of these changes would alter Jewish attitudes toward Judaism. Even prayer, often thought to be "unmanly" by sophisticated Jewish youth, acquired a new-found respect in the military, especially for men under fire.[35]

Given the opportunity and requirement to defend their country, American Jews would discover not only how American but also how deeply Jewish they felt. "They learned," Saperstein explained to his congregants, "that unless you stand up for yourself, nobody is going to stand up for you."[36] Standing up for oneself as a Jew turned out to be the American thing to do. Military service strengthened Jewishness in part by changing its meaning. Jewish GIs would realize that their Jewish identity lived inside of them, as part of their personalities. They were Jews in all sorts of complicated ways that had relatively little to do with faith and observance and a lot to do with dignity, fellowship, and humanity.

Dash began his journey to the armed forces from New York City. Close to half of American Jews, over two million, called New York City home.[37] More precisely, most of them would say they came from Brooklyn or the Bronx. Large enough to be cities in their own right, these outer boroughs contained dense and diverse Jewish neighborhoods.[38] Other major American cities — Chicago, Philadelphia, Cleveland — claimed Jewish populations in the tens of thousands.[39] But if the overwhelming majority of Jews lived in urban America as did Dash and the Dragons, many towns had at least some Jewish families: a dentist or druggist, perhaps, an owner of a liquor or drygoods store, on occasion a self-employed professional, or salesman, or manager. Dash had cousins who lived in small towns in western Massachusetts. For them, the simple fact of not being Christian excluded them from many public as well as private aspects of small-town community life. Bigotry did not shock them. They would bring into the armed forces a deep sense of their religious difference from the majority and an inbred tendency for self-protection.

For Dash and the Dragons, the process of Jewish differentiation was more complex. The rhythms of urban life led to an understanding of America as a nation of immigrants and their children.[40] Dash recognized both what he shared with his Christian neighbors and where he differed. Everyone went to school, but Jews always went to public school. Parochial education, adopted by Catholics, had no broad basis of support among Jews. As laws extended the age of compulsory education to sixteen, neighborhood high schools prospered and secondary education spread in American cities. Dash attended one of these new schools, Abraham Lincoln High School on Coney Island. Caught up in its rigors and rewards, he was less aware of its ethnic enclaves. What mattered were extracurricular activities: sports, journalism, arts, and politics.[41] He edited his high school paper and played on the tennis team. Choosing the academic rather than the commercial or vocational tracks, he studied in classes largely with other Jews. When he graduated in 1937, increasing numbers of Jews throughout the city were not only graduating but also continuing their studies in college. Few of them went to a private college as he did. But in New York City where college education was free, approximately 30 percent of Jewish sons attended college.[42] Most of the Dragons could not afford to continue studying. Like other Brooklyn boys, they went to work after high school.[43] Still, they knew that political and religious differences separated them from their Irish and Italian neighbors, not to mention the Germans.[44] Several of the Dragons played baseball on a team with other Jews. In their America, while everyone drank from the same water fountain, friendships rarely crossed ethnic and religious lines.[45]

Dash and the Dragons imbibed both urban cosmopolitanism and provincialism from their Brooklyn childhood. The latter existed in the web of family and friendships, school and work, that bound their lives. It also served them as a compass as they navigated the city. The former resulted from their living among many cultures different from their own. As the Dragons traveled to Manhattan, explored neighborhoods, strolled through parks, and rode subways and trolleys, absorbing the cityscape's expressive power, they moved through shifting contexts of possibility and risk.[46] A meal out in a cafeteria or a Chinese restaurant presented the opportunity to eat *treyf,* unkosher food. And the Dragons didn't need to observe kosher norms to know what was exotic and forbidden. They also picked up elements of cosmopolitan style — how to dress and walk in all neighborhoods — that made them New Yorkers and not just Brooklyn Jewish boys. The pace of the city and the multiplicity of its cultures and languages thus shaped their identity. They savored the pleasures of movies and occasional nights on the town in Times Square; when they had a few extra dollars to spend, they attended theaters or nightclubs or concerts. Along with his friends, Dash listened regularly to national radio programs and enjoyed recorded music.[47]

Although cosmopolitanism characterized increasing numbers of Americans growing up in large cities, religious and ethnic differences also colored their experiences.[48] Judaism, provincial and intimate, punctuated the Dragons' calendar year and guided their tastes. Irrespective of their degree of piety, the Dragons' practices were typical of Judaism's urban folkways. For them, Hanukka and Passover mattered more than Christmas and Easter, and September always brought a new year, both the beginning of the school year and the Jewish New Year, Rosh Hashana. In fact, September 1939 began a new century in the Jewish calendar, 5700. The High Holy Days ushered in a period of celebration and reckoning, communal worship and family reunions. It was a time to purchase new clothes to be worn initially to synagogue. In cities across the United States where Jews lived, preparations occasioned sales in clothing stores and intense activity by women to ready their homes.[49] Summer slipcovers were removed; rugs were returned to their accustomed places. Windows were washed and foods purchased.[50] Enterprising cantors rented halls and movie theaters to cater to the synagogue overflow of Jews who came to services at this time of the year. They were called "three-day-a-year" Jews,[51] only attending services on the mornings of the two days of Rosh Hashana and then ten days later for the fast day of Yom Kippur. Rabbis might preach the importance of going to synagogue, but most American Jews remained unmoved.[52]

Martin Dash and his family never entered either a regular synagogue or the satellite varieties that sprang up. They joined other secular Jews who merely donned their new clothes, closed their workshops and stores, kept their children home from public school, and enjoyed the holiday with a promenade up the main thoroughfare of their neighborhood. At midday, synagogue Jews and secular Jews alike would gather at home for a hearty family dinner of gefilte fish and chicken soup, brisket and vegetables, topped off with honeycake, a sweet confection of doughballs and nuts called taglach, and the requisite apple slices dipped in honey. The latter dish symbolized hopes for a sweet year ahead.[53]

By the time Rosh Hashana arrived on September 14, 1939, American Jews were contemplating a far from promising year. The German military machine had so overwhelmed the Polish armies that journalists had coined a new term to signify the rapidity of the German victory: blitzkrieg.[54] Although Warsaw held out until the end of the month, only bad news emanated from Europe. At the end of the fall holiday season, most of Poland's three million Jews were living under Nazi rule. When the Soviet

Union occupied eastern Poland, some American Jews breathed a sigh of relief.

Dash returned to Yale that September to finish his junior year. Observing World War II from the safety of the United States and unsure of what would happen, he concentrated on academic matters.[55] Still, he contemplated leaving school in May of 1940 as the German blitzkrieg on the western front forced the British to evacuate the European continent at Dunkirk. His social psychology professor invited him to come to Washington to help set up an office to deal with inter-American affairs. Dash had gotten straight A's in psychology and was flattered, but he resisted the offer. He feared that if he went, he would not graduate, and college took priority over preparations for America's involvement in the war. On June 17, France surrendered to the Germans, bringing all of western Europe except for Switzerland under Nazi control. That summer, Hitler launched unprecedented air attacks against Britain. Dash watched with dismay. He favored the Roosevelt administration's interventionist efforts to help England.[56] But in the fall of 1940, he returned to Yale to complete his senior year.

Akiva Skidell saw the events of late 1939 and 1940 through his ideological commitments. As *mazkir* (secretary) of Habonim, he viewed the unfolding Jewish tragedy in Europe as the central fact of his world. He tried to imagine how intolerable Jewish life was under Nazism. He believed that even those without relatives abroad should feel a sense of responsibility for their beleaguered co-religionists. Zionist American Jews, repeatedly urged to give money to bring "thousands of homeless and oppressed men and women" to Palestine, opened their pocketbooks in response to the European crisis.[57] Skidell regularly read the newspapers and listened to stirring live reports on the radio: William Shirer from Berlin, Eric Sevareid from Paris, Edward R. Mur-

row from London. Although he did not realize it, those news-
casts were an "emotional down payment" on the coming war.[58]
For now, he increased his organizing efforts to convince young
American Jews that a Jewish national home in Palestine was essential. Peace increasingly seemed a mirage after the fall of
France in June 1940. Nazi Germany controlled almost all of Europe, free to pursue unhindered its barbaric persecution. Skidell
could not fathom how Jewish radicals could ignore the terrible
disaster overtaking European Jews.[59]

The prewar British White Paper drastically limiting Jewish
immigration to their mandate in Palestine complicated Skidell's
attitudes toward England. It was not, as Dash might have put it,
just a question of defending freedom. As the mandatory power
in Palestine, Britain controlled the fate of Jews. Where were
millions of refugees from the ever-expanding reach of Nazism
going to go if not to Palestine? Yet even after the war broke out,
Britain refused to modify its anti-Jewish immigration policy in
Palestine. Skidell and other Zionists faced a dilemma: should
they support the British in the fight against Germany, or should
they fight the British over the exclusion of European Jews fleeing to Palestine?[60] Skidell followed David Ben Gurion's leadership and adopted his policy of fighting Hitler as though there
were no White Paper and fighting England as though there
were no Hitler.[61]

Harold Saperstein shared Skidell's commitment to Zionism
and concern for the fate of European Jews, but he struggled for
many months over whether to abandon his total dedication to
pacifism.[62] Despite the unpopularity of pacifism among his congregants, Saperstein had boldly preached his beliefs. Born in
1910, he remembered World War I and the violent postwar
years when Jews suffered from warring armies in eastern Europe. His commitment to pacifism had taken shape during his

youth in Troy, New York. By the time he graduated from Cornell University in 1931, Saperstein was passionately devoted to peaceful means of resolving international conflicts.[63] But as Rosh Hashana approached in the fall of 1940, Saperstein reluctantly admitted that he feared "a peace on Hitler's terms, a peace of submission to the forces of barbarism." There were some things worse than war, he concluded, and some things "more important than peace."[64] Truly the outlook was grim. For fifty-seven consecutive days, beginning on September 7, hundreds of tons of German bombs rained down on London.[65]

"What can a religious leader say to his people in times like these," Saperstein asked, "when ideals as well as worlds are being shattered?" Appealing to the long and sad course of Jewish history, he assured his listeners dressed in their holiday best that Jews were on the side of righteousness. He saw no end to Jewish suffering, but he was convinced that "our suffering is not meaningless." Whatever "forces of decency" remained in the world, they stood "side by side" with "us."[66] Given how embattled those forces were, it was not much comfort. But Saperstein stopped short of endorsing war.

Like most American Jews, Saperstein, Dash, and Skidell addressed their anguish over German victories in Europe by lining up behind Franklin Delano Roosevelt's bid for an unprecedented third presidential term in 1940. Although only Saperstein could vote (Dash was not yet twenty-one and Skidell wasn't a citizen), all three supported FDR and whatever policies he proposed to help Britain after the fall of France. The initiation of the first peacetime draft in October 1940 brought the possibilities of armed conflict closer. A couple of the Dragons were drafted into the army. They considered the initial requirement of one year's service a not unreasonable demand. They had to resist the Nazis. Most American Jews preferred FDR's anti-

Nazi, pro-British politics to Wendell Wilkie's cautious stance and applauded Roosevelt's strong support of England during the Battle of Britain.[67]

Listening to the President articulate his vision of "a world founded upon four essential freedoms" in his annual message to Congress on January 6, 1941, American Jews felt confirmed in the rightness of their choice. "The first is freedom of speech and expression," Roosevelt declared, words that resonated deeply for Saperstein, Dash, and Skidell. This freedom protected minorities, like Jews, who often dissented from majority opinions. "The second is freedom of every person to worship God in his own way — everywhere in the world." One didn't have to be religious, Dash understood, to recognize the significance of religious freedom. It included not only the right to pray to the God of Israel in synagogues with other Jews, but also the opportunity to slaughter meat according to the kosher laws, to circumcise Jewish sons, and to observe the Jewish sabbath and holy days. "The third is freedom from want . . ." Skidell knew well how poverty eroded human dignity. He championed democratic socialism along with Zionism because of its guarantees of a decent standard of living. Saperstein saw the welfare state as a modern expression of the Hebrew prophetic tradition and applauded the President when he described "economic understandings which will secure to every nation a healthy peacetime life for its inhabitants." In these phrases, Saperstein and Skidell heard a shorthand for the New Deal's social welfare provisions securing the rights of workers and the most vulnerable members of society. The fourth freedom, "freedom from fear," meant, the President explained, "a world-wide reduction in armaments . . ."[68] Saperstein eagerly agreed. But Skidell imagined "freedom from fear" differently; to him it implied an end to discrimination and persecution. In a world free of fear, Jews would no longer cower and hide, tremble and flee. Skidell thought that a nation dedicated to a world free of fear would also support the dream of Jews for a state of their own. The commitment of the United States to the four freedoms—freedom of speech and worship, freedom from want and fear—promised Jews a future of dignity, as individuals and as a community, at home and abroad.

The German invasion of the Soviet Union in June 1941 dramatically changed perspectives on the war. Now Soviet Jews too were threatened by Nazi persecution. Saperstein abandoned his pacifism after almost two years of "soul-rending struggle."[69] He accepted the fact that the United States stood on the verge of war. Dash also recognized that war was imminent and knew that he would enter military service.[70] And Skidell found himself on the same side as a newly formed popular antifascist front, although he stopped short of advocating, along with communists, that the United States open up a second front. Saperstein, Dash, and Skidell could not know that when Hitler launched Operation Barbarossa in the East, he also initiated systematic mass murder of Jews by specially trained units. The regular war news of German savagery on the eastern front was sufficiently alarming. By October 1941, the German army threatened the outskirts of Moscow.[71] Saperstein's Rosh Hashana sermon that year reflected his mood of confusion and despair. He could only summon Job's conviction amid his suffering that though God might slay him, yet he would trust in Him.[72]

Although they had anticipated the entry of the United States into the war, when it struck, Saperstein, Dash, and Skidell were stunned. Each man acted upon his convictions and entered military service. Not surprisingly, its challenges were always double-edged, forcing them to respond as Jews as well as Americans. "The experience of the war years," writes the historian Lucy Dawidowicz, "has had a transfiguring effect on American Jews and on their ideas of themselves as Jews." For countless numbers, induction into the armed forces during World War II "launched their discovery or rediscovery of themselves as Jews."[73] Jewish self-understanding evolved within the context of military service. Dash and the Dragons grew to comprehend the interdependence of their Jewish and American identities and accepted military service as their duty. Thus they came to internalize their Jewishness as a private aspect of their personalities rather than a public dimension of their culture. In the process of training them to defend their country, the armed forces would also teach them how to defend themselves and their people. This is not to say that the Dragons did not assume the rights of citizenship prior to the war. They felt at home in America, but their America was urban and, in many ways, provincial. After the war they would feel at home in a much larger and more diverse America, and in cases where other Americans might challenge their right to feel at home, Jewish veterans were ready to meet and overcome that challenge.[74] Yet as Dash, Skidell, and Saperstein negotiated the demands of military service, they would recognize only dimly that their participation was changing the American national story as well as the course of American Jewish history.

The American national chronicle had ignored Jews in the nineteenth century and had positioned race as the critical issue dividing the American people, optimistically assuming the integration of millions of ethnically and religiously diverse immigrants into a largely Christian United States.[75] After World War I, a deep pessimism and fear of foreigners and non-Protestants vanquished such optimism and led to drastic quotas on immigrants.[76] Although the New Deal coalition welcomed the children of immigrants, mitigating anti-immigrant sentiment, many Americans opposed the arrival of Jewish refugees fleeing Nazi

Germany and dismissed the value of religious diversity.[77] Jewish participation in military service during World War II would help to transform this opposition by demonstrating that Jews and Judaism were integral to American democracy and that Jews and Catholics were equal members of a distinctly American religious tradition. The war would make Jews visible, not as objects of scorn and hatred, but as subjects participating in American culture, politics, and survival.[78]

The history of World War II as experienced by American Jews in the armed forces is one of difference amid similarity, of exclusion amid integration, of transfiguration amid routine, of triumph amid catastrophe. It is also a story of courage despite fear. American Jews struggled to maintain the cohesion of their American and Jewish selves throughout their service, from the first decisions about whether to enlist or wait to be drafted, to the initial encounter with military norms at induction centers, through basic training, and on to the tour of duty. The mobilization of the United States for war catapulted American Jews into a radically different world from the one they had known. As the world of home receded, their identities shifted from "New Yorker" to "American." American Jewishness developed legs. The saga of American Jewish fighters might begin in Brooklyn or Chicago, but it ended in the vast diversity of a pluralist United States.

2

JOINING UP

One generation past, two days by plane away,
My house is dispossessed, my friends dispersed,
My teeth and pride knocked in, my people game
For the hunters of man-skins in the warrens of Europe . . .
Now I wait under the hemlock by the road
For the red-haired postman with the smiling hand
To bring me my passport to the war.

—STANLEY KUNITZ, "Reflection by a Mailbox"[1]

DECEMBER 7, 1941. Victor Geller had just ducked into Harry's luncheonette uptown in Manhattan's Washington Heights. At Yeshiva High School he had third periods free on Sundays, a normal school day for him and his fellow orthodox Jewish students. Geller regularly patronized the neighborhood hangout, with its gleaming metal counters, mirrored walls, and tempting soda fountain. Harry always welcomed the boys and turned up the volume on the radio when there was a football game at the Polo Grounds so everyone could hear the WOR broadcast. This Sunday was not going to be an ordinary day; it was Tuffy Leaman's Day in recognition of the Giants' outstanding fullback. The weather was cold and gray, perfect for football. Geller took a seat at the counter on one of the revolving stools with several of his friends. A couple of guys sat in the booths, taking in the game. Early in the second half, as the Giants were getting an unexpected drubbing, the announcer interrupted with a special news flash. Japanese planes had just bombed Pearl Harbor.

The surprise attack stunned Geller, a well-informed high school student. Despite its mutual defense agreement with Germany and Italy to form the Axis Powers in 1940, and despite its ongoing aggression against China, Japan did not seem to be a threat to the United States in 1941 — until that infamous Sunday. Geller had eagerly followed the war news, but he focused on Europe, deeply concerned about the fate of European Jews under Nazi domination. He knew that Hitler's armies had swept in a blitzkrieg through Poland in September 1939, had moved across western Europe in similar lightning fashion the following spring, and had plunged deep into the Soviet Union in 1941, reaching the outskirts of Moscow before the cruel Russian winter struck. He watched newsreels, finding some consolation in the evacuation of Dunkirk following the devastating defeat in France. Hungry for even more news, he discovered the compelling immediacy of radio's newspaper of the air. CBS's worldwide news coverage transported him to London, Paris, Rome, Berlin. He paid more attention to the war news than most of his friends, perhaps because his mother's brother and uncle and their families still lived in Hungary. The attack on Pearl Harbor sent shivers up his spine. War was "no longer a spectator sport for Americans," he realized, no longer just a matter of rooting for the "good guys."

Still only sixteen, Geller knew that he had time to figure out what he would do. He had choices. He was on track for a 4-D deferment as a theological student if he decided to continue after high school at Yeshiva's rabbinical college. By the time he graduated, the war might be over. Such a decision would please his widowed mother. But Geller was not a brilliant Talmudist; so he poured his energies into sports and being popular. He became athletic director of the Talmudical Academy's basketball team and coached them to a victorious season that year. And he

News of Pearl Harbor stunned Americans. Everyone knew it meant war, but listening to President Roosevelt's speech in a crowded Times Square made New Yorkers realize how different their future would be.

pondered what he, still a *yeshiva bochur* — a bookish youth, the traditional ideal Jewish male — should do now that the United States was at war.[2]

Sy Kahn, a year older than Geller, couldn't wait to turn eighteen to be eligible for the draft. He was anxious to be inducted because he "felt the war was the most important event of our century." He wanted to be a part of it. Monday morning after the Japanese attack, Kahn sat with his classmates in the auditorium of George Washington High School in upper Manhattan listening to President Roosevelt address the Congress. It seemed as though the President spoke to him personally. Kahn wanted to do his part. Although far from religiously observant, he was conscious of his Jewishness. He hoped to "be sent against Germany." It was the German enemy that mattered to him, not Japan. Impatient to fight, Kahn knew that he hardly excelled in those masculine attributes associated with soldiering. He was a bright New York City boy, born and bred in Manhattan, who loved English literature. He was not "particularly strong or athletic." As he later admitted, "at eighteen I was infinitely more comfortable with a book or violin in my hands than I was with a rifle, or any other weapon or tool." To his chagrin, he could scarcely distinguish a face across a room or, more important, identify more than the giant "E" on the first line of the eye chart without glasses. He lacked physical skills, stamina, and strength. Unlike the men he would meet in military service, he possessed no experience tinkering with motors or hunting. Yet he desperately wanted to do his part as a soldier in the armed forces. He was determined to remake himself into an American fighter, even if that meant losing his life. Indeed, Kahn was pretty sure he wouldn't survive since he was a secular version of a *yeshiva bochur,* but he didn't want to miss out on the epic struggle against Nazism.[3]

Kahn's and Geller's feelings at this time — their sensitivity about their physical capabilities coupled with their political awareness of the war's significance — reflect two distinctive dimensions of Jewish attitudes toward the question of military service.[4] Most Americans in December 1941 considered Japan the archenemy, unlike American Jews, who targeted Hitler as the important foe. Though neither Geller nor Kahn thought of himself as political, because neither espoused any left-wing ideology, their shared animosity toward Nazi Germany included a profound revulsion against fascism. By contrast, "Americans were fighting because they had been attacked," writes the historian William O'Neill. "Their war aims did not extend beyond defeating the enemy and ensuring peace."[5] This was perhaps the least ideologically motivated military machine in American history. Estimates suggest that only 5 percent of American soldiers fought for ideological reasons.[6] Paul Fussell goes further in his assessment. "If the Jews, like those in New York, like to think the war was in some way about them," he writes with a dose of sarcasm, it was clear from wartime advertisements "that most people didn't want to be like them in any way or even reminded of them. You could spend your life studying the magazine ads of wartime without once coming upon a yarmulkah or prayer shawl, or even features suggestive of Jewishness." Fussell argues that "to most American soldiers and sailors the United States, at least, was pursuing the war solely to defend itself from the monsters who had bombed Pearl Harbor without warning."[7] The slogan, he notes, was "Remember Pearl Harbor," not "Remember Poland." "The primary objective of our war is to defeat the Jap—not Hitler, and certainly not Nazism," one Jewish recruit wrote in disgust about his gentile comrades.[8] For Geller and Kahn it was the European conflict that counted, not the war in the Pacific. They knew why they would put on an American uniform even as they worried about how they could transform their teenage Jewish selves into fighting men.

The history of their concern about becoming a warrior stretched back over a century to antisemitic accusations questioning Jewish masculinity and ability to fight. European experiences in soldiering influenced Jewish attitudes toward military service, especially since those experiences included a strong dose of anti-Jewish bias. Jews had been drafted into modern armies during the French Revolution. Then during the nineteenth century various European nations, including the Russian and Austro-Hungarian empires, conscripted Jews into their armed forces. In World War I Jews fought with armies on both sides of the conflict. But antisemitic regulations prevented them from becoming officers in the armed forces of some states, and there were frequent caricatures of popularly perceived weaknesses.[9] Pervasive canards focused on Jewish bodies, claiming that flat feet, bowed legs, asthmatic lungs, and stunted stature made Jews physically unfit for the rigors of army life, especially in the infantry. Given the link between citizenship and military service in the modern state, denigration of "the Jew's body" accompanied attacks on the right of Jews to participate in the body politic. The eagerness with which some Zionists championed Jewish sports clubs and physical fitness emphasized the anxiety among Jews over these biased assumptions about their bodies.[10]

Antisemitic attitudes crossed the Atlantic and found expression among some career soldiers in the United States. Although Jews volunteered for military service in all of the wars of the United States, "the American cultural panorama," the historian Joseph Bendersky observes, "simply did not include the image of Jews as soldiers."[11] In a society that valued "a good left hook" and decisive action to end potential conflict, a perceived physical weakness coupled with verbal skill damned Jews as poor military material. Jews served as citizen soldiers when America mobilized to fight a specific war, and a few joined the regular army. Yet career officers often suspected them of physical weakness, selfishness, cowardice, and dishonorable behavior. On occasion these prejudiced assumptions even influenced official military guidelines. Until it was changed in March 1918, the Army Manual of Instructions for Medical Advisory Boards stated: "The foreign born, and especially Jews, are more apt to malinger than the native born."[12]

Some Jews worried that there might be a grain of truth in the image of the Jewish weakling. Behind their self-doubts lay not only decades of antisemitic slanders but also the reality of an alternative ideal of masculinity. Jewish society "had long associated the pale, slender Jewish body with Torah study" and nobility.[13] Nineteenth-century European Jewish reformers had criticized this male ideal as effeminate, passive, and cowardly. Yet secularized versions of the traditional model endured even in the United States. In a sense, Sy Kahn's book and violin substituted for the previously normative Talmud folio. Victor Geller's refuge in sports, especially basketball, which was enormously popular among urban Jewish youth, provided another alternative expression of masculinity for young American Jews, as did the hero worship of Hank Greenberg, the Detroit Tigers' King of Swat.[14]

Herbert Walters, a newly minted lawyer, entertained few qualms about his physical ability to serve in the armed forces. In his assumption that he could fight as well as any man, he typified the attitudes of many other young American Jews. But Jewish familial concerns restrained him from rushing to join up. He could not enlist because it would hurt his parents too much. The youngest son of immigrant parents, Walters occupied a special position in his large family. His older brothers were married, as were several of his sisters. Single, living with his parents at home in Borough Park, Brooklyn, he felt obligated to them. Walters clerked in downtown Manhattan at the prestigious German Jewish law firm of Marshall, Bratter, and Seligson. On Sunday, December 7, he had been doing some legal work when his friend came running up the stairs, breathless, with the news of Pearl Harbor. They both raced down to tell his parents to turn on the radio. The Monday morning after Pearl Harbor, as Walters walked from the subway to his office, he eyed with envy the long line of men stretching for four blocks around the Federal Building waiting to enlist. He wanted to join the men who were free

Jewish youth growing up in American cities embraced sports, especially basketball and baseball, as badges of their American identity. In addition to playing the games, young Jewish men rooted for local teams and followed the statistics of their favorite players.

to volunteer. Men in suits and men in overalls stood ready to sign up at the Naval Recruiting Station. Periodically, an Army recruiter would come by, promising "No waiting to get into the Army — no waiting to get into the Army."[15] Walters did not want to sit out this war. Still, he knew that enlisting would devastate his elderly immigrant parents. But all of his friends on the block were going.[16] So he struggled with multiple tensions: his strong desire to enlist, the unspoken pressures of his peers who were joining up, his parents' fears that he would not return alive, even the expectation of his boss that he would prefer a desk job in Washington that was appropriate for a young lawyer as his form of military service.[17]

Jewish immigrant families traditionally looked on military service as a misfortune. Uniforms distressed them. Herman Kogan remembered that his parents refused to let him join the Boy Scouts. It didn't matter that all the kids in the neighborhood were doing it. "They said once you're in khaki, you'll never get out."[18] Such folk wisdom harked back to the misery of Jewish conscription into the tsar's army. Jewish memories preserved horrifying tales of military service from the previous century when recruiters would snatch poor young Jewish boys for twenty-five-year terms, during which time military officers tried to convert them to Christianity.[19] Military service in the tsar's army meant the loss of a child to his people, faith, and family.[20] "Parents of recent conscripts would light mourning candles, as for a deceased relative," writes the historian Benjamin Nathans, "on the assumption that they would never see their sons again, at any rate not as Jews."[21] Although these harsh long terms of service ended before mass immigration began to the United States, even regular military duty dismayed Jews. To avoid conscription, young Russian Jews married early, maimed themselves, or fled across the border and then on to America. America was not Russia, but armies were still armies. An older generation of Jews viewed military service with terror because of their old-world memories. Still a child, Jerold Auerbach watched the family drama of generations with acute discomfort. "My mother's brother had just been drafted into the army," he recalled. "Our extended family gathered in my grandmother's living room in Philadelphia to lament his fate." Then, after "hushed conversation over tea, brewed in the Russian samovar that was the family icon of my childhood, my grandmother and her sisters . . . spontaneously burst into tears and began to shriek and wail in Yiddish." Their outburst shocked him. It expressed a "primal fear as though my uncle was about to be impressed into the czar's army." However, the American-born generation accepted what had to be: "No less startling than their volubility was my parents' controlled silence." To Auerbach it represented Americanization, the stoic acceptance of "what provoked terror in their elders, still haunted by old country fears."[22]

American-born and bred, Martin Dash and the other Dragons didn't worry particularly about their physical ability to serve in the armed forces. They were healthy — a bit overweight perhaps, but nothing that a military regimen couldn't fix. Nor did they consider any alternatives to military service. They did not intend to seek deferments. They didn't even fret about their parents. They were young American men, as patriotic and adventuresome as the next guy. They accepted their duty to defend their country. Jewishness really wasn't an issue. Joining up was only a matter of time and the question of whether to enlist or wait to be drafted. They were all the right age and unmarried. Many already had a draft number, although until Pearl Harbor few were called. Working in commercial, service, or light urban industries and living at home with their parents, without dependents, they were prime candidates for the draft. Some, like Dash's buddies Wilton Hilowitz and Lester Klauber, were already in uniform. Hilowitz had been drafted in January 1941, almost a year before the attack.[23] Klauber had entered the army a week before Pearl Harbor. What he thought was going to be one year of military service suddenly became a question of how soon he would be sent into combat.[24] The draft also caught his fellow Dragon Henry Baker, who ended up bumping into Klauber at Fort Lee in Virginia.[25] Unlike Klauber and Hilowitz, Herbie Jawitz, yet another member of the gang, received his draft notice on the day after Pearl Harbor. He went into the Army on January 12, 1942.[26] Ralph Jackson didn't wait for the draft, although he had his number. On Monday morning, December 8, he walked into the office at MGM and gave them two weeks' notice. Swept up in the patriotic fervor, he enlisted in the Army Air Corps before the New Year. Like so many Americans, Jackson had no desire to get personally involved in the war until Pearl Harbor. But the attack changed him, as it did so many others.[27] They might not have ever heard of Pearl Harbor before the attack or even realized that it was United States territory. (After all, Hawaii was halfway around the world from Brooklyn.)[28] No matter. They were Americans, and this was their war. They would join up.

But other Americans did question the willingness of Jewish men to serve. Contemporary stereotypes portrayed such typical Brooklyn Jews as quintessential draft-dodgers. As one professor at City College joked, "The Battle Hymn of the Jews is 'Onward Christian Soldiers, we'll make the uniforms.'"[29] Softened by time, jokes may seem harmless, but in fact serious calumnies circulated throughout the country in 1942 and 1943. The slanders accused Jews of causing the war, benefiting from defense contracts, and even serving as a dangerous Fifth Column undermining America as they avoided military service. As the war progressed, antisemitic libels claimed that Jews in military service stayed stateside, in the "Zone of the Interior" as it was called, or found cushy jobs behind the lines. The jokes and ditties that people felt free to repeat represented popular expressions of a deep-seated animus. Needless to say, the military did not consider a Jewish trade like garment manufacturing to be defense work, unlike farming or heavy industry. There were no classifications exempting clothing workers from the draft. The crude antisemitism that portrayed them as cowards and war profiteers angered most Jews. They demanded police protection when members of the Christian Front, followers of Father Coughlin, vandalized synagogues. Still, even as they fought Christian Front toughs, they bitterly resented their need to defend themselves on the streets of Boston or the Bronx when the United States was engaged in a war against Nazi Germany.[30] Aware of anti-semitic attitudes, the Dragons tried not to let these stereotypes influence their own behavior. Nevertheless, the decision to en-list instead of waiting for the draft was in part a way to prove just how willing they were to get into the armed forces.

Martin Dash decided to enlist. Enlisting had distinct advan-tages: he could choose his branch of service or try out for a par-ticular program. He chose the Navy. A recent college graduate, he didn't anticipate any difficulties. Dash was studying insurance to be certified as a broker in the fall of 1941, but after Pearl Har-bor he immediately went down to the Naval Reserve office to enroll in their ninety-day midshipman's program. A petty officer looked over his college record and told him that he lacked the math requirements. It was true: Dash had majored in psychol-ogy at Yale University and hadn't bothered taking math courses. So the rejection made sense. Dash enrolled in two six-week crash courses in spherical trigonometry and solid geometry at City College. A good student, he scored grades of 92 and 94. Then he went back down to the Naval Reserve office. This time, it was a different story. The navy officer, a two-striper, lieutenant senior grade, wanted to know: had he ever been a Boy Scout?[31] No. Did he know where Lake Okeechobee was? No, he did not. Well then, he was not qualified to be admitted for midshipman training. They were full up at this time.[32]

Dash interpreted the second rejection differently. The excuse that "they didn't have room for anyone" after questions about the Boy Scouts and an obscure lake in Florida didn't sit well with him. Five foot eight with brown eyes, dark skin, and black curly hair, Dash could pass as Cuban, as he had in the summer of 1939 when he'd sold maracas at the World's Fair. On a Brook-

Martin Dash in Navy uniform. Crashing the Naval Reserve midshipman program turned out to be Dash's first skirmish of the war. Sharing the photo with his Brooklyn buddies helped maintain their friendships during three long years in military service.

lyn boy, those "Latin from Manhattan" looks also announced that he was Jewish. Was it possible that the Navy wasn't interested in a potential Jewish officer?[33] It was the type of exclusion that Jewish boys growing up in big cities across the United States knew about. There were quotas on college admissions and in medical and law schools.[34] Many large companies refused to hire Jews. The Kings County Lighting Company, Brooklyn's public utility, asked job candidates on the application what church they attended — and at that time, "church" was not a generic term that included synagogue.[35] Then there were neighborhoods where Jews couldn't rent an apartment, let alone buy a house. Dash remembered what had happened when he tried to join the tennis team at Yale.[36] He had been a member of the Abraham Lincoln High School team and wanted to continue to play the sport. But he was turned down not because he wasn't good enough but because he didn't have the "right" shoes. So the "no" he now encountered from the lieutenant was not unfamiliar. He had given up playing varsity tennis in college, but he was not ready to accept the Navy's rejection.[37]

Despite their significant differences, Geller, Kahn, Walters, and Dash all faced a similar dilemma: how to overcome barriers confronting them as Jews who wanted to join the armed forces. For Geller, Kahn, and Walters, those obstacles derived from Jewish attitudes toward family. Loyal sons, they had sought to fulfill their parents' ideals of study. Now they confronted a powerful alternative male model. American notions of masculinity included not only strength, stamina, physical skills, and the proverbial good left hook but also an individualism and independence expressed outside familial boundaries. The Japanese attack raised the question of military service. For these loyal Jewish sons, mobilization for war clashed with their families' expectations and values. It forced Geller, Kahn, and Walters to consider self-consciously their identity as Jews and Americans and to prioritize their loyalties. All three reached the same answer. They wanted to become American men and leave behind their families' constraints so that they could defend their country. That the enemies of the United States included Nazi Germany, the bitter foe of the Jews, only reinforced their desire to serve. Paradoxically, their Jewishness simultaneously restrained them and motivated them to act upon their wish to enter the American armed forces. Each man negotiated his ambitions differently. In contrast with the other three, Dash confronted an external adversary—antisemitism in the very military he wanted to join. Crashing the Naval Reserve would be his first skirmish of the war.

Dash had decided early on that he preferred the Navy, considering it a more elite branch of the service. Living on a ship seemed cleaner, although he hated the water and couldn't swim. Because he wanted the Navy, he went on a grapefruit diet to lose weight. And he neglected to tell the Navy about his asthma and other ailments. So when he received the second rejection he was upset and angry. He had just spent six weeks studying mathematics to qualify. Frustrated, he turned to his family for help. How about the relatives in Baltimore? He could go down to Baltimore, use their address, and sign up there. It seemed like a good plan. The best way to deal with such individual antisemitism, he figured, was to outflank it. So he went down to Baltimore's Naval Reserve office. There were no questions about the Boy Scouts or Lake Okeechobee; they were happy to have him. Dash's status changed in the context of a city in which blacks were segregated from whites. In Baltimore, despite its religious and ethnic divisions, he appeared more white than Jewish. No longer identified as a Brooklyn Jew, he shed the associated antisemitic stereotypes. He received an added bonus: the chance to choose where he wanted to do his midshipman's course, in Chicago or New York. Dash chose New York, of course. He came home, knowing that he would do his officer training at Columbia University. He had won his first contest for acceptance in the military.[38]

Herbert Walters couldn't turn to his family for help, but he could use a similar circuitous strategy. Unbeknownst to his parents, he typed a letter to his draft board asking them to call him. This way he had an excuse for his parents: when the draft notice came, they would have to accept the hand of fate. He could join his peers. But he sacrificed the choice that came from volunteering. Walters, enticed by a chance for adventure, had wanted to enter the Army Air Corps. Having lived what he considered a sheltered existence, bounded by the tight-knit worlds of office, home, and neighborhood, he sought to escape. When the notice arrived from his draft board, a senior partner in the firm told him that since he had recently passed the bar, he could join the Army's legal branch, the Judge Advocates. The partner had contacts in Washington to whom he would speak for Walters. Walters demurred. He thanked the partner for the offer, but he was "not going to sit in Washington during the war and have to say that to my grandchildren."[39] Walters wanted more than to serve. He wanted to fight. A short man with a slight build, fair skin, and blue eyes, Walters never did get the opportunity to become a cadet in the Air Corps. The army discovered weakness in his eyesight. Nor did he end up as an officer: the army rejected his application because of his height.

Walters' refusal to accept the offer by his firm to use its connections on his behalf also reflects the pressures of class. Although he clerked in a respected Jewish law firm, Walters had come to his position through hard work and professional competence. He began at the firm as an office boy after graduating from high school. Deciding to study law, he continued working while he took enough evening courses at Brooklyn College to qualify for law school. Then he remained with the firm as he attended St. John's Law School at night. Even as he moved up, he never felt comfortable around wealthy and prominent lawyers and their rich clients. Using connections to secure a respected but soft job in the Judge Advocates department didn't sit right with him. He believed, along with most of his neighborhood buddies, that it was his duty to get into this war.[40] Like most Jews, he went with the mainstream to wherever he was sent.[41] He became a Sergeant Major in an anti-aircraft artillery unit.

Sy Kahn, well aware of his own physical limitations, decided to use his intellectual skills to get into the army. Stripped naked, he waited in line with men of various ages and physiques on a

A necessary ritual to enter military service, the physical examination prompted Sy Kahn to memorize the eye charts so that he could serve his country in uniform. Others hoped the doctors would find some disqualifying disability that would give them their pick of jobs in the accelerating wartime economy.

cold February evening in 1943. The lines moved slowly, so he memorized as much of the eye charts as he could. When his turn came he took off his glasses and "read" the letters as clearly as though he actually saw them. He passed, or so he thought. Then after his physical exam, "papers in hand and still naked," he stood before three officers on a platform behind a long desk. "In front of the colonel seated in the center were two large rubber stamps, a blue one for 'Accepted' and a red one for 'Rejected.' After the three officers briefly examined my papers," he recalled, "the colonel nonchalantly picked up the red marker and stamped a large 'Rejected' across the first page, and handed the packet down to me. Stunned, I stared at that red word stamped diagonally across the page. I turned back and said, 'Sir, why am I rejected? I think you may have made a mistake.'" Surprised at the naked man's challenge to his assessment, the colonel shifted his gaze. "After glancing through the papers, he said, 'You are right. I picked up the wrong stamp.'"[42] Kahn was inducted into the army that day. Few, Jewish or gentile, would have challenged fate as Kahn did. It was normal for a young man to think of his life and future. In the context of universal conscription, those who were rejected "were considered lucky." As Raymond Groden pointed out, "They could have their pick of jobs." He admitted that among his Brooklyn friends, "if one was physically or mentally handicapped," he was envied.[43]

Victor Geller's strategy evolved slowly. During the spring semester of 1942, he savored the war excitement at high school, now abuzz with blood drives and air raid drills. He noticed, too, the presence of men in uniform on the streets of his Bronx neighborhood and then the thinning ranks of men who regularly gathered in the park. But what really captured his imagination was a newsreel. At the elegant Loew's 167th Street theater in the Bronx, Geller intently watched a documentary on the Army Chaplaincy School at Harvard University. Among the men featured in the film was a young rabbi ordained at Yeshiva's own Rabbi Isaac Elchanan Theological Seminary. The movie depicted Rabbi Herschel Schacter preparing for his new role as chaplain in the U.S. Army. Geller thought he looked very impressive "with the Ten Commandments in his lapels." Paradoxically, the film confirmed Geller's decision that he would not "hide out" at Yeshiva during the war. A 4-D deferment was not for him. When the time came, he decided, he would serve. He knew his widowed mother "would be very upset. Her anger would be hard to deal with, but, just as I couldn't blame her, I couldn't back away." Still not yet seventeen, Geller figured that he would keep his plans to himself "until it was time to act."[44]

Geller's Jewish politics included an almost visceral repugnance toward Nazi antisemitism. It fueled his sense of purpose as a Jew and an American. His attitudes and activism had taken root in an orthodox immigrant household. Adversity at home — especially his father's death at an early age — propelled the teenager into a position as the "man" of the household. His religious education included Zionism, and he regularly carried a Jewish National Fund (JNF) box to raise money to help settle Jews in Palestine. Standing by the news vendor at the subway stop with his blue and white JNF box, Geller discovered comic books for Sabbath reading. His enthusiasm for American popular culture nourished a strong patriotism not shared by his Hungarian-born mother. Nazi antisemitism angered him even as American culture emboldened him.[45]

By September 1942, Geller had formulated his plan. He enrolled in Yeshiva College. His action pleased his devout mother, but it was only the first step in what he had determined to do. He soon initiated dinner-table discussions to prepare her for his decision to study secular subjects at CCNY and then continue his religious studies at Yeshiva.[46] Geller intended to give up the 4-D deferment that would be his as a Yeshiva student when he turned eighteen the following year. He wanted to sign up for R.O.T.C., which would help transform him, a *yeshiva bochur*, into a soldier. His mother finally acquiesced in his plan, allowing him to take his "psychological step" toward American "manhood." Once at CCNY, Geller learned about the Army Specialized Training Program (A.S.T.P.), which selected college students and others in the army for engineering, language, and other types of college-level training. To be eligible, he had to join the Army Reserves. Since he was still seventeen, he needed his mother's permission. For two days his younger brother did his best to persuade her. Finally she agreed. She signed the papers, freeing him to pursue his patriotic passion and his American manhood. Geller entered the Army Reserves on March 1, 1943.[47]

The next day the *New York Times* carried a rare front-page headline that read "Save Doomed Jews, Huge Rally Pleads."[48] The headline confirmed for Geller the rightness of his decision. Time was running out. Day and night, Nazi SS were gassing Jews in death camps. Two million already were dead. The Jews of Europe could not fight Hitler, but as a GI in the U.S. Army, Geller could. He felt an extra obligation as a Jew to fight Nazism and antisemitism. In volunteering, he merged his enthusiastic, "teen-aged, starry-eyed" American patriotism with his pride in his Jewish identity.[49] Jewishness strengthened his resolve to be a good soldier. Geller was lucky in this regard. The army sent him to the battlefield he most cared about: the European theater.

Jewish political activists calibrated their response to Pearl Harbor, the war, and military service according to a different calculus than that of Geller, Kahn, Walters, or Dash and the Dragons. Just as Dash's opposition to antisemitism did not depend upon politics, Geller's political consciousness did not sprout from a left-wing ideology. However, socialist, communist, and Zionist ideologies dictated the reactions of an articulate minority of American Jews. Outspoken and self-conscious about their actions and the meaning of what they did, they were willing to agitate on behalf of their beliefs. Hitler, Mussolini, and Hirohito all represented the face of the Axis powers and a reviled fascism, but Nazism occupied a primary position because it explicitly linked fascism and antisemitism. This linkage made defeat of the Third Reich the crucial struggle. Liberating Europe concerned these ideological activist Jews more than avenging Pearl Harbor. However, other related political issues also influenced their assessment of what they should do.

The attack on Pearl Harbor made the Soviet Union, a formerly suspect government, an ally of the United States, a situation that simultaneously amazed and heartened many Jewish communists. Now their commitments as radicals, Americans, and Jews converged. They were eager to fight: as political radicals dedicated to revolutionizing the world, as loyal Americans devoted to defending their country, and as Jews suffering persecution.[50] In an unanticipated but certainly not unwelcome development, the war moved Jewish communists from what had been a dissenting fringe in American politics toward its liberal wing. Aspects of the popular front reappeared. At a "progressive" nightclub frequented by left-wing Jews, the kind that boasted an integrated audience of blacks and whites, a song caught on: "Open up that second front, that second front."[51] Communists and fellow travelers vociferously advocated the opening of a second front in Europe to ease the intense pressure on the Russians who were fighting Germany. Many left-wing Jews enlisted with enthusiasm.

Harold Freeman's left-wing political commitments gradually overcame his initial reluctance to fight. Married but without children, he drew a high number in the army draft lottery and breathed a sigh of relief. In 1942 he managed to get a civilian job with the Army Signal Corps. He expected that he would be among the fortunate ones who would never be drafted. But in the middle of 1943, as he watched the war from afar, he slowly had a change of heart. As he put it, "After years of shooting my mouth off about fighting fascism I now felt I should be fighting fascism by shooting with a gun."[52] Freeman acted on his convictions. He went to see his draft board in Brighton Beach, Brooklyn, to inquire when he could expect to be called up. They checked his records and told him he had an exemption. Freeman had never applied for an exemption, but his office had. With manpower at a premium, Freeman's superiors wanted to hold on to him to train new personnel, mostly women, and provide a measure of stability. Learning of his status made Freeman uncomfortable, and he told the draft board that he did not want the exemption.[53] Without it, he was quickly called up. In December 1943 he was inducted into the Army and got his rifle.[54]

Leftists like Freeman rejected the isolationism and pacifism that anti-Stalinist socialists maintained even after Pearl Harbor. He spurned the arguments that World War II was "a war between two great imperialist camps" for world domination, a view popular in some socialist circles. Although Freeman recognized that the United States and Great Britain were capitalist countries, he emphasized their common opposition to fascism, a demonic evil far greater than capitalism. But dedicated socialists insisted that this war was not their war. When Philip Rahv, editor of the left-wing literary journal *Partisan Review,* questioned that analysis in the issue of November-December 1941, he was upbraided by Irving Howe, a younger and more doctrinaire socialist. For the twenty-two-year-old Howe, the war remained an imperialist one, with little discernible difference between the Allies and the Axis.[55] The real choice was socialism or barbarism.[56] The poet Delmore Schwartz called the war "obscene" in 1942. The eagerness of "hundreds" who rushed "to wrap themselves in the flag" revolted him. "Now we will have a war until every Chinaman has to buy Gillette blades or lose his self-respect," he lamented.[57] These Jewish socialist ideologues did not lose sight of their Marxist analysis even in the face of Hitler and even after some of them entered military service.[58]

Unlike radicals on the left, a cadre of American Zionists thought not only about fascism, communism, socialism, and imperialism, but also about Jewish national liberation. The war against the Axis was only the initial battle in their pursuit of Jewish political independence. Once the Nazis were defeated, there would be a second fight for a Jewish state. "It seems more and more apparent that after Victory," wrote one young Zionist soldier in December 1943, "we Jews will still have to face a long and bitter struggle to establish Palestine as our national home and safeguard the rights of Jews everywhere."[59] A few self-conscious Zionist activists thought of entering military service in part as training for the second difficult conflict yet to come. They could learn skills in the American armed forces, not just how to fight but also how to fly planes, operate tanks, and navigate ships. Then, after the war, they could apply their knowledge on behalf of the future epic campaign for Jewish sovereignty.[60]

Consciousness of events in Europe depended not only on politics but also on age. Jews who entered military service early in the war, in 1942, could recall Kristallnacht, the Nazi rampage in November 1938 that sent synagogues throughout Germany up in flames and shipped Jews by thousands to concentration camps. They could also remember hearing of Nazi roundups that forced Polish Jews into ghettos in 1940. Politically engaged Jews recruited in 1943 or 1944 were already aware of Hitler's war against the Jews. News of the Final Solution had been broadcast widely in November 1942. Then in April 1943 they heard stories of heroic resistance by doomed Warsaw Ghetto fighters.[61] By contrast, younger recruits possessed a more fragmentary knowledge of the history of Jewish persecution by the Nazis, unless they were politically aware teenagers.

Jewish attitudes toward military service ran the gamut from fervent patriotism to elaborate efforts to avoid a uniform despite the influence exerted by politics and prejudice. Although Jews saw issues concerning the war differently from other Americans, the vast majority, like most Americans, knew that if they were the right age, they would be drafted. They might hope for deferments and pray that the war end quickly, but relatively few actually sought out defense work or exemptions. A handful chose the security of the 4-D deferment scorned by Victor Geller. Studying medicine was an attractive alternate path to service during wartime if one had the aptitude. "Half the student body at [Johns] Hopkins during World War II was pre-med," Robert Kotlowitz wrote with candor; "it was a respectable way of evading the draft."[62] Yet a disinclination to volunteer and a certain envy of those who escaped military service did not translate into avoiding one's duty when called. Many American Jews preferred to leave the decision about whether and when to don a uniform to fate.

Fate meant the draft board. When the call came they went, or they raced to enlist. One Dragon, Artie Kolin, delayed his decision until October 1942. Then, with the draft breathing down his neck and most of his buddies already in uniform, he took the subway to Grand Central Palace on Lexington Avenue and 44th Street to enlist. The Army Air Corps appealed to him, even if he didn't have the college education to apply for cadet training. Kolin figured he would be a mechanic. He was good with his hands; he had worked with his father in his window cleaning business and with his brother waxing floors. He joined up because he didn't want to get drafted into the Army. He was sure they would put him into the infantry — not an unreasonable assumption — and he didn't want an infantryman's lot. Tall and athletic, with red hair and freckles, Kolin "wasn't about to look to carry a gun" on his shoulder. Nor did he want to start shouldering a pack on his back. He figured that if he went into the air corps, at least he would be sitting down in an airplane.[63]

Just as the draft drove Kolin into the Army Air Corps, it

pushed Merv Reines into the Marines. Initially Reines had wanted the Navy's V-12 program because he thought he would acquire a good education there. But his widowed mother wasn't eager to see him in uniform, so he deferred to her wishes. Then in February 1942 she called him up at Penn State where he was studying engineering. "I got draft cards," she told her son. They summoned him to report on a future date. So she said, "You do what you want now." Free to enlist, Reines went to New York to try for the Navy but, like Dash, he didn't succeed. When Reines returned to Penn State's campus, however, he discovered that the Marine recruiter was interested. He told Reines to "meet me in Pittsburgh," where he could take the physical exam for the Marine officer candidate class. Accepted as a Marine, he went home to Long Island and reported to his draft board. When he explained the situation the board was furious. "You can't do that!" "Well, I did it," Reines replied. He took his card out and showed them. They had lost a draftee and the Marines had gained a future officer.[64]

Such scenes were replayed over and over throughout the United States. A little more than a year after Pearl Harbor, all of the Dragons were in uniform except for Bernie Miller, who was working for Pan American Airlines in Miami as a mechanic. (The draft would soon snag him too.)[65] Several joined up for the choices offered rather than taking a chance with the draft. A few were training to be officers. Most were in the Army. Aside from Dash, only two other Dragons joined the Navy, one as a pilot. Uncle Sam recruited Jews whose grandparents were born in the United States as well as recent refugees from Nazism not yet eligible for citizenship. As in the population as a whole, scarcely a Jewish family existed that did not have a son or a brother, a father or an uncle, in the service.[66] Quite a few had sisters or daughters in uniform as well.[67] Jews served their country, as did other Americans. This war was their war as much as anyone else's.

By 1943 the pace of mobilization reached boys who had been teenagers when they heard the news of Pearl Harbor. By 1945 the draft recruited Jews who had celebrated their bar mitzvah when the Germans invaded Poland. Jerome Minkow graduated from DeWitt Clinton High School in the Bronx in January 1945 to a steady stream of parental tears. Fear and anguish filled the hall, distressing the graduates. Middle-class parents, well aware of the frightful casualties in the recent Battle of the Bulge, watched their sons graduate into military service. Over three-quarters of the commencement class of 450 boys were going into the army the next day. Minkow had turned eighteen in December. For his birthday he received a Magen David (Star of David) to wear around his neck. Six weeks later, he was inducted into the military. The change happened so quickly that he could scarcely comprehend it.[68]

Both the draft and the enthusiasm of their peers pushed Jews to join up to defend their country. Patriotism inspired them. Adventure lured them. A new masculinity beckoned them. They left their Jewish families and the neighborhood ambience with its communal values. Most of them departed with their parents' blessings and prayers.

For Jews like Geller and Kahn, Walters and Freeman, politics and Jewish identity figured in their decision to fight. Jewish imperatives honed the edge of their American patriotism. Some of them deliberately subverted their family's desires to keep them out of military service. They overcame obstacles to fulfill their ambition to become American fighters. Such Jews understood the war as a battle against a generic oppressive fascism, but even more against a specific Nazism. It was a war for freedom and democracy, a just war, and thus a good war. Most important, it was their war. Hitler's Jewish survivors would be freed, his victims avenged. Watching newreels of Nazi soliders humiliating and abusing Austrian Jews, Artie Kolin fumed. "As a Jew, naturally," he confessed, "you'd like to see this guy dead."[69] Now he was going to put on a uniform that would turn such sentiments into action. The beast's heart should be cut out. Even as metaphor, such fury was new to these young men. It would be tempered by the imminent reality of basic training.

Both groups of Jews, those pushed by peers and those pulled by passion (and some by a mixture of both), entered military service and moved from their civilian individuality to military sameness. In confronting the demands of the armed forces, it did not matter how they had been recruited or what political beliefs they held. The transition from civilian to soldier dominated all who traded the constraints of family for the regime of the barracks. They left behind their peer group of friends for one of strangers. Although most would make new friends among their comrades in arms, some would never overcome completely the alienation from their former selves that military service entailed. The armed forces lifted Jews out of their familiar neighborhoods and transported them to sections of the United States they barely knew existed. In the process, their sense of what it meant to be Jewish would change. No longer would Jewishness be a natural part of the air they breathed, the food they ate, and the words they spoke. No longer would Jewishness pervade the rhythms of work and leisure. Inducted into the vast American military world, Jews would begin to discover their difference.

3

EATING HAM FOR UNCLE SAM

Ikey, Mikey, Jakey, Sam
We're the boys that eat no ham.
We're all in the Army now
So we're eating ham for Uncle Sam.

—Basketball Cheer[1]

JULY 11, 1942. Family, friends, and neighbors gathered at the modest attached house on 44th Street in Borough Park, Brooklyn, to say goodbye. As mobilization reached into intimate neighborhoods and summoned young men to military service, what would become a ritual still seemed new and awkward in the summer of '42. In the morning Herbert Walters would be leaving for Fort Dix. He sat on the front porch with some of the guys who hadn't yet gone into the service. Smells from the flowers blooming in the backyard garden filled the air. His sister Rita was in the kitchen with the women. Though he joked with his friends, the atmosphere was tense. Walters was eager to enter the armed forces, but was nervous nonetheless, especially around his family. His departure was difficult for his immigrant parents. Over the male talk and banter he could hear sobs drifting through the kitchen window. Then Mrs. Levy, his next-door neighbor, came over. She brought a gift, a gold chain with a Jewish symbol. It looked like a mezuza, the small narrow object that Jews affix to the right-hand side of the doorframes of their

49

home. A mezuza contains a parchment scroll that holds several verses from the Torah. Mrs. Levy's present had no scroll inside but was meant to provide protection, like an amulet. Jewish women pressed such gifts upon young men heading for war, just as their Italian and Irish neighbors gave medallions of guardian saints.[2] The amulet was meant to keep the young man unharmed and to bring him home alive. Mrs. Levy insisted that Herbie put it around his neck. He did, although he had never worn anything like it.[3] The gift, a tangible connection to family and neighborhood, would help, in times of need, to remind him of his people.

A month before he was called up for his midshipman's course, Martin Dash received a very different gift from his American-born father, Charles. He convinced Marty to join the Masonic order in the belief that the fellowship that came from membership in the brotherhood could fortify him if there should be incidents of antisemitism abroad. His father was an active Mason and favored its fraternalism over any religious alternative. Marty agreed that it might be useful, an extra shield.[4] Going into military service as a Jew, it was impossible to anticipate whether one's peers would accept one.[5] A little extra protection, whether from a mezuza or a Masonic membership, could not be spurned by young men.

"Greetings." An envelope in the mailbox changed everything. "You are hereby ordered for induction into the Armed Forces of the United States . . ."[6] Anticipated or not, these envelopes jolted recipients and their families. It didn't matter if the notice came early in the war or during what would be its last year. Every young recruit had to prepare to say goodbye to an accustomed past. Jews entered military service without any precedents to guide them. So their parents improvised, doing their best to prepare their sons for the unfamiliar ordeal by giving them gifts of Jewish connections.

Artie Gorenstein said goodbye to his parents, Saul and Lillian, and his little sister Judith on a hot summer day in July 1944. He knew the moment was coming because he had enlisted in the Army Reserves when he turned eighteen in February. That decision allowed him to complete his freshman year of Hebrew studies at the Teacher's Institute of Yeshiva College while he took a battery of Army tests. Gorenstein hoped to qualify for cadet training in the Army Air Corps. Although math and physics were not his strong suit, he scored well enough to be accepted into the cadet program with its long preflight training period. His parents were happy about his achievement, but nervous. He was their oldest, and their only son. Despite his slight build, at five feet eight he stood taller than his foreign-born father. With brown straight hair and sparkling blue eyes, Gorenstein appeared to his proud parents to be the very image of an American pilot, or navigator, or bombardier.[7]

Like all parents, Saul and Lillian worried about their son. They wanted him to succeed in the military as he had in school. More than that, as socialist Zionists they feared the isolation he would encounter as a Jew in the armed forces. They had experienced discrimination in the workplace and outside it. Many Americans did not like Jews, even if they had never met one. So his parents scoured the mimeographed list of forty other sons called up to report on July 24th. They were looking for Jewish-sounding names from Brooklyn. When they found one, Saul got on the telephone with Lillian standing beside him. It didn't take long to get to the point. You have a son going into the service. We have a son going into the service. "Why don't we have the sons meet?" Mr. Fiedelbaum agreed: "We're gonna drive our son down to the reception center at Fort Dix in New Jersey. We could all go down together." The Gorensteins were ecstatic. So the two families piled into the Fiedelbaums' car for the trip across to Jersey. The Fiedelbaums were clearly more prosperous; after all, they owned a car. But class took a back seat in the face of military service. More important was their common denominator. Both Allen Fiedelbaum and Arthur Gorenstein were going to be Jewish GIs.[8]

Walters, Dash, and Gorenstein all received parting presents designed to protect them that reflected their families' different understandings of Jewishness.[9] Mrs. Levy's mezuza amulet summoned the God of Israel to shield Walters. It assumed that his Jewish identity was primarily religious, although Walters did not consider himself observant. By contrast, Dash's special Masonic membership put its trust in a formal fraternalism that crossed religious and ethnic boundaries, a secular notion of brotherhood open to Jews and gentiles alike. It assumed an ethnic Jewish identity that could be subordinated to a more inclusive and universal fraternity. The Gorensteins placed their faith in an explicit sense of Jewish peoplehood, where Jewishness overrode personal differences. Each gift represented a common recognition on the part of parents that their sons were leaving a safe Jewish home and entering a potentially perilous gentile world. Jewishness, which had suffused the atmosphere of neighborhood and work, friends and family, now would shrink to a solitary identity. Military service involved dangers more threatening than living among gentiles, of course, but parents could do little about those perils. So they focused on what was possible, as they saw it: how to protect their sons from the inevitable difficulties of making their way as Jews among strangers. The sons, far more at ease in America than their parents, accepted the presents without a great deal of thought, much as they had always taken what their parents had given them for granted. They were leaving home as American men, ready to do their duty and serve their country. They did not imagine that they would need the extra protection, not realizing that they were embarking on a journey that would transform their understanding of themselves as Americans, as Jews, and as men.

As soon as he arrived at Fort Dix, Artie Gorenstein began to write letters home. "With only ten hours under my belt, I can't really give you a fair impression of 'army life,'" he acknowledged. Still, he recorded his observations of the reception center. First he noted "the immensity of things." Only four companies used one mess hall with a seating capacity of five hundred. But he waited in line three-quarters of an hour before finally getting into the hall. Then he tried to allay his folks' concerns. "People are human," he wrote. "They are naturally friendly."[10] And he wanted to stay in touch. Letters became a lifeline to loved ones, to family and friends, helping to relieve the loneliness. Lillian and Saul spoke and wrote English well, which made communication with their son relatively easy. But for immigrant parents who were often more comfortable in Yiddish than English, military service separated them from their second-generation sons, who rarely knew how to write Yiddish. This was Herbert Walters' situation. In his eagerness to leave his law firm to join the army, Walters hadn't thought that the written word would be a problem. Since his youngest sister still lived at home, he addressed all his letters to "Mom, Dad, and Naomi." Naomi was the one who replied. His mother couldn't write English, and although his father knew English, he did not take up the task of writing letters.[11] Martin Dash's father Charlie, a skilled typist, eagerly shouldered the responsibility for staying in touch. He wanted to maintain his son's ties with home and neighborhood. So he started to write a weekly letter to all of the Dragons, keeping them up to date with one another's fortunes.[12] *The Dragon Weekly* connected the far-flung friends with news of promotions and furloughs, milestones passed in basic training, courtships and marriages. It reinforced bonds of boyhood friendship despite the separation necessitated by military service.[13]

Artie Gorenstein wanted his parents to share his experiences, and they were eager to know how he was doing. So he chronicled the daily routine. Reveille sounded at 5:30 A.M. "The dawn came and the bugle blew and in the fifteen required minutes your son had dressed washed made his bed put his personal stuff in order and was out in formation," he breathlessly wrote on his first day in camp. Gorenstein hadn't received his uniform yet, but he did eat breakfast. And breakfast proved to be his first ordeal in becoming a soldier. Facing the new recruits were "orange juice, milk, coffee, wheaties, toast and ham 'n' eggs." A regular, hearty American breakfast. He "plowed through everything except the ham and eggs. Hesitated a minute and remembered the five long hours until lunch." And then he dug into the *treyf* (forbidden) combination. "It was horrible," he admitted to his parents, "but with the help of the coffee I swallowed it much as one would an aspirin."[14]

If reveille awoke young American men to the reality of military service, army food alerted many Jews to the fact of their difference. "Eating ham for Uncle Sam" challenged identities absorbed in their mother's kitchens. Forcing down *treyf* food like ham and pork was only the beginning of the problem. If one habitually or ritually observed the prohibition against the mixing of meat and dairy dishes or various kosher strictures, the complications multiplied.[15] Jews who had grown up in kosher homes often found unkosher food revolting. Although Gorenstein was hardly an observant Jew, he found it difficult to swallow pig products. So he tried another strategy with pork chops, gener-

Artie Gorenstein outside the barracks at Appalachicola, Florida, 1945. Until that first Army breakfast, Gorenstein, like many Jewish recruits, had not realized how his Jewish identity was lodged in the mundane realm of food. He was ready to pass into the ranks, but at mealtimes the Army kept on reminding him of his difference.

ally served on Sundays. Pretending that they were lamb chops, he carefully cut away all of the fat. He identified fat with pig. Then he cut into the chop. After several bites, he gave up. He wanted to resemble other GIs and enjoy the Sunday fare, but neither masquerade nor self-deception worked. Much as he tried to overcome an aversion no longer sustained by religious belief, he couldn't.[16] The experience surprised him. He had not expected that it would be so difficult to violate the bounds of ritual purity. Until that first American breakfast, he had not realized how firmly his Jewish identity was lodged in the mundane realm of food. A socialist Zionist and activist in the youth movement Habonim (the builders), Gorenstein had assumed that ideology and politics determined his American Jewish identity.

Observant Jews self-consciously steeled themselves for the ordeal of violating the commandments.[17] They knew, as Paul Steinfeld did, that eating kosher food in the army was out of the question. The son of Lithuanian immigrants, Steinfeld had grown up in the Bronx and spoke both fluent Yiddish and Hebrew. His comprehensive religious education included Zionism and emphasized intellectualism and culture. When the draft caught up with him in 1944, he was twenty-four, a college graduate, married to his high school sweetheart, Lillian, and employed by the Bureau of the Census in Washington, D.C. Steinfeld brought the same pragmatic skepticism to military service that had characterized his outlook as an undergraduate back in the Great Hall of City College. At that time he had taken the Oxford Oath but questioned its meaning. Now he prepared to vault another hurdle. "You're gonna learn to be a soldier and that's it!" he admonished himself. The test occurred immediately, while he was at Fort Dix, the reception center. As he came through the still unfamiliar mess line, the server threw something down on his plate. Steinfeld recalled thinking, "This must be a pork chop." He reminded himself, "You gotta learn to live with this stuff." The next thing he knew, a KP server took a pad of butter and dropped it onto the pork chop. That was too much. Steinfeld "had trouble not vomiting." He had girded himself to face down the pork chop. But the butter, as he politely put it, "really violated my sensitivities."[18]

Getting over the pig was often the first hurdle that Jews confronted in their transformation into military men. American soldiers didn't flinch at pork chops. Nor did they swallow their ham and eggs as if it were medicine. Gorenstein and Steinfeld were ready to serve their country like the other GIs, but at mealtime the army reminded them of their Jewishness. They sought refuge in the ritual behavior of the regular guy. The recruits they chatted with over breakfast or dinner would not know that they were struggling to consume *treyf* without complaint. A man with such grit was strengthened to navigate the obstacle course of military training. Ready to pass into the ranks, Gorenstein and Steinfeld appeared to be like any other soldier. Or so they thought. However, they did have foreign-sounding names. Moreover, they came from the city, not the country. But their goal was integration. They knew they needed to be accepted by the men in their unit. Ultimately, their life might depend upon it.

Herbert Walters had no problem with ham or pork. He reveled in his new American identity at Fort Dix. There were a couple of college guys in his barracks, and one of them had brought a football. To pass the time they all went outside and tossed the ball around. Walters enjoyed talking to these college guys and playing football together. Educational background mattered more at the reception center, he thought, than where you were from, since most of the men came from the New York metropolitan area. After the football they came back inside to shower. Walters walked down to his barracks bed, naked, with just the mezuza hanging around his neck. One of the fellows asked, "What's that?" Walters tried to explain what it was and in the process revealed his Jewish background. "From that point on they turned away." Walters found their behavior incomprehensible.[19] Bewildered and hurt, Walters didn't take the mezuza off, but the incident made him wonder about Jewish difference. He had gone into the service as an American. Now his fellow GIs were reminding him that he was a Jew.

Jerome Minkow had received a similar gift from his aunt for his eighteenth birthday. A good-looking, tall, self-confident teenager, with thick black hair and brown eyes, he entered the service right out of high school wearing the gift, a Jewish star, around his neck. For the next two years he found himself in a fight "every ten days." The Magen David provoked antisemitic remarks, and Minkow had a short fuse. But like Walters, he didn't take it off. To do so would be to repudiate his family and his Jewishness.[20] Still, the antagonism provoked by the amulet disturbed him. He struggled to figure out what his fellow GIs expected him to do.

The Magen David and mezuza marked Jewish bodies more effectively than circumcision. In Europe, the practice of circumcision had distinguished Jewish men from Christians.[21] In the United States, by contrast, because middle-class parents, Christian and Jew alike, favored routine medical circumcision for health reasons, Jewish bodies bore no singular characteristics. "There is very little affect attached to circumcision in branding a man as a Jew," reported a study of Jewish soldiers in 1951. "Rather it has become a class point in America and most middle class men under the age of forty have been routinely circumcised in infancy." Furthermore, *"In terms of physical appearance,* young Jews who have grown up in the orange juice and codliver oil tradition are no longer undersized, underweight or stoop-shouldered in the stereotype manner of fifty years ago."[22] When all this was combined with Jewish participation in sports, little in their physique set Jews apart from their barracks mates. The average height of GIs in 1943 was over five feet eight inches, although infantrymen averaged almost an inch less.[23] Basic training built Jewish bodies. Writing home to his parents in Sioux Falls, South Dakota, Ira Koplow enthused over the large meals and the weight he was gaining: five pounds in a couple of weeks, eight pounds even before basic training started, twelve pounds in two months, and eventually twenty-two pounds, bringing his weight up to 130.[24] Jews at the other end of the physical spectrum, tall and hefty, soon learned how military service brought their physiques closer to the norm. When Merv Reines, a big man, received his Marine Corps uniform he was puzzled. "Lieutenant," he said, "this uniform doesn't fit me." "Don't worry," the lieutenant replied. "In a few days that uniform will be just right." The lieutenant was wrong. Under the rigorous regimen of basic training, Reines lost a lot of weight. The uniform was soon too large.[25]

If Jewish physiques proved less different than some Jews had feared before entering the armed forces, Jewish ethnic culture loomed larger than anyone had anticipated. All those aspects of urban life that Jews took for granted, that had shaped their understanding of themselves as young men, acquired new meanings in military service. Jews encountered regional stereotypes at odds with their own experiences and self-perceptions. As mobilization gathered momentum and scattered the population across the continent, regional differences entered military culture, with New York City typecast both as ethnic and as cosmopolitan. By 1943 war movies pictured the ideal infantry platoon as a melting pot, with at least one person each from Texas, the

Midwest, and Brooklyn.[26] Brooklyn represented a typical urban community. Someone from Brooklyn was surely a white ethnic, which usually meant either a Catholic or a Jew. New York Jews were supposed to be loud-mouthed smart alecks, talkative and brainy, but incompetent around machinery. Jerome Minkow, who had grown up in the Bronx, quickly learned to his surprise that GIs thought of New Yorkers as sophisticates. At eighteen, he didn't consider himself particularly cultured.[27] Sure, New Yorkers lived in a big city, with theaters and museums. Many loved classical music, tuned into Philharmonic broadcasts over the radio when they could, and read books and poetry for the fun of it.[28] But most of the Dragons preferred swing and popular music to classical concerts.

Jewish GIs' actual experiences of New York collided with popular perceptions that saw New York as synonymous with the skyscrapers of Manhattan. The truth, as Minkow understood it, was that "most of us who were raised in the boroughs, really lived in small towns. You lived in a small neighborhood that was generally influenced by your high school, your schoolyard, a candy store, a shopping street."[29] Minkow's account charts the geographic and emotional coordinates of a Jewish teenager growing up in the city. Religious or secular, it made no difference. Minkow went to public school, Victor Geller to Yeshiva. Still, Geller estimated that "outside of school, we spent most of our time within an area of twenty-four square blocks, from 161st Street north to 167th Street and from Jerome Avenue east to the Grand Concourse." On those streets Jewish teenagers "had little access to anonymity," supposedly one of the premier traits of urban life. These young men were constantly visible to the close-knit community; as Geller put it, "our accountability followed us like a shadow."[30] In contrast to the Bronx, "Manhattan existed as a place your parents worked in," Minkow recalled, "or a place

Jerome Minkow outside the switchboard exchange of his regiment in the Philippines, 1945. "Basic training was an incredible revelation," Minkow acknowledged. It taught him to see himself as an American Jewish man through the eyes of others.

you went when you cut school, or if you went on a prom." So "when you went into the service and they knew you were from New York, they expected amazing things from you," Minkow reflected.[31] It was hard to live up to expectations, especially contradictory ones.

It was also difficult just to blend in with other soldiers because Jewish notions of masculinity were seemingly dissimilar. As Minkow put it, "now just speaking sexually, you would run into kids from Iowa and Kansas who had been having sexual relations since they were fourteen." Minkow exaggerates a bit to make a point. Most of the guys that he knew, "at eighteen were still virgins because there's no place to go. So it's basically a very naive, unsophisticated group of kids that go into the service during the war," he concluded.[32] Barracks talk abounded in sexual exploits and vulgar bravado, especially after a night off in town. What kind of a man could a Jew be if he hadn't had sex by the age of eighteen and didn't know how to drive a car? As sophisticates or as loud ethnics, New Yorkers were supposed to be experienced, worldly; but in fact many Jews had lived relatively sheltered lives in the big city.[33] Even sports figured differently for urban Jews. Minkow remembers once playing a game of baseball when he slid hard into second base. "Why d'you do that?" the guys asked. "You could hurt somebody." "Well, it's the game," he replied, confused by their criticism. This was how he had played baseball in the Bronx, hard and competitive.[34] It was a way of demonstrating one's masculinity. But it didn't sit well with his fellow GIs. He, and many other New York Jews, were seen as different. And those differences lay as much beneath the surface, in attitudes and experiences that had shaped their personalities, as in external characteristics. External behaviors could be changed.[35] One could forgo music or books, learn to bite one's tongue when tempted to make a glib remark, not insist on driving home a point in an argument in an effort to fit in.[36] But the sense of being a Jewish man with all its attendant values was harder to relinquish, especially when the armed forces appeared to send mixed messages to Jewish recruits, integrating them on the one hand and on the other reminding them sharply of their difference.

America turned out not to resemble the country that Jewish GIs knew from civics classes, geography books, news reports, and movies. New York was not America. Coming to grips with this basic fact challenged their assumptions of where they fit into the American panorama. Artie Gorenstein, who had lived in Chelsea, Massachusetts, and Washington, D.C., as well as New York City, kept a log of his impressions on the forty-nine-hour trip in an Army Air Corps troop Pullman down to basic training in Mississippi. Pennsylvania was familiar, but the industrialization around Columbus, Ohio, including "an airplane factory that took a good ten minutes to pass it was so long," warranted comment. So did "one-street towns" and the hills of Kentucky, "like the choppy ocean or the dunes on Revere Beach. The crowns of the hill are brown, rock and dead grass. But the valleys are filled with trees and greeness [*sic*]. The result is almost a checkerboard." Then came the backwoods of Kentucky with its "primitive farmhouses — a ramshackle clapboard hut with a series of additions, each one about a generation older than the previous, as if the house was being expanded as the family brood grows. A dirt yard surrounds this with a pigpen near that. The pigs run around and it seems as though the liter [*sic*] of children run around much the same way," he commented. The comparison was telling. Gorenstein had been around, but this was not life as he knew it. In Alabama, near the Gulf of Mexico, he wrote about the "thick foliage. It's all swampy and every so often we pass over a wide muddy river." The contrast and injustice of "beautiful southern homes" near "the most wretched sharecroppers' hovels" also caught his eye. A socialist Zionist like his parents, Gorenstein paid attention to disparities of class.[37] The trip gave him a broad and detailed sense that much of America was foreign to his experiences and alien to Jewishness.

Herbert Walters vividly remembered his trip to basic training in the Army Air Corps because, like many GIs, he had not journeyed beyond his hometown before he was inducted and shipped across the United States. He referred to life before the service as "secluded," consisting of home, school, and work, and not extending much beyond Brooklyn and Manhattan. When the army assigned him to the Air Corps, he "took the first train ride" of his life. He "had never been on a railroad before," and was "excited about traveling. We didn't know where we were going." Curious, he stayed up all night because he was sleeping in a real Pullman for the first time. The trip to basic training remained with him for the rest of his life. Every time the train pulled into a station, he lifted the little blind on the Pullman "to see where the hell" he was. He read names like Harrisburg, Pennsylvania, and Richmond, Virginia. He was thrilled. Early in the morning the train pulled into a town called Clearwater, a short distance out of St. Petersburg on the west coast of Florida. The men "trucked to what must have been the most palatial, rich, fancy resort area surrounding a golf course with individual bungalows and swimming pools which the Air Corps had taken over." Walters was stunned. This was the Army? "The golf course became our first training ground and we lived in these bungalows. Of course all the furniture had been cleared out and the Army had put up the double deckers." But that was home. Palm trees, utterly new to him, amazed him. "Gorgeous!" he exclaimed.[38]

The incongruity of basic training in an elegant resort heightened Walters' sense of dislocation. He "had never been exposed

*Herbert Walters in Manila, the Philippines, 1945. As a mi-
nority of one, the only Jewish man in his unit, Walters
struggled to fit in with the other men, his comrades, fellow
Americans. He felt doubly displaced as an urban, working-
class Jew.*

to living with gentiles like that, or even associating with them."
Now he was doing basic training among gentiles in upper-class
surroundings. He felt doubly displaced. The situation brought
back echoes of his discomfort around the wealthy men of his law
firm. Soon enough, the singularity of his minority status was

clarified for Walters and for every other recruit. The moment came when "they had to get information for the dog tags." The men assembled, "about 150 guys under a shady tree." Then the training sergeant announced that he needed to know the religion of each recruit. Walters didn't think much of it. But when the sergeant called out for the Jews, no one stood up except Walters. Out of 150 guys, he "was the only Jew."[39] Most of the others were southerners. They stared at him. No matter what he did, he remained a curiosity to them. As a minority of one, Walters struggled to fit in with the men in his unit, his comrades, his fellow Americans. It was difficult, but he managed.[40]

"Basic training was an incredible revelation," Jerome Minkow acknowledged. It taught him to see himself as an American Jewish man through the eyes of others. The mirror held up to him seemed terribly distorted, but Minkow couldn't figure out how best to correct his fellow GIs' perceptions. He remembered an older guy — and "older" in the army meant mid- to late twenties — from Memphis. The man asked Minkow to sign his name "because he wanted to show the people back home what a Jew's signature was like." What could that possibly mean? Minkow didn't understand why a Jew was such an oddity. He had imagined himself in the American grain. He grew up on Andy Hardy and John Wayne movies. Doing basic infantry training at Camp Blanding, Florida, and living with men recruited from across the country undermined many of his assumptions. The men were not as he had imagined from the motion pictures. At times their accents were so thick that a fellow from Maine could barely communicate with a guy from Texas. He struggled to fathom his fellow GIs' attitude toward Jews. And he suffered as a distinct minority. In his "company of 200 guys there were two Jews. The other guy hid someplace," he recalled with bitterness. As he remembered, "Everything sort of centered on me." But he had "gone into the Army with a great deal of self-confidence" and it "really kicked the shit" out of him. Every time he thought he had the Jewish issue figured out, that he knew what to do in the Army, he got sideswiped.

One night on maneuvers Minkow was on guard duty when out of the blue, "a bunch of the Irish kids" surprised him, attacked him, and tied him up. When the Lieutenant found out about it, he asked Minkow, "Why didn't you hit 'em with your gun?" Shocked, Minkow replied, "What?" So the officer repeated his suggestion. "Yeah," he said. "Why didn't you hit 'em with the gun?" Minkow was flabbergasted. It hadn't occurred to him. They weren't the enemy but fellow American soldiers. "You know how heavy a gun butt is?" he asked rhetorically. But the officer's query was so natural, implying "that's what a man would do. Ya know, ya just hit the other person with a rifle." As Minkow realized, "Good God, you could kill somebody if you hit 'em with a rifle." Of course, he "hadn't been taught yet to kill."

That came later in basic training at the point when "you do a particular exercise with live ammunition. And what you do is you run and you fall down. You aim your gun." Well, Minkow ran, fell down, and aimed his gun, "right in the back of a head" of one of his worst enemies. The guy turned around and pleaded, "Minkow don't! Minkow don't!" And Minkow smiled. It was just a moment, but it left a sweet memory.[41] Minkow was not yet ready to settle any grudges with such force. But he was learning new ways of thinking about himself as an American man. The army was teaching him to be a tough soldier even as its version of masculinity produced a heightened awareness of his own Jewish difference.

Basic training thrust Jews into what Minkow calls "a peculiar situation."[42] They had to learn how to live as an inconspicuous minority — a difficult task for most New York Jews, whose occa-

sional directness tripped them up in the military. How could
they subordinate their Jewishness when it infused their speech
and body language, their cultural preferences and tastes, their
whole sense of self?

Antisemitism further complicated matters. Jews knew the
anti-Jewish stereotypes: they were not reputed to make good
soldiers; they were accused of being cowardly and manipulative;
they had a nasty reputation for slyness; they supposedly lacked
leadership skills. Stereotypes were layered in complex combina-
tions. Rural Protestants tended to locate their opinions about
Irish and Italian Catholics as well as Jews along a common urban
axis. But many Jews had a separate history with Irish guys. In
Minkow's previous experience, antisemitism "mostly came from
one group and that was the Irish kids." No matter the neighborhood, "there always seemed to be one or two blocks of Irish
kids."[43] Conflict between Jews and Catholics erupted on the
streets of Brooklyn and the Bronx in the 1930s. But this basic
"part of growing up" mattered less on an individual than a collective level. The Jews were "us" and the others were "them."

Now military service was reconfiguring "us." Jews had to live
with Catholics around the clock, not to mention southern Protestants. Many Jews held their own unpleasant stereotypes about
Catholics and rural southerners and would have to learn to suppress or change their attitudes. Jewish recruits would have to
posit a sufficient difference between themselves and African
Americans to allow them to identify with their barracks mates,
finding in a shared white American identity a basis of kinship
and friendship with Catholics and southerners.

Not all Jews felt singled out during basic training. Some discovered a sense of their own competence and liked their comrades.[44] The experience of acceptance impressed many Jews, as
did the feeling of being a citizen soldier in a democratic mili-

tary.[45] Arthur Gorenstein enthusiastically described a conversation on the train down to basic training with the captain, who "sat down with the group and we all gathered around and just talked." Being treated as one among many pleased him greatly. He concluded, "a thing like that is extraordinary in this army, and in a way it is typical of the air corps."[46] Attempting to fit in was harder for some than for others. Often it was a matter of luck, age, or temperament. Lillian Gorenstein praised her son for his "good personality." She summed up two approaches among her neighbors' Jewish sons in the armed forces: "Mrs. Weinstein's son is very unhappy and constantly complains," she wrote in an early letter. On the other hand, Mrs. Chaplin's son "grins and says 'oh well' or 'what do you expect' and does the best he can anyway."[47] Artie Gorenstein, for his part, credited luck for his relatively successful "fitting in," a fairly widespread view among GIs. Then again, he did basic training with Fiedelbaum, and they became friends. Saul and Lillian's strategy had worked. Their son was not completely alone. He had someone to go into town with. Knowing another Jew was a comfort and helped ease the isolation that Jews often felt as minorities of one or two or three in their unit.[48]

Jews who came from small cities usually had fewer difficulties. They had grown up as a minority and were used to living among Christians. Ira Koplow, whose father had served in World War I, spent two years at the University of Missouri before enlisting in 1942. He understood that he lived in a predominantly gentile world in the army as he had all his life in Sioux Falls. He had nice words about his boss, "really swell," a tech sergeant who was even shorter than Koplow. But he also identified Jews in a picture of his battery cadre that he sent home to his folks. There was "Staff Sergeant Weiss — supply sergeant of the Battery and a swell guy," and Corporal Testa. Testa was "a yehudi [Jew] and really funny at times."[49] Out of twenty-seven men, three were Jews like Koplow. Such a minority experience compared favorably to the world of his youth in Sioux Falls, with its Jewish population of less than five hundred out of more than forty thousand—about one percent.[50]

If basic training taught Jews that they were a tiny minority in a vast sea of gentiles, the southern setting of many of the camps aggravated Jewish discomfort. Although military exercises took up the entire day, enlisted men had evenings and Sundays free. After completing a portion of their training, GIs were eligible for longer passes when they could go into the nearest town. And the nearest town offered its own surprises. "The impression I got of this other America and soldiers," recalled an eighteen-year-old from Brownsville, Brooklyn, who did his infantry training at Camp Shelby in Mississippi, "was that they would like to drink and fight, get beat up, come back, bloody, and claim they had a great time." The alternative to drinking and brawling and sex was to walk from one end of Hattiesburg to another, and then walk back again. "If you had a couple of dollars, you went into one of the restaurants and had a gigantic steak that you'd never seen in your life."[51] Food may have been comforting, but it did not necessarily relieve a sense of alienation.

Southern women, the proverbial shiksa or gentile female, struck Herbert Walters as plain. Their simple cotton dresses set them apart from New York City girls even before one heard their accent. A forbidden female could be alluring, but she could also make a man nervous about how he appeared to such an alien kind of woman. Jewish GIs from Brooklyn soon discovered that their borough's reputation preceded them. Walters recalls one unusual encounter with "town girls" at a USO dance in Florida. "Where you from?" "Brooklyn," he would answer. Coming to the point, she would ask, "What are you?" That meant she wanted to know his religion. So he told her. "Oh, I'm so glad," she said. "You're a Jew. I thought you were an Irish Catholic."[52] Walters was amazed. Revealing his Jewishness usually exposed him to curious prodding and occasionally led to unfriendly responses. Being a Jewish man rarely attracted women. Not all Jews owned up to their religious identity;[53] some avoided the question, or lied.[54] Yet Walters was lucky to get someone to dance with him. "One begins to dance with one of the southern belles," Artie Gorenstein wrote his folks, "he takes maybe two steps and three others are tapping him on the shoulder waiting to cut in."[55] The ratio of five hundred servicemen to twenty "girls" at a Sunday afternoon dance in Biloxi, Mississippi, overwhelmed him. Retreating, Gorenstein watched the others for a while and then settled undisturbed into a chair to listen to the N.B.C. Symphony on the radio. But once Fiedelbaum set them up on a blind double date with two shiksas while on a Sunday pass in the Mississippi town next to Keesler Field. Fiedelbaum had a "gorgeous shiksa," while Gorenstein got stuck with her plain-looking cousin.[56] Still, it helped to make basic training endurable even though neither Walters nor Gorenstein, unlike most of the Dragons, felt particularly comfortable around shiksas.[57]

Many Jewish GIs ignored the fact that both the Army and civil society in the South were segregated, but some northern Jews did remark on Jim Crow. Segregation taught Jews forcibly that despite whatever animosity they might meet, they were still white. "Past Sunday I went into Charlotte, and had two Pastrami sandwiches," wrote Louis Gruhin to his Orthodox family in Jersey City. "The thing that gets you when you first hit the South," he observed, "is the multitude of signs 'White' and 'Colored.' Nowhere except breathing the same air are they allowed to mix. That is on the surface, and you see it in stations, and rest rooms, and busses." It distressed him. "It's taken for granted. Of course, everybody from up north says hello and good morning to the colored as well as the whites, [but] the colored kids are afraid to wave back." Gruhin empathized with them. "It must be horrid to live thru life always looking into someone else's face (such as the colored due [*sic*] to the white) and see if you see therein, love, or hate, or respect."[58] As a northern Jew, Gruhin imagined a minority experience that was foreign to him. But training in the south gave Jews "an education in bigotry," as one Brooklyn Jew put it.[59]

Racial practices existed to teach everyone a lesson, many Jews learned. Some noticed not only the separate rest rooms and drinking fountains for blacks, but also the degrading street rituals of race, enforced by soldiers as well as civilians. Howard Sachs remembers his uneasiness over trips into town with his buddies at Fort Benning, Georgia. He quickly learned that "Columbus was not an antisemitic town but it certainly was an anti-black town." On occasion he'd spend a weekend with guys in town. These were "good friends," men he "was ready to die for because that's what" being a soldier in the war meant. They were his comrades, and they were all in the fight together. Then one day, "walking on the street," they saw some blacks. Southern etiquette required a black person to step off the sidewalk to let Sachs and his buddies pass. This time, one African American didn't move quickly enough for his friends. They punched him to force him off the sidewalk. Sachs was shocked. He challenged his friends, but they came right back at him, claiming that blacks had no right to walk on the sidewalks. He was stunned — and silenced. "Well, who was I to argue with those guys?" he asks rhetorically in retrospect. "I was in no position to."[60] Conscious of his own vulnerability, Sachs retreated. He wanted to have buddies. It was enough to be Jewish. He didn't think he could handle the isolation that might come from his censure of the GIs' racism. In the bright glare of racial distinction, his Jewish difference seemed to fade. Like many Jewish GIs, Sachs was learning to adapt. He would need the support of his fellow recruits after training ended. So he suppressed his shock at their behavior toward blacks and accepted their willingness to consider him, a Brooklyn Jew, as a fellow white American deserving of respect.

Military life exposed Jewish recruits to social practices that challenged many of their assumptions about the nature of their Jewishness. The armed forces distinguished not only between blacks and whites, but also among religions. Service identification requirements for burial and opportunities for religious observance included four choices: Protestant, Catholic, Hebrew, or "blank," signifying no religious affiliation.[61] "Hebrew" stood for "Jew," a system of classification derived from 1899 federal immigration records. Many Jews thought the term had racial overtones.[62] The military used it to designate Jewish religion. This practice did coincide with Reform Jewish usage: both the Reform rabbinical seminary, Hebrew Union College, and its congregational organization, Union of American Hebrew Congregations, employed "Hebrew" to indicate "Jewish." In the nineteenth century when these institutions were established, "Hebrew" harked back to biblical times, before the Middle Ages made "Jew" a term of rebuke. "Hebrew" inspired respect and suggested a common religious heritage with Christians in the Old Testament.[63]

Most Jewish servicemen opted for an "H" on their dog tags. Less visible than a mezuza or Magen David worn around the neck but more visible than circumcision, an H on the dog tag placed Jews within the military's classification system of religious difference. Not all Jews chose one. Chaplains thought that officers were less likely to identify themselves as Jews.[64] Many men must have felt as Sy Kahn did. "I made no attempt either to hide or to deny that I was a Jew, but neither did I make a banner or cause of it," he wrote. "Within myself I was comfortable with my heritage and religion, though relaxed in its practice, and I was pleased to have H indented on my dogtags."[65] Jerome Minkow thought that "there was something strange about the H." He had been called a Jew before but had "never been called a Hebrew." It bothered him.[66] The H might single one out as different from the other men, as happened to Herbert Walters. Most important, it assured that a Magen David would mark a Jewish grave in case of death. But that did not necessarily offer much solace for the living.

The Hebrew dog tag divided Jews from non-Jews as well as from Jews who declined to be labeled as such. At the same time, the H reminded Jews wearing it that they were "am Yisrael" (the people of Israel) and emphasized their common bonds across denomination, class, and ideology. It united them in a collective identity joining religious and secular Jews in one category for the military's convenience and religious observance. "It has become apparent to me that any organized attempt to further Zionism or Labor Zionism among the Jewish boys in the Armed Forces must center around the religious services," wrote a secular Labor Zionist, a sergeant from McClellan Field in California. "It is no coincidence that so many of our *haverim* [comrades] have been attending services regularly and encouraging others to attend. It is not that we suddenly have found religion," he explained. "We recognize almost intuitively that our way of life and Zionism in general cannot exist in a vacuum. Hence we participate in the only organized activity in the Army relating to Jewish life — the religious services."[67] Military policy had no place for Jewish secularism and forced secularists to pursue

The Henrietta Sterne Sisterhood of Anniston serving refreshments in 1943 for soldiers stationed at Fort McClellan in Alabama. Jews from diverse parts of the country met for the first time in the armed forces and when they attended religious services off base. Although rural Jews often appeared unfamiliar to urban Jewish GIs in their ways and speech, they warmly welcomed the Jewish soldiers.

their Jewish commitments under a sacred canopy. Commanding officers assumed a religious unity among Jews that didn't exist.

Ironically, under army auspices Jews achieved a group cohesiveness they never had as civilians. Not only did Jews from diverse parts of the country meet for the first time in the armed forces, they also met when they attended religious services off the base. There GIs often encountered other Jews who appeared unfamiliar in their ways and speech. Still, the Jewish GIs were welcomed warmly by small Jewish communities in relatively isolated parts of the South and West. Some families in fact hoped that romance might blossom for their Jewish daughters of marriageable age. Among strangers, the dog tag served as a generic certificate of Jewishness. One of the Dragons, Ralph Jackson, attended a Passover seder in Denver, when he was stationed at Lowry Field in 1942. When he walked in, the family eyed him with suspicion: "Jackson, what kind of a Jewish name is that?" they asked bluntly.[68] Only the H on his dog tag persuaded his hosts. From their point of view, he did not resemble any Jew they had ever seen.

Occasionally, a GI could discover not only community but exactly the sort of Jews one knew back home. Artie Gorenstein managed to do this in Biloxi, Mississippi. Observing the Jewish New Year turned into the high point of basic training at Keesler Field. "As a Jew," he could "get off Rosh Hashana" but was only entitled to a 36-hour pass because he "was in basic training." He couldn't "negotiate for much more than that," as a private.[69] Gorenstein's request for leave reflected a mix of homesickness, a sense of entitlement stemming from his socialist Zionist activism, and a desire to get off the base.[70] The closest place that promised a Jewish community was New Orleans, a six- or seven-hour trip by train. He arrived in the city late in the afternoon of Erev Rosh Hashana, the evening of the Jewish New Year. He knew he had to be back on the train after midnight and could only spend a few hours in New Orleans. "But yet it was terribly important to go."[71] This was his only chance to connect with other Jews. It was his taste of Jewish time, that important moment in the calendar when a new year began. As soon as he got off the train, he went to the Jewish Community Center where the local women had arranged hospitality for the holiday. One woman inquired, "Well, what kind of a family would you like to spend the evening with, Erev Rosh Hashana?" And Gorenstein, in his naiveté, answered with his ideal: "Well, if possible, a Zionist family and traditional." The woman looked at him and glowed. "Well, there's one family like that in New Orleans, but I think they're full," she said. "Wait a minute." She called them up and whoever answered must have said, "Send him over." He got instructions to the house, a private family dwelling. As Gorenstein climbed the stairs of the modest home, a "tall, elderly gentleman" met him at the door. "You're the soldier who wanted a Zionist and traditional family," he said in a deep voice. "Welcome." Gorenstein entered the house. Out of the corner of his eye, he glimpsed on a daybed a copy of *The Jewish Frontier.* This was more than he'd bargained for. The family were not just Zionists, but Labor Zionists. Just like him. Only later did Gorenstein realize that this was Ephraim Lisitzky, the "great Hebrew poet."[72]

Gorenstein wrote home, describing the festive meal. He asked his parents to send the family some tree certificates, indicating a contribution to the Jewish National Fund. But his mother Lillian determined on her own the proper gift. In gratitude for hosting her soldier son, she promptly sent Mrs. Lisitzky "a beautifully engraved" wooden box. On the bottom "it had stamped 'Made in Palestine,'" and carved Hebrew letters indicated that it was a product of the Bezalel Art School. The interior was lined with silk. Lillian filled the box with candy and signed a blue card, "with greatefull [sic] appreciation, Aryeh Gorenstein."[73] Bertha Lisitzky replied promptly: "Thank you very much for the beautiful Palestinian box and the sweets that came in it. The candy we enjoyed and the box we shall treasure as long as we live." Then she told Lillian what every Jewish mother longed to hear. "You have no idea how happy we were to have your son with us. He is everything a mother can hope and wish for."[74] Such encounters strengthened the bonds of community among all American Jews.

For a minority of Jewish recruits, including most of the Dragons, army service opened unexpected doors. Working-class men without college degrees could apply for officer training, especially if they entered the service early, either in 1941 or 1942. The military regularly scoured its ranks for qualified enlisted men with potential for mobility. The increased responsibility, prestige, and pay of officer status attracted both Jews and gentiles. But training to be an officer raised the stakes because one could fail as well as succeed. Anxiety among Jews was often heightened by an internalized sense of collective responsibility for the reputation of all Jews. Still, several Dragons decided to take a chance. *The Dragon Weekly* kept the boys informed of each Dragon's progress as either commissioned or non-commissioned officers and encouraged them to move up in the ranks. It assumed that each Dragon could succeed and ignored widespread attitudes among gentiles that Jews would not make good officers.[75] *The Dragon Weekly* optimistically demonstrated that these Brooklyn Jews could be model American military men.

But *The Dragon Weekly* did not chart the more private struggles that each Dragon endured. Prejudice affected opinions on whether Jews could be officers, just as it poisoned views on whether they would make good soldiers.[76] A common assumption was that the less Jewish one appeared in language and looks — that is, the less obviously different from other Americans — the better leader a man would be.[77] Nor did *The Dragon Weekly* deal with gentile officers' fears that Jews would not do well in combat and the related issue of whether a Dragon's eagerness to enter combat reflected a desire to prove himself as a Jew above and beyond his expression of his patriotism and enthusiasm. N. Jay Jaffee reflected on both of these issues. He had given up his rank as staff sergeant in the Timberwolf Infantry Division to volunteer for combat as a private first class. He received a furlough home, but when he returned, the army had rescinded the call for volunteers. Restored to rank as squad leader, he recalled that his men "could not understand why" he had volunteered for overseas combat. Nor could they comprehend his "burning desire" to put his "life on the line for the ideals of democracy" that he so "fervently believed in. What was difficult for the men to appreciate," Jaffee acknowledged, was his uncommunicated "belief that being a Jew and having certain political convictions meant setting an example for others." That was his "underlying reason" behind his "desire to get into the fray," aside from a romantic notion he had about combat.[78]

Internalizing the values of the surrounding society, Jewish servicemen struggled with antisemitism and bias. Individual incidents had to be sorted out against warnings given, stories told, experiences in other contexts, and, in the end, the issue of consequences. Many recalled no encounters with prejudice or discrimination. Others remembered bitter incidents that colored all their years in service. Reflecting on their memories, some thought that they had misinterpreted flash points — such as conflict between regular Army and Navy men with enlistees and Naval reserves — as instances of antisemitism. Others thought that regional and educational differences exacerbated friction.[79] To complicate matters further, norms and expectations regarding anti-Jewish sentiment in the 1940s differed from later assumptions. As Howard Sachs put it, "It wasn't antisemitism in the sense that you would regard antisemitism today. Today if they call you a 'jewboy' you'd feel insulted. In the army," he thought, "it's not the worst thing in the world to hear."[80] After Americans and Jews learned about Hitler's extermination program and death camps, they recognized antisemitism as a dangerous and deadly form of racism. Some even perceived a slippery slope leading from disparaging remarks to murderous hatred. Sensitized to the dangers of antisemitism, American Jews would later adopt an openly critical posture even toward social slurs. But during the early years of the war, the same slurs might be acceptable as simply military language.

At Camp Blanding in Florida, Sachs felt he could talk to the other men. As he explained, "spending time with them, it meant that there wasn't any real antisemitism." Given the opportunity to socialize with his fellow GIs, Sachs was ready to ignore the prejudiced remarks around him. "They didn't bury you with any of that stuff," was how he put it. Occasionally someone might have said to him, "hey jewboy." And so he responded in kind, "hey dago, or wop," he recalled. These slurs did not "make any-one angry."[81] They reflected a form of guys' talk. Growing up in multiethnic cities, boys mastered ethnic slurs as part of matura-tion into manhood. Convention dictated that women didn't use such language, only men.[82] The terms were part of army life. Looking back, Sachs contextualizes what he experienced as a kind of ethnic prejudice that affected all the men. In his view this pervasive form of American bias united GIs more than it di-vided them.

No etiquette book guided Jews in responding to antisemi-tism.[83] Each individual Jew had to decide how to react.[84] Jews knew what words hurt and which behavior threatened them. But what, if anything, a man should do about it was less clear. The problem was far from abstract; it was deeply personal. And it came when you least expected it. Paul Steinfeld was shaving in the latrine at the Indian Gap camp. Next to him in the mirror stood another GI. He happened to be one of the A.S.T.P. boys who were integrated into Steinfeld's infantry unit in 1944. He came from rural Pennsylvania. As they stood there shaving, he turned to Steinfeld and asked: "Steiney, how come you're in the infantry? I thought all of your race were in the Quartermaster."

Steinfeld recognized the accusation that Jews only served in supplies behind the lines as an antisemitic canard. Although rear-echelon positions included a complex array of logistical support, only one area was identified with Jews: the quartermaster corps, which supplied the troops. Jewish representation in the quartermasters paralleled army norms, but antisemites suggested otherwise. The quartermaster corps seemed to be the closest to wholesale and retail trade, a "Jewish" speciality according to antisemites. Steinfeld dropped his razor, ready to fight. "What's the matter with you? Take it easy," the GI said. Then he confessed, "How do I know? I never saw a Jew in my life until I met you." Steinfeld cursed the GI and called him an ignoramus. "First of all," he said, "we're not a race." Then they got into a discussion of what a Jew is. Steinfeld explained, "We are a nationality but we're not a race. Furthermore, you see me here. Obviously I'm not in the Quartermaster." Eventually, the two men came to an understanding. Steinfeld thought he "became sort of my friend."[85] However, antisemitism left Steinfeld, like most Jews, frustrated in the face of such stereotypes.

Occasionally an antisemitic encounter unexpectedly led to gratifying results. Artie Kolin, a Dragon, when in preflight training in California met a towering man, "about six feet six," who apparently hated Jews, because he used to walk around their barracks yelling, "Heil Hitler, Heil Hitler." There was also a Lieutenant, a very nice guy, "a Swede," perhaps. Kolin, a working-class ethnic who had waxed floors and cleaned windows before entering the service, was comfortable with the men. Neither vulgarity nor ethnic slurs bothered him, and he freely used them. But this guy's provocations were a more serious matter. However, Kolin felt he couldn't do anything on his own. Then the Lieutenant called him in. "I understand you are having a little trouble in the barracks," he said. Kolin was surprised the of-

Artie Kolin in Army Air Corps uniform. Neither vulgarity nor ethnic slurs bothered Kolin, but with his commanding officer's tacit approval he took to the boxing ring to give a persistent antisemite a serious drubbing. Most antisemitic encounters left Jewish GIs feeling demoralized.

ficer knew what was going on. "No, I'm not having nothing that I can't handle," he replied. And the Lieutenant responded, "Well, we have a gymnasium for these things." Kolin understood. The officer was telling him what to do. But Kolin hesitated, explaining that "after all, I've spent a lot of time getting up to where I am . . . to be a bombardier navigator." "Well, in the gym everything goes," the Lieutenant countered.

So Kolin decided to act. The gym had boxing gloves, and he had done a lot of boxing as a boy at the Jewish Community House of Bensonhurst. One day he took some gloves and threw a pair at the antisemitic GI. And then he insulted him in front of all the other guys. "Come on, you gutless Dutchman." The GI didn't know much about boxing but he rose to the bait and put on the gloves. Kolin promised himself, "I'm not going to make him bleed. I won't hit him in the face. But, I'll fix this guy real good." Since he couldn't move his hands, Kolin "could hit him at any time." He "beat his stomach in so bad." Then he paused from giving the GI a drubbing. He looked at the bleachers on the side of the gym and saw the Lieutenant sitting there. Kolin "could just see him smiling." Finally, after a particularly hard punch in the stomach, Kolin "gave him one shot in the face and knocked him down." Maybe he got up. Maybe he didn't. But Kolin "gave this guy a terrific beating" — in front of an audience that appreciated the show. The guy never bothered him again.[86]

Kolin's story about antisemitism ends well. But most antisemitic encounters did not result in a similar triumph but rather left Jewish GIs feeling demoralized. Those who ignored prejudiced remarks, as did Howard Sachs, and those who fought antisemites, as did Jerome Minkow and Paul Steinfeld, recall little satisfaction. Prejudice gnawed at a man's sense of self-esteem and diminished his masculinity.

At the same time, the confrontation with antisemitism in the military strengthened many Jewish recruits because it happened en route to becoming soldiers. Trained to carry guns, Jews learned how to defend themselves not just as soldiers but as Jews. From brainy, smart-aleck, urban, talkative ethnic recruits, Jews became disciplined, physically fit, skilled in handling weapons. As assertive soldiers, they would manage somehow to deal with antisemitism even as it caused them anguish. They determined to prove themselves as soldiers and as men. Their Jewishness became integral to their individual identity. No longer taken for granted, part of the intimate environment of home and neighborhood, Jewishness became a private piece of who they were. And since they were GIs, Jewishness became a part of being an American soldier. One fought as an American. That meant one stood up as a Jew. A new type of Jew was being forged in the military.

Most Jewish recruits did not reflect on these subtle changes. For the majority, military service was only incidentally about being Jewish. The move from civilian to soldier involved so many adjustments — mental, social, and physical — that the issue of Jewish identity usually took a back seat to the more obvious shifts in personal status. Following orders, being told when to get up and what to eat, what to do with one's time and with whom — all this absorbed a GI's attention. Larger issues of individuality and masculinity, of fear and bravery, were uppermost in their minds. Howard Sachs vividly recalled a lecture at Camp Blanding. The officer mounted a platform and turned to the recruits sitting before him. "Now you guys," he said, "I want you to look at the guy next to you. Look at him." Slowly Sachs turned his head to look, as did the other men. "One of you are going to come home," the officer said. "The other one of you is gonna be dead." Shocked, Sachs said to himself, "The dead one's certainly not gonna be me, that's for sure."[87] But maybe it would be. You never knew. It was a standard lecture, but it drove home the point. The United States would win the war, of this virtually all GIs were confident. But what their own fate would be was far less clear. Few GIs, Jewish or gentile, had tested their own limits or knew how they would be tested. Some, of course, would fail to make the transition. Others would end up at desk jobs. Still others would surprise themselves by becoming officers and leaders of men. Many would fill the ranks of enlisted men. Most would acquit themselves decently.

Although Jewishness lingered at the edge of consciousness for Jewish soldiers, it was present wherever they went. The transformation of their physiques accompanied a transformation of their identities. Under Uncle Sam's commands, Jews renegotiated their self-understanding. Although the issue rarely appeared in stark terms, either at the time or in retrospect, military service taught Jewish GIs to defend not only their country, but also their religion and people. Whether they wanted to or not, they could not help experiencing the war as Americans and as Jews.

4

CROSSING OVER

You went with me
Into the army, where
One night in a foxhole
On Leyte a fellow soldier
Said where are the fuckin' Jews?
Back in the PX. I'd like to
See one of those bastards
Out here. I'd kill him!
I decided to conceal
You, my you, anyway, for a while.
Forgive me for that.

—KENNETH KOCH,
"To Jewishness"[1]

SEPTEMBER 26, 1943. The troop ship slowly sailed under the Golden Gate Bridge and headed west, part of a huge convoy. As the vast expanse of the Pacific Ocean swallowed the horizon, Sy Kahn pondered his future. "I am leaving the U.S.A. quite girl-less and do not regret it," he confided to his diary. He would be away for a long time. "A girl on my mind would not help matters," he mused. "It is easier this way. Missing my family and home is quite enough to take." He worried particularly about his mother, hoping she would understand that his silence for a month meant that he had shipped out. On September 15th he had just turned nineteen. Less than two years earlier he had listened in his high school auditorium to President Roosevelt's speech to Congress condemning the "day of infamy." Eager to reach eighteen to be eligible to fight, Kahn wanted to do his part. Once he finished his basic training, he applied for the Army Specialized Training Program (A.S.T.P.), since he had had a taste of college. He waited to hear for four months, only to learn that his application was marked ineligible. His unit, the 244th Port Company, part of the 495th Port Battalion of the Army Transportation Corps, was scheduled to depart for the Pacific Theater. The dry-run days were over.

Despite his disappointment over the lost opportunity to attend A.S.T.P., Kahn couldn't suppress his excitement. "It gives me a strange feeling that I am going overseas," he wrote in his diary. He remembered nights when he used to sink into his "battered armchair at college and dream of far-off places." Now his dreams would be realized. Here he was "on a ship headed for 'somewhere,' liable to attack at any moment, men constantly on the alert at the various guns on board, the radar spinning from the mainmast, here is drama, and one hardly realizes it." He marveled at the endless blue of the Pacific, as well as the constant dice games on the ship where hundreds of dollars changed hands. Kahn was ready to do his duty. He had packed several spare pairs of glasses, including one in his gas mask, because he knew how blind he was without them. Unlike many teenagers, he felt vulnerable. He realized it was "not going to be easy," and he doubted he would survive if he faced battle or disease. But like many his age, he was idealistic. He was "anxious to get there and be a part of the telling blow that shall smash the enemy and forever end war." Although the main job of the 244th Port Company, part of the Army Service Forces, was to load and unload ships, Kahn sensed that he was starting an adventure.[2]

Hyman Samuelson left for the same destination more than a year earlier, in March 1942. Older than Kahn, Samuelson had graduated from college in 1940 at the top of his class, with an engineering degree and a commission from the R.O.T.C. Growing up in New Orleans, the sixth of nine children, Samuelson had known a very different world from Kahn's Manhattan. Although "Jewishness became very natural" to him as part of a large extended family, most of his friends were gentiles.[3] Called up in the fall of 1941, he was out on maneuvers in North Carolina with the 96th Engineering Battalion, a segregated construction battalion, when he heard the news of Pearl Harbor. The next day Samuelson listened to the President declare war. Then he wrote to his high school sweetheart, Dora — a serious letter "free from emotion and sentimentality" — to propose that they not wait any longer to get married. "We are in a long war, perhaps for another five years," he told her. "But we are on the stronger side and, God willing, should eventually come out on top." Samuelson was pretty confident. He hoped for a year in training before he would be sent abroad. When he got a furlough for Christmas, he went home and married Dora. "The best thing about being married is being in love," he told his diary seven weeks later. "Love is pretty good stuff before you're married, but if a man gets the right girl for himself, he doesn't know what love is until after he is married." Samuelson and his wife, intoxicated with each other, decided to have a child despite their uncertain future. Two months later Samuelson received orders to leave Fayetteville. He learned that Dora was pregnant while he was traveling north to ship out.[4]

Samuelson embarked from New York City on a cold March day. Despite the gloomy weather, he was excited about his "first time on the ocean." He even acknowledged that he "was enjoying the heavy seas." Although officer quarters were crowded, they were spacious compared with accommodations below deck. The ship left New York harbor and headed south. It passed through the Panama Canal, part of a large convoy that included the battleship USS *Hornet.* Blimps flew overhead, giving the trip a festive air.[5] Samuelson was thrilled to see the extent of the convoy. But time passed slowly in the Pacific. They seemed to be sailing "on a sheet of glass." He did his best not to think, passing the time with bridge, checkers, chess, poker, blackjack, and reading. "Thinking of home at a time like this is the worst form of torture that I can subject myself to," he confessed.[6] He missed his wife. But he did not regret his decision to marry and bind himself closely to his beloved Dora.

Samuelson and Kahn, as they headed out across the Pacific Ocean, understood that they were beginning another life, one that they could scarcely imagine as American Jewish soldiers. Both men kept diaries, although they knew this was illegal when they were overseas in wartime. Kahn wrote for the sake of history and his family; he wanted his parents to have something to remember him by if he were killed.[7] Samuelson wrote out of an old habit and a desire to stay sane. He had started keeping a diary as a boy, and continued to write regularly for the rest of his life.[8] Neither man wrote much about his Jewishness, but neither tried to hide it. When they reached New Guinea, they learned to accommodate themselves to the harsh conditions of life there. Their recorded impressions and feelings reveal how they were gradually changing as days added up to months and months to years overseas. Both men would come to acquire an American masculinity that would help to bind them to their comrades; both would also nonetheless endure loneliness as they struggled to do their jobs and not succumb to feelings of isolation as Jews.

Shipping out overseas during the war marked the climax of stateside training. Herbert Walters, who had been so eager to fight that he asked his draft board to take him, spent two years training in the United States, long enough to have seen movie versions of the war. In the movies, soldiers board the troop trains heading overseas while their families watch, tears in their eyes. Walters learned to his surprise that "when you go overseas, nobody is supposed to know about it." But the trains carrying soldiers to the piers passed by houses where people living on each side of the tracks figured out that these boys were going overseas. "So they would be waving" in an effort to cheer up the troops. Walters got off such a train in September 1944. He was excited finally to be heading for the front lines. As he marched onto the pier he suddenly noticed a familiar face in uniform. It was his cousin, Aaron Gross. Gross had a stateside assignment. Like over two million other soldiers, 40 percent of the Army's Ground Forces, he wasn't shipping overseas.[9] Their eyes met. Walters couldn't say anything, but he knew that his family, who had been kept in the dark, was going to find out that he had left for the Pacific Theater. His old concern about his elderly parents momentarily returned. Then, as he climbed the steep, narrow gangplank, carefully balancing all his gear, an Army band struck up a beautiful popular march. A piano player himself, Walters thought, "This is one piece of music I'll never forget." A week later, he couldn't remember it.[10] The familiar world of the United States quickly slipped out of his consciousness as a new and foreign universe took its place.

Kahn, Samuelson, and Walters were crossing the Pacific Ocean as Americans. They were heading for an area that held no Jewish associations for them, to fight an enemy that bore no special significance for them as Jews. The Pacific Theater was an enormous expanse of never-heard-of islands, devoid of cities or familiar populations. In these foreign islands, they could let their uniform assimilate them into the fellowship of other white soldiers. No longer oddities to the men in their units, they expe-

rienced a measured acceptance overseas as comrades-in-arms.
They even received invitations from fellow soldiers to pass as
Christians or from chaplains to convert to Christianity. Kahn
and Walters declined these offers, but Samuelson was tempted.
Thinking of themselves as Jewish Americans, they discovered
that their American identity proved more powerful overseas
than stateside training would have led them to anticipate.

Jewishness, identified with home and family, now seemed a
vital but largely hidden element of their identity. In this "lonely,
dangerous, insecure, and violent world," Jewishness needed to
be submerged and protected.[11] Kahn and Samuelson admitted
that their distance from home increasingly made their former
civilian lives feel irrelevant. Even their previously negotiated
identity as Jewish American soldiers required effort to sustain in
the Pacific. All three needed fellowship, but it was difficult to
find a feeling of connection to other American men in their units
despite the soldiers' offer of acceptance. Kahn and Walters may
have felt accepted as fellow Americans, but they didn't feel accepted as Jews. Although they could not forget their own sense
of difference from their comrades, they did their best to dis-
guise it.

By contrast, Jews in the European Theater, where relatively
large numbers of American soldiers served, rarely experienced
feelings of isolation. They all knew Europe from their school-
books. And for many, it was also the continent their families had
left for America. When Harold Freeman gave up the draft exemption that came with his Army Signal Corps job to fight fascism with a gun, he knew the Nazi enemy was waging war
against the Jews as well as the Allied armies. Jewish identity
could not easily be ignored or repressed in Europe. Although
Jewish GIs had left their country as Americans, crossing the Atlantic into the shadow of the Third Reich involved specifically

Jewish issues that would complicate further their quest for fellowship.[12]

"Embarkation is dramatic, particularly the actual boarding of the ship. It is the climax of soldiering in the U.S.," Harold Freeman wrote to his wife Bea. "It is the beginning of another life," he observed in June 1944 after arriving in Tilshead, England. Freeman had shipped out from his native New York City. Before leaving he had hoped to get back to Brooklyn for the farewell dinner of spaghetti and meatballs that Bea had prepared. But he never arrived, and she began the long, lonely wait for mail and news. "Most of the drama" of leaving the United States, he wrote, came from "the hustle and bustle of embarkation" which left little time for thought. "Handling all your equipment absorbs most of your attention."[13] The steep gangplank seemed both narrow and precarious, a bridge to another world. But there was more than drama in the details. A vast unknown faced these soldiers.

For enlisted men like Freeman, the trip had few amenities. Inducted into the service just before Christmas of 1943, Freeman first trained as a rifleman at Camp Blanding, Florida. Six months later, after instruction in infantry communications at Fort Meade, he took a ferry across New York harbor and boarded what had been an Italian luxury liner before the war, the *Conte Biancamano*. He slept on one of the bunks, arranged four high and located deep in the cargo hold, which he reached by descending four steep flights of steel steps. It was rather like the steerage passage of so many immigrants decades earlier, only in the reverse direction. Fortunately, he did not suffer from seasickness. Since he was not a gambler or interested in card games, popular pastimes among the soldiers and sailors, he spent time reading, writing, and talking with a couple of the men.[14] Like many GIs, Freeman found it "difficult to convince

myself of the reality of the situation. The ocean, Europe, War —
all geography and history heretofore is now becoming a part of
my personal experience."[15]

But Freeman also thought about his pending ordeal as a Jew.
"Last night, lying on my bunk — a piece of canvas stretched taut
— I pondered over my fate," he wrote to Bea. "I found myself
considering this trip as a *return* to Europe. I considered how
narrow the margin was between my being born in Pietrakov
rather than in N.Y. and how tenuous the hold of the 2nd generation is on the adopted fatherland."[16] Going to Europe in uniform
involved more than American patriotism. Freeman recognized
the personal and political dimensions of his voyage. He understood his good fortune in not having been born in Europe,
in having escaped the lands of antisemitic persecution. He acknowledged, too, emotions connecting him to Jews who remained in the old country. Some American Jewish soldiers, like
Akiva Skidell who had grown up in Poland, had family members
still in Europe; others possessed a diffuse empathy or a sense of
collective responsibility for their coreligionists. American Jews
were coming to fight both an American and a Jewish battle
against Nazism.

Relatively few of them ever made it to the front lines. Most
soldiers who went overseas, Jewish or gentile, never came
close.[17] They knew a different kind of war. All sorts of men —
and all of the 350,000 women — served behind the front lines
and never saw combat. The contrast between battlefield soldiers
and those in the rear was dramatic. "When we got a quarter of a
mile behind the front line," one GI recalled with a touch of hy-
perbole, "we might as well be in Brooklyn."[18] Behind the lines
was not exactly Brooklyn, but the amenities available, including
such basics as cooked food and water for washing, surprised the
front-line troops. "We were always amazed, and riled," Harold

Freeman admitted, "when on pass or circling around through a rear area, to see so many American soldiers walking around neatly and cleanly dressed — and wearing ties."[19] Despite the dramatic contrast with the front lines, dangers existed for those engaged in logistics.[20] Sy Kahn characterized the tensions of his work as ricocheting between tedium and terror, the unrelenting boredom of unloading ships by day and the frightening bombardments of Japanese planes at night. Soldiers behind the lines were as vulnerable to the vicissitudes of weather and illness as were those at the front. In the Pacific islands, harsh jungle terrain and tropical diseases threatened all military personnel. Bombs and artillery on occasion landed behind the lines, especially when a unit followed close on the heels of an invasion. But there were also opportunities to explore European and North African cities, to meet the peoples of Southeast Asia and the South Pacific.

In the jungles of the Pacific islands, there were no Jewish civilians and few Jewish GIs. So Jewish soldiers searched elsewhere for fellowship. Hyman Samuelson, comfortable around gentiles, discovered that his position as a white officer of a segregated black company gave him a group of Christian Americans as companions. He regularly attended Sunday services on New Guinea with his men and listened to Chaplain C. Herbert Dubra's preaching. Dubra impressed Samuelson. As a southerner, Samuelson had known other Negroes, but never on terms of equality. Dubra's status as a chaplain made him an officer, and Samuelson discovered that he enjoyed talking with him. "I like his views on religion," he reported. "I like his ideas about race problems. He is one of the most intelligent men I have ever met. His grammar isn't very good, and a 'picture' is a 'pitcher,' but his sermons to these colored boys are wonderful. I seldom miss any of them."[21] Samuelson's distance from Christianity

*Hyman Samuelson in 1942.
In New Guinea, isolated as
a Jew, Samuelson sought
out companionship in the
forms available on the island
and succeeded in finding it
among Christians. As a white
American officer of a Negro
engineering company, he
considered his Jewishness
largely irrelevant.*

gradually narrowed as he grew to know and appreciate his soldiers.

As time passed he came to identify more deeply with his men
and to defend them against slander. He wrote to his wife, Dora,
about the Easter services in the new recreation building that his
men had just constructed. He had had to fight for authorization
even for a segregated building for his Negro troops. Samuelson
explained how he had a "squad of men install benches and decorate the interior with palm leaves." It looked beautiful. Chaplain
Dubra dedicated the building to the men just before he began his sermon. "When I looked around at them all, I couldn't
help feeling happy. . . . Nearly the whole company was present. They sang the hymns beautifully, and, little girl, you have
never heard hymns sung right until you hear these boys sing.

They put real meaning in it."[22] The spiritual power of black music uplifted him.

Thread by thread, Samuelson's ties with home and Jewishness loosened. He began an affair with a nurse whom he had met when he was hospitalized with malaria. She gave him a Saint Christopher medal to protect him. A month later Chaplain Dubra offered him Holy Communion at Sunday services. Despite his regular attendance at church services, Samuelson had never before taken communion. "This morning, for the first time in my life I did. It made me feel strangely happy."[23] Slowly, Samuelson was coming to feel an intense connection not only with his men and with the nurses but also with their Christian practices. Sharing Christian fellowship brought him a measure of peace and happiness that he did not quite fathom. Isolated as a Jew, he sought out companionship in the forms available on the island and succeeded in finding it among Christians. Despite his wife's pleas and his own longing to see his baby boy, he did not seek a transfer to return to the States because he was ambitious to advance in rank. No longer alone and estranged in the jungle, respected by his troops, enjoying the intimacies of women, and making money running a dice game, Samuelson had adjusted to life in New Guinea. His Jewishness, deeply buried, seemed irrelevant and very far away. Here he was simply a white American officer.[24]

Had Samuelson stayed with the 300 men of the 96th Battalion who were under his command, he might have drifted further from his Jewish roots. Instead his wife's serious illness called him home. While waiting for his papers to leave Hollandia, New Guinea, for New Orleans, he observed some Jewish soldiers praying. He didn't realize it was Rosh Hashana, the Jewish New Year. He joined the men in services. It was the first time he had participated in over three years. "I was surprised that I could still read — with difficulty of course — Hebrew. I'd like to study Hebrew when I get home," he wrote. Samuelson hoped that his study might help him cope with Dora's cervical cancer.[25] The presence of a small Jewish community of military personnel in Hollandia, makeshift as it was, brought him back to Judaism. Released to return to his dying wife in New Orleans, he turned to the traditional Jewish solace of reading and studying.

Ten days later, still waiting for a plane ride and orders to return to the United States, he observed the Day of Atonement, Yom Kippur. "I didn't write my diary last night because I was keeping Yom Kippur as I have never kept it before. Not only did I fast, as I have done many times before, but I didn't write or lift a finger to work. I spent last evening and all day today in the chapel. I read Hebrew with its English translation hour after hour. I followed the services closely. I tried and tried to pray — to get some divine soothing inspiration." Samuelson admitted that he "just wanted to feel near Him, to tell Him that I understood what He was doing and that I'd make the most of life regardless of what happened. Sometimes I felt that He heard me, but then I knew that He didn't hear — or else, He wasn't interested." In the end, he concluded that God mattered less than Jewish companionship. "My comfort lay in the people I know — in Papa, Dotsy, Beryl, Ethel, other friends and relatives. More comfort in them than in God."[26]

When Samuelson left New Guinea in the fall of 1944, he had been in uniform for three years, more than two of them overseas. His wartime experience had partially submerged his Jewishness, which seemed irrelevant to the demands of serving as an officer of a segregated Christian company. Although some might find a Jewish attribute in his sympathy for his African American troops, Samuelson never connected the two.[27] Instead, his diary suggests that the remoteness of the Pacific is-

lands and the integration of Jews in the military marginalized
Jewish aspects of his personality. Samuelson never went as far as
embracing religious conversion, but other Jews did. "Wartime is
good for converts," a priest explained. "The Jews felt kind of
lonely, you know, because they were so few, so they picked out
what they thought was the best, as far as services were concerned, and they stuck with that."[28] The nurses, his fellow officers, and his troops had mitigated Samuelson's loneliness. They
ignored his Jewishness, and in his ease around Christians, something he had acquired growing up in New Orleans, he took comfort from them.

Not all Jews could or wanted to submerge their Jewishness.
Even when they might have preferred to ignore it, others reminded them of their responsibility to live up to their Jewish
identity. As a Marine officer, Merv Reines was assigned to get
equipment and supplies to the docks when his unit left New
Zealand. In charge of a working party to clean out the camp, he
had to deal with drunken and rowdy Marines who challenged
his authority. Cursing, they swore that "they'd be damned if
they'd take orders from a goddamn Jew." It was "the first time"
Reines had ever heard such remarks, so he decided to overlook
them. After all, the men were drunk. Two of his non-commissioned officers observed the insubordination. Both NCOs were
Irish, one from Boston and the other from New York. Watching
in disgust, the Sergeant turned to Reines and asked: "Lieutenant, what'a you gonna do about it?" Then the Corporal chimed
in with the same question. "I'm not gonna do a goddamn thing
about it," Reines replied. But these two men wouldn't accept his
answer. "Well, if you're not gonna do anything," they responded,
"we're gonna do something about it." Reines didn't pay them
any attention. He focused on the task ahead and got the camp
emptied. They loaded the trucks up. Finally, he headed for the

Two Coast Guard–manned LSTs off Leyte Island beach, 1944. Relatively few soldiers ever made it to the front lines; most soldiers who shipped overseas knew a different kind of war. Still, dangers existed for those engaged in logistics.

ship and supervised as the Marines stowed everything on board. They sailed for Guadalcanal, and Reines put the matter out of his mind.

Then, "lo and behold," he was summoned to testify in a court-martial. True to their word, the Irish NCOs brought charges against the two non-coms who had cursed Reines. With the Sergeant and Corporal testifying against them at the court-martial, the men were convicted, reduced in rank, and fined. The experience shook Reines up and "left a bad taste" in his mouth — so bad, in fact, that "even after it was all over," he went over and shook hands with the offenders, saying, "I'm sorry this happened." The Irish NCOs were furious. "Lieutenant, you're too goddamn easy!" they told him.[29] They wanted Reines to receive the respect due his rank as an officer. The personal affront — the antisemitic slur — was insubordination and undermined Reines as a Marine officer. Reines could not afford to place his identity as a Jew above his status as a Lieutenant and Marine. It was incumbent upon him as a Marine officer to take offense at such slurs.

The issues were no less complicated for enlisted men. For Sy Kahn, antisemitism was a moral puzzle he could not fathom. Antisemitic comments seemed to carry the same weight as obscenities in the armed services.[30] Apparently antisemitic cracks, like curses, were generally uttered impersonally, part of the unreflective banter that strengthened camaraderie among men across social and military ranks. Such words kept at bay the awkwardness and anxiety that often lurked in silence. But antisemitic remarks stung Kahn whether or not they had been said ignorantly or without malice for him personally. He felt helpless before them, so much so that he didn't even tell his diary about what he endured. The pain he "felt in encountering anti-Semitism is nowhere directly noted in the journal," Kahn observed. "Even in so private a record," he discovered to his surprise over forty years later, he "could not bring" himself to deal with his "anger, fear, and bewilderment, or a curious sense of shame for the perpetrators of prejudice," when he encountered antisemitism.[31]

Kahn's reflections help to illuminate Reines's dilemma. The silence in Kahn's diary revealed to him how deeply antisemitism had disturbed him. No other subject "was sacrosanct." As if indirectly addressing the slurs from men in his unit, Kahn labeled them "'crude' or obnoxiously loud, or narrow-minded and insensitive." In this way he "castigated their prejudices, and particularly the anti-Semitism" he "detested so deeply" that he "could not call it by name." He "was keenly sensitive to the common anti-Semitic assumptions that Jews could not be good soldiers or stomach hard physical work," and he "determined to give the lie to these opinions" by making friends with the men in his unit despite their slurs.[32] It would not be easy, especially given the difficult conditions on Cape Gloucester.

As enemy planes flew bombing missions overhead, alerts increased and Kahn learned to be prepared, to protect not only himself but also his buddies. "At 1:45 A.M. I heard three horn blasts," he wrote in his diary. "I never heard the guns go off; they must have jarred me awake." He had clothes, shoes, glasses, and helmet handy. "Wide awake in a second," he dressed in twenty. Unable to rouse his partner by yelling, he ran into the tent and shook the bed. Kahn's "nerves were raw to every sound." He could feel the thud of bombs exploding on the airstrip, six miles away, under the moonlight. Alone in his foxhole, he regretted his isolation. But he had chosen privacy, a chance to read and write, over shared camaraderie. "Bombs began to explode, but they were distant . . . Then a plane began to roar, getting louder and louder. . . . The buzzing sounded ominous . . . I was thoroughly scared, crouching, waiting for the Z-Z-Z and the thud of a 500-pounder, and oblivion. Pictures of home, family, Carolyn pounded through my mind, like raging water down a gulley. I crossed my fingers, and waited." Kahn definitely was not the praying type. "What else was there to do?" he queried rhetorically.[33] After the raid he inspected the captain's foxhole to learn how to make a better one for himself. Gradually he mastered survival skills.

Military service was changing Kahn, both physically and

Sy Kahn in Luzon, the Philippines, 1945. Military service changed Kahn, both physically and emotionally. As he learned to operate a winch, a complicated piece of machinery that had intimidated him, he retained his private Jewish identity, which was intimately bound up with his love of reading, poetry, writing, and discussion.

emotionally. For almost a year he worked at the boring job of checker, loading and unloading ships. To his surprise, he grew to be a muscular guy, weighing over 180 pounds. As if to match his new physique, Kahn grew a curly beard. His new strength brought an unexpected bonus. Not keen for "arguments or fighting," he discovered that his size saved him from much of this. "I am rarely belligerent," he admitted.[34] Then he learned to operate a huge winch, a skill that gave him satisfaction in part because machines had always mystified him.[35] His youth (he was the youngest in his outfit), his size, perhaps even his diary and his reading gradually helped him to get along with the diverse types of men in his unit. In his company of 225 men, there were only four Jews. (Two percent of the company was about half of the average Jewish distribution in the American military.) The Jewish soldier he liked best, Seth Hillsberg, was "quiet, unassuming, cool, slightly built and meek-looking."[36] Most of the men in his unit came from the south and southwest, including "two Spaniards" as Kahn called them, Sanchez and Morales from Florida.

For amusement he went swimming regularly, often with a fellow GI named Denison. Lounging on the beach, they talked about everything from "sex to the machine age." Kahn thought they got along well. Denison "has a willing intelligence. However, we disagree on nearly everything." That pleased Kahn "because there are few things I enjoy better than a good discussion, whether it is on the shores of New Guinea or in a living room off Central Park West."[37] But Kahn did not speak about the poetry he read or about intellectual issues. These were matters he connected with his inner Jewish self. After a year on New Guinea, Kahn confided that he had "been getting along wonderfully with everyone. I don't know whether this is a reflection of my own amiability, my being able to make the fellows laugh, or quite what it is. For some reason I am more at peace with the whole world and, for the most part, happy."[38] Like Samuelson, Kahn had found a kind of serenity. Unlike Samuelson, however, Kahn never moved toward Christian fellowship, perhaps because he remained acutely conscious of antisemitism. He retained his private Jewish identity, which for him was intimately bound up with his love of reading, poetry, writing, and discussion.

In the Pacific Jews fought alongside other Americans in a war that mattered to them as Americans, but in Europe many Jewish GIs felt that they were also in combat as Jews.[39] The Nazis were fighting the Americans, who dared to oppose them; they loathed Jews. Many American Jewish soldiers knew that European Jews must be living in dire circumstances but had no reasonable cause to expect the ghastly reality that would subsequently be revealed to them. Europe's geography was mapped by Jewish associations — birthplaces of aunts, uncles, cousins, grandparents, parents. Some soldiers would even point "that way" to their own childhood homes. A man's Jewish identity was felt more insistently in Europe than on a remote island in the Pacific. At unexpected moments, anger might well up and explode, surprising a Jewish GI at the power and depth of his emotions.

Most vulnerable were Jewish physicians and medics, trained to heal and care for all, friend and foe alike. Physicians moved from their status as Jewish civilians, where they often faced discrimination in medical schools and hospitals, into positions of authority and respect within the military.[40] Rank and responsibility counted, and their Jewishness often stayed in the background. Irving Fishman entered active duty after completing his medical internship in January 1944. He expected to go to the Pacific Theater but ended up in France with the 220th General Hospital. Occasionally he worked on wounded enemy soldiers, but felt that he was not compromising himself as a doctor or as a Jew. Antisemitism did not surface. He understood his medical work as vital to the war effort.[41]

While Fishman remained behind the lines, Herman Hellerstein moved forward to the battlefield. "I am sitting in a nice comfortable kitchen in a Dutch house," he wrote in February 1945 to the woman he would later marry. "The stove is perking merrily, heated by a briquette of peat. Our light is the rather dull but mellow light of kerosene lamps. The civilians have long abandoned this area because of the fierce battle" in the vicinity. Hellerstein's aid station was ideal, steel-girded and cement-reinforced. But his job was not to treat patients at an aid station. He was responsible for retrieving the wounded from the battlefield and administering medicine at collecting points just behind the front. "We move forward to our goal, several wounded tankers. They had crawled about one hundred yards from their tank in the middle of a small village. Good first aid had been applied by their fellow tankers. Hasty inspection, load them, and dash to the collecting point and to the aid station."[42] Hellerstein was convinced that antisemitism had sent him and Schwartz, Goldberg, and Cohen to the front-line combat medical units. Colonel Boland didn't like Jews. He kept the safer jobs for gentile medical officers. But Boland's prejudice ironically enhanced Hellerstein's status. Jewish physicians in the medical company performed well; Hellerstein never heard antisemitic remarks in combat. The men of the 40th Tank Battalion knew that soldiers with Jewish names were good doctors.[43]

Fishman did not have to contend with such a colonel. He stayed with the hospital, removed from combat, until he was sent on detached service into Germany. Then he saw a different side of the war. Reporting to the office of the Surgeon General,

Fishman took over arrangements for captured German military hospitals. He let the Germans run their own hospitals with supplies from captured German warehouses. At this time, Fishman carried a gun, although he knew that as a non-combatant he was supposed to be unarmed. Still, having only one other doctor and four enlisted men with him, two of whom drove ambulances, he preferred to risk being armed than to have no protection. Even though he had bodyguards, he felt uneasy.[44]

Once he came into a prison camp near Köthen, south of Berlin. A bunch of bodies lay in a common grave. Among the dead were two American fliers, apparently killed by the local farmers. Their bodies had been punctured with what looked like a pitchfork. Hitler had encouraged farmers to murder airmen on the grounds that they were all *Luftgangsters,* "terror fliers," and not legitimate prisoners of war.[45] What Fishman saw incensed him. He decided to do something about it. So he got into his "little ambulance and drove a good ten miles or fifteen miles and found an American outfit." He went "stomping into the commanding officer of this outfit," demanding some men to go to the mass grave with him. "I can't spare them," came the response. But Fishman persisted. Finally the officer agreed: "Well, you can have 'em for four hours."

Fishman headed back with a weapons carrier and perhaps a dozen GIs. They rounded up all the people in the surrounding farming community and brought them to a big field with their shovels. Then he "told them to dig graves." The Germans were petrified. They imagined they were digging their own graves. Fishman stationed the soldiers all around the area, standing guard. The people came up to him on their hands and knees. They crawled up to his feet, begging, "Please!" Unmoved, he shouted, "No! Go back and dig the grave." When the graves were finally dug, he ordered: "Now, go into the pit. Bring out those bodies, and bury them."[46] A palpable feeling of relief swept through the farmers as they followed the orders. Still, Fishman felt a small measure of satisfaction.

Fishman's rage, fueled in part by his Jewish identity, had compelled him to act. His unnerving encounter made clear that his American uniform did not necessarily shield him from his Jewish self. He forced the German farmers to dig graves, just as the Nazis had forced Jews. He created a situation in which the farmers' own guilt would terrorize them. Despite Fishman's anger, he treated the civilians correctly, within the conventions of war. The German farmers would go back to their homes unharmed, unlike millions of Jewish civilians who were rounded up and forced to dig their own graves and to die in them. Later when Fishman entered a death camp, his outrage would turn against God, not man.

Fishman didn't seek this harrowing encounter with enemy civilians, but ideologically committed Jewish soldiers, like the socialist Zionist Akiva Skidell, deliberately sought out Jewish civilians. Drafted in November 1943 as a married man with a young daughter, Skidell served as a radio operator with the 2nd Armored Division in Europe. He arrived in France in the fall of 1944 and then quickly moved up toward the front. By the end of October he had reached Holland. Waiting his turn to take a shower in a Dutch coal mine, he inquired if there were any Jews in town. It happened that a Jewish family lived nearby, so he asked if he could visit them.

This first contact with European Jews moved him deeply. He found "besides the residents, parts of three more families there, from other parts of Holland, still German-held. It appears that the residents are one of three Jewish families in the town in the pre-war days. Of those three, one was deported to Poland and probably fixed for good, and two, including this one, disappeared from the surface and lived underground." Skidell thought they had probably been "a fairly well-off middle-class family, but what's left now I don't know. I do know that there is some cognac left, because I tasted some, and it was good. Other things they showed me were not so good, such as the Yellow Badge with the word Jood [Jew] on it." This part of Skidell's report to his wife Ettie is laconic; she understood the stigma of the yellow star and the murderous persecution that stalked its wearers. But Skidell was surprised and delighted because he "had walked in — of all things — on a Hebrew lesson! A young woman, in her late twenties; attractive, quite grey-haired tho, was teaching the Hebrew alphabet to one of the boys . . . who said to me: It is for Palestine! He is planning to go there to join some of his family, and so is the woman." Skidell was thrilled to find a child alive and a family committed to Zionism, preparing for postwar redemption. Stumbling upon other Zionists appeared too good to be true. But he reported news that "of some 150,000 Dutch Jews, about 30,000 managed to hide out when the deportation order came." Skidell found a measure of hope in these depressing statistics. "If the same ratio holds for Poland," he wrote, he might "still have a chance" to find the family he had left behind.[47]

A European Jew by birth and education, Skidell never expected to discover that several years in the United States had remade him. Revelations both Jewish and American came during a three-day pass in Brussels, a trip that combined ordinary tourism with Jewish sociability. Billeted in a hotel, Skidell reveled in his own room, "with a bed, an actual bed with two white sheets and a white pillow case," he wrote to Ettie. "The furniture is modernistic, tho a bit neglected during these years, but the whole thing is a dream." The Allied Expeditionary forces ran the facility, and the Army probably subsidized the cheap rates. On his first day in town Skidell visited the Jewish Hospitality club and bumped into a woman who asked, "Efsher a yid? [You a Jew, by any chance?]"[48]

Jewish civilians in Europe and elsewhere persistently looked for American Jewish soldiers.[49] They were eager to connect with individuals from the one large Jewish community unscathed by war. It gave them hope for the future. As a Zionist, Skidell answered such queries affirmatively and learned that there were Jews alive in Brussels. But all had tales of woe: "The things we've been reading about — deportation, living in hiding, afraid of one's shadow, night raids by the Gestapo, denunciations, miraculous escapes."[50] This brought home to Skidell the difference his uniform made. He had been a European Jew. Now, as an American soldier, he could fight the Nazis and defeat them. The Allies were winning the war, but not quickly enough to rescue his brethren in Poland. How many Jews would be alive when the war ended?

Before Skidell left Brussels a friend connected him with the local Labor Zionist movement, a group invisible to Jews not of this persuasion. Skidell visited a room where around thirty young people were dancing. All the different Zionist factions had merged in 1942 under the pressure of the deportations and then went underground. When they reemerged in late 1944, the wartime unity folded. Skidell was surprised that the decimated Zionists would drift apart. "Is all this necessary? Is it justified? Wouldn't it be better to continue in one unit?" he asked. No, "perhaps it wasn't absolutely justified, but it was inevitable that the old differentiations should re-emerge," came the answer. "They insist on their identity, have their emotional ties to specific spots in Palestine, argue the differences of kibbutz forms and seem to thrive in the process," he was told. In America, where you have to start from scratch, his guide informed him, "it is easy to have a broad base. Here, on the other hand, all that you have to pound away at — Jewish identity, Hebrew, aliya — is taken for granted, and if you take away the inner differentiations, you take away the spice of life."[51] Fragmentation, rigorous ideological debate, placing party commitments over common goals: these were the living practices of Belgian Zionism. Hitler's relentless effort to destroy Jewish politics and culture along with his annihilation of Jewish men, women, and children had failed.

As an American, Skidell could not grasp why unity in the face of an unremitting foe lasted only as long as the struggle for survival. It seemed that European Jewish Zionists had not learned anything from their underground experience. The Nazis made no distinctions among Jews slated for destruction. But they had manipulated internal divisions among Jews, even among Zionists, to weaken them. Still, Skidell was delighted to share a copy of the Labor Zionist weekly, *yidishe kemfer* (Jewish Fighter), as well as the new Jewish National Fund calendar mailed to him by American Zionists. The latter included a map depicting the thirty-eight settlements established in Palestine since 1940. The Belgian boys' eyes bulged. Cut off from news for four years, these young people knew nothing of what had happened in Palestine. Skidell concluded his letter with a dose of realism. "That they are able to be hopeful and of good cheer is a tribute to a strong spirit, because they have suffered terribly," he wrote, "and to say that they are down-trodden proletarians is merely a fancy way of saying that they are poor, unspeakably poor, without work and without any outlook for the future other than *aliya* [immigration to the land of Israel]. In this hope they are sustained so completely, as our people will never be." Committed as he was to the Zionist dream of *aliya* and the establishment of a Jewish state, Skidell nonetheless added a final sentence. "And, let's hope," he wrote, "will never need to be."[52]

Skidell did not wish such suffering on American Jews to propel them to Palestine. The decision to settle in the land of Israel should not rest only on the absence of any other alternative. Meeting these young European Jews, Zionists as he was, made him realize how different "our people" were. Although thrilled at their steady devotion to Palestine, Skidell recognized a gulf between European Jews and himself, now an American. Compared with European disunity, the American penchant for consensus looked appealing. Skidell was impatient with ideological rigor. Nevertheless, he confronted the stark fact that Europe had no room for Jews. In retrospect, Zionist analysis seemed to have foreshadowed this awful truth. But fortunately America was different.

Opportunities to meet other Jews often came from Jewish families who extended hospitality to servicemen, even in remote parts of the world. David Macarov was stationed in India for two years. In Calcutta he enjoyed a weekly tea "at the magnificent home of Lady Ezra, and a kosher chicken dinner" each Friday at Mrs. Gubbay's house. A Zionist activist in Young Judaea, Macarov believed in Jewish solidarity as well as the importance of building a state in Palestine. Writing to his parents in Atlanta, he emphasized how his Jewish ideological commitment overrode his American upbringing. "Born and bred in the South, it didn't matter what I *thought*, I *felt* an instinctive prejudice against dark skins. Given the choice," he admitted, "I would invariably sit by or talk to a white person, rather than a colored person, even though I knew such an attitude was wrong."[53] Macarov was convinced that his prejudice was so deeply rooted by conditioning that he could not overcome it. Then he met these Indian Jews. Yes, he explained to his folks, they are Indians. "One girl tells me that her family has lived in Calcutta for seven generations." But more to the point, he knew that his par-

David Macarov with members of the Calcutta Jewish community, 1943. For Macarov, stationed in Calcutta, meeting Indian Jews and Jewish soldiers in the Allies' armies stretched his understanding of Jewishness. Eventually he came to question his American assumptions about diaspora Jewish life.

ents really were asking: "Are they dark-skinned?" The question angered him. He was tempted to answer: "What difference does it make?" But he wanted his parents to realize what a remarkable accomplishment such sentiments represented for him. Now he no longer felt the prejudice against color that was so ingrained in him as a white southerner. In fact, he couldn't "see how it could have existed." Yes, these Indian Jews were dark-skinned, ranging from "what we would call 'white' to a very dark copper tan, with the majority merely a sunburned brown."[54]

For Macarov, meeting other Jews stretched his understanding of Jewishness and eventually led him to question his American assumptions and identity. The strangeness of Indian Jews challenged much of what he thought he knew. Their differences appeared not just in skin color and customs but also in their ignorance of Yiddish, *the* Jewish language from his Ashkenazi point of view. Speaking "Jewish [Yiddish] in a foreign country," one GI mused, was "like falling in love in springtime. Sweet music."[55] That didn't happen in India. Instead of Yiddish in his English, Macarov found that Hindustani phrases were creeping into his speech. Occasionally the two would get mixed together in expressions such as "Pucca Goy" (Real Gentile) and "Maluum Yiddish?" (Understand Yiddish?). Then Macarov discovered the local Zionist group. A visit to the synagogue led to an invitation to supper from the cantor, where one of his daughters sold Macarov a ticket for a school play. At the play he met one of the teachers, who in turn introduced him to her cousin, the Zionist group's secretary. Such a chain of connections drew him ever deeper into the web of Jewish community. He discovered that Americans were "looked upon with suspicion," as were any soldiers. The American GI practice of repaying a dinner invitation by asking the daughter for a date did not sit well with these patriarchal Jewish families. Not only did the soldier "not get the date, but he also never gets invited again," he explained to his parents. As Macarov learned about Jews in this remote section of the world, he probed his self-understanding. His encounter with Indian Jews changed his "attitudes and feelings toward life."[56] Rather than affirming his own Americanness, his contacts generated a Jewish solidarity that gradually dominated his Jewish American identity.

While stationed in Calcutta, Macarov planned a Zionist meeting for servicemen and local activists. The cross-section of soldiers represented a taste of the diversity of Jews fighting the war for the Allies. "Present at the Pegisha [meeting] was Gabby Bick, a Chalutz [pioneer] from England, who has been fighting with Wingate in Burma. Also there was Dov Sinclain, a Scotch Chalutz, who bears scars on his face from the razor gangs of Scotland, similar to our Ku Klux Klan. Solly Marcus, of English Hashomer Hatzair [The Young Guards] was present, as was Ted Sassen, a South African sailor." Then "there was Harold, who worked for the Communist underground in Germany, during Hitler's regime, for two years, although not a member of the party." And Nat, from Poland, instigated "the revolt against anti-Semitism in the Polish Forces." The Polish government-in-exile imprisoned Nat for this; then they pardoned him and transferred him to the British forces, which sent him to India. For the purpose of the meeting, the men buried their intramural ideological differences. Macarov, like Skidell, wished "that such a situation could exist permanently."[57] Jewish experiences covered a vast range, but political commitments usually drew Jews together.[58] Zionists, especially, made Jewish nationhood a concern that overrode other differences.

As rewarding as the Zionist gathering was, other confrontations with diverse Jewish servicemen elicited frustration. Macarov at times felt annoyed with the superficial hospitality of

Lady Ezra's tea party. "You just come in, get your tea and cake, and pass out into the yard." Such noblesse oblige irritated him. Even more bothersome were several Jewish soldiers who had been in Calcutta a long time. They "came swaggering in as though they owned" Mrs. Gubbay's house. "They treated the house as though it were a restaurant, and they were going to pay for their meal." Their bad manners offended Macarov. How could these men criticize the food in Yiddish when their hostess didn't understand the language? "One of the boys, who is in Special Services and is a radio announcer, commented that he was sure the proposed Jewish Brigade [soldiers recruited from Palestine to serve as a separate unit within the British military] wouldn't get anything done, since if they were all Jews, they'd all be entertainers and office workers." Macarov was disgusted. "If anyone else had said that, I'd consider it anti-Semitic," he told his folks. The remarks reflected prevalent antisemitic assumptions that Jews could not make good fighters, and it was particularly depressing to hear another Jew spout such prejudices. This soldier was sounding off about the fighting potential of an all-Jewish brigade even though he had seen no combat at all. Macarov thought of "Gabby with the Chindits, and Monty in Upper Assam." He remembered his own combat time. And he recalled exploits of the "new Jews" among the Palestinians he had met.[59]

By the end of his stay in India, Macarov had completely reversed his point of view toward American Zionism. It no longer seemed sufficient. "Our chalutzim are leaving this week for Palestine," he wrote to his folks. "How I envy them! Now the wheel has come full turn. I came to India with faith in the Galuth [diaspora], and now I have seen enough to negate it entirely." Only "those Jews who go to Palestine are doing all they can for Zionism," he concluded.[60] Macarov did not change his mind again.

Although he assured his parents that he would wait until he returned home to make such a major decision, he did subsequently settle in Palestine, heading for the Hebrew University on the GI bill. His two years in India had transformed him. Looking at the Jewish diaspora in India forced him to reexamine his own comfortable American existence and allowed him to overcome his deep-seated color prejudices. Meeting other Jews from the Allies' armies convinced him of his primary Jewish loyalty. He seized the possibilities of "new Jews" — those Palestinian fighters whose exploits he knew. His years in an American uniform erased his provincialism and strengthened his Jewish self-determination.

Crossing overseas thus initiated journeys that encouraged American Jewish soldiers to explore not only new and foreign worlds but also more personal ones. Integration into the military forced Jews to search hard for comradeship. They could not take for granted the friendship of the men in their unit. Loneliness and isolation often accompanied their military service overseas, especially in the jungles of the Pacific islands. To their surprise, many Jews like Sy Kahn "slowly discovered a surprising physical and emotional resilience." Although Jewishness lay deep in the recesses of his consciousness, Kahn did not abandon it. Others, like Hymie Samuelson, put their Jewish identity aside for the duration. Samuelson's family was far away, and the warmth of Christian fellowship cheered him. But both Kahn and Samuelson found a measure of happiness and satisfaction in doing a job well. And they learned, as did many Jews, how to live and work with diverse types of men. "We had all kinds of men," Martin Dash recalled, "some who would get into problems, some who would get thrown into jail, and some who were difficult to control aboard ship."[61] Their years in service encouraged Jews to assume responsibilities that they had only imagined as civilians. Their encounters with the men they met sharpened their perceptions of their American and Jewish identities.

Committed Zionists like Skidell and Macarov deliberately sought out Jewish civilians. They believed in Jewish peoplehood, assuming common connections among an internationally dispersed people. Yet their wartime encounters surprised them. Macarov came to appreciate how Jewishness helped him transcend his color prejudice, an aspect of his American identity that he disliked but had accepted as instinctual. Imbued with a new passion for Jewish solidarity, he vowed to jettison his Americanness at the first opportunity. Skidell, by contrast, learned that the handful of years he had lived in the United States had actually influenced his perspectives. He viewed European Jews differently, especially their penchant for ideological schisms. Crossing over reconfigured the American and Jewish components of both men's identities. The experience of meeting Jews who differed from them taught them the fluidity of their own self-understanding.

Much as Jews were integrated into the service, so Jewishness was assimilated into their identity as American soldiers. The armed forces created a world that enabled Jews to be different if they wished. Then they were shipped overseas. Once they crossed over, they had to decide where and when they differed, how and with whom they would seek companionship. Sometimes others made the decision for them, but often their situation allowed for flexibility. Regardless of what choices they made, their wartime experiences transformed their personalities.

5

WORSHIPPING TOGETHER

The bugle sounds the measured call to prayers,
The band starts bravely with a clarion hymn,
From every side, singly, in groups, in pairs,
Each to his kind of service comes to worship Him.

—KARL SHAPIRO, "Sunday: New Guinea"[1]

FEBRUARY 3, 1943. Past midnight, everyone except the crew on duty was asleep as the USAT *Dorchester* churned through the freezing Atlantic waters. The converted coastal liner was crammed with servicemen bound for Greenland. Over nine hundred filled its holds, sleeping on canvas bunks stacked one above the other. The trip was treacherous. German submarines freely roamed the Atlantic. Only three months earlier, in November 1942, they had torpedoed a record 509,000 tons, more than a hundred ships.[2] Part of a small convoy that included three Coast Guard Cutters, the *Dorchester* did its best to elude the U-boats. Ninety miles from Greenland, its luck ran out. The torpedo hit at 1:00 A.M. Its explosive force killed hundreds and smashed two lifeboats. Men staggered from their bunks, shocked by the blast. They raced to the deck as the ship began to sink. In the confusion, many forgot to grab their life jackets, belts, and gloves. No one could survive without them in the frigid ocean.[3]

Four officers, chaplains, also ran to the deck. They were among the first to arrive because their sleeping quarters were nearby. Hearing the command to abandon ship as the few remaining lifeboats were launched, the chaplains distributed jackets, belts, and gloves to the panicked soldiers. Together they tried to calm the men who were confronting catastrophe. When Lieutenant John Mahoney turned back to the cabin to retrieve his gloves, Rabbi Alexander Goode stopped him and insisted that he take what the chaplain claimed was his extra pair. "Just before the ship went down," testified Daniel O'Keefe, a nineteen-year-old merchant marine from the Bronx, "the chaplains gave their life preservers to members of the crew. They were standing on deck praying when our lifeboat drifted out of sight."[4] As the ship sank into the dark sea, the chaplains linked arms and offered final supplications. The Latin, Hebrew, and English prayers of the Catholic, Jewish, and Protestant chaplains blended into a common invocation. The deaths of Protestant Chaplains George L. Fox and Clark V. Poling, Catholic Chaplain John P. Washington, and Jewish Chaplain Alexander D. Goode would come to symbolize the nation's democratic religion.

Alexander Goode's path to the *Dorchester's* doomed deck seemed in retrospect to be *bashert,* his intended destiny. He actively promoted the interfaith cause that his death would exemplify. Goode followed his father into the rabbinate. Born in Brooklyn, he grew up in a traditional Jewish home in Washington, D.C., where his father served in a Georgetown synagogue. He attended the Reform Hebrew Union College on a scholarship supported by the sisterhood of his father's congregation. Deeply disturbed by the segregation of African Americans in the nation's capital, Goode championed equality. "We are fighting for the new age of brotherhood," he wrote, sounding one of the themes of worshipping together.[5] He also articulated a critical role for Judaism in the antifascist struggle. Goode's commit-

Iconic image of the four chaplains: Protestant Chaplains George L. Fox and Clark V. Poling, Catholic Chaplain John P. Washington, and Jewish Chaplain Alexander D. Goode. The four chaplains of three faiths worshipping together exemplified the creation of a Judeo-Christian tradition.

ment to Judaism and democracy, brotherhood and equality, and his hatred of Nazism inspired him to volunteer for the chaplaincy even before the attack on Pearl Harbor. He had protested his posting to Greenland with the Army Air Corps because he wanted to be closer to the men in action.[6] Now he stood in the midst of a disaster in which close to seven hundred men would lose their lives. As he felt the boat keel toward starboard, he saw hundreds of red lights from the men's life preservers bobbing in the sea, "like a long neon sign."[7] Then he recited the words of the *Sh'ma,* the affirmation of the unity of God, before the waters silenced him forever.

The four chaplains of three faiths worshipping together exemplified the creation of a "Judeo-Christian tradition" that would come to express American ideals guiding the country's wartime mission. In the face of death, religious differences no longer mattered. However one prayed, the same God heard the prayers. Similarities outweighed differences. All Americans, the "tradition" proclaimed, believed in the Fatherhood of God, the Brotherhood of Man, the individual dignity of each human being, and "positive ethical standards of right and wrong" existing apart from "the will of any man."[8] Throughout the war, chaplains would preach these values as emblematic of both American democracy and the Judeo-Christian tradition. What had formerly been three distinct religious traditions were now part of a collective tradition. The lifeboats of the survivors of the *Dorchester* catastrophe carried a waterproof package of pocket-sized Protestant, Catholic, and Jewish Testaments. The Jewish Scriptures included selections from the Torah, Prophets, and Writings.[9] The Protestant Bible contained the King James Version of the New Testament; the Catholic Testament held the Douay Version of the same text.[10] But the latter included the sentence "Jews are the Synagogue of Satan," which Jewish chaplains protested. Worshipping together in life, under the stress of future and past combat, would require dedication to mutual understanding beyond sharing a lifeboat and different versions of scripture. Both chaplains and enlisted men would have to work together to establish a Judeo-Christian tradition as Standard Operating Procedure in the armed forces.

Press accounts about the story of the four chaplains articulated some of the core values of this new Judeo-Christian tradition.[11] The deaths of the chaplains exemplified faith confronting adversity, the triumph of fellowship over religious strife, the spirit of self-sacrifice by officers for their men, the power of love over death. But it took almost two years for the chaplains' heroism to receive official public recognition. In December 1944, the chaplains were awarded Distinguished Service Crosses posthumously for their bravery.[12] Brigadier General William Arnold, chief of chaplains, praised "the extraordinary heroism and devotion of these Men of God." They were "an unwavering beacon for the thousands of chaplains of the armed forces." He called "the manner of their dying . . . one of the noble deeds of the war"[13] and observed that "the churches of America can be proud that such men carried their banners." Then he alluded to Jews, remarking that "men of all faiths can be proud that these men of different faiths died together."[14]

Such sentiments reflected efforts by Clark Poling's father, Dr. Daniel A. Poling, a leading Baptist minister and editor of *The Christian Herald,* to create an Interfaith Memorial within a year of the *Dorchester* tragedy. The chaplains' courage demonstrated to Poling the strength of religious conviction, while their deaths signaled the special ecumenical character of religion in the United States armed forces. He wanted to enshrine this new democratic faith as a guiding light for all Americans.[15] Without his efforts to publicize and interpret the death of his son, the sinking of the *Dorchester* would not have been transformed from tragedy to triumph. Poling drew upon a blend of politics and religion that harked back to his struggles during the Depression against anti–New Deal racists, conservative Christians, and antisemites. To his dismay, these men of the right "had appropriated 'Christian' as an identifying mark."[16] He had watched Christian Front supporters of the radio priest Charles Coughlin rally against communism, the New Deal, and American Jews.[17] After the sinking of the *Dorchester,* "Judeo-Christian" increasingly became "a catchword for the other side." That "other side" included liberal Christians and Jews like Poling and Goode, as well as American communists, especially during the popular front years.[18]

Poling's work on the home front complemented practices developed by the military. For the armed forces, the notion of Judeo-Christian universalist ideals promised to build morale among the troops. It was the spiritual side of the democratic ethos. In February 1943, the same month as the *Dorchester* tragedy, the Army adopted a new plan of room assignment at its Chaplains' School at Harvard University "as a means of promoting understanding among men of different faiths," according to the Army's official history. "At that time four men were being quartered in most dormitory suites. So far as it could be arranged, a Catholic, a Jew, a Protestant of one of the liturgical churches, and one from an evangelical body were billeted together. This plan did much to promote cordiality and personal friendship."[19] It also replicated the template dramatized by the recent deaths of the four chaplains. The military was moving gradually to create a Standard Operating Procedure (SOP) for the Judeo-Christian tradition that would make worshipping together not only possible but also practical. It would not be easy: formidable religious differences had to be both respected and surmounted; doctrinal disagreements had to be accommodated and subordinated to the demands of war and military requirements.[20]

Rabbis approached chaplaincy training with trepidation, fearing that they would have to compromise their beliefs. As his one-month course at Harvard neared its end in August 1943, Harold Saperstein wrote to his Lynbrook congregants about his experience. "The army has no room for theories or individual opinions or new slants," he observed, ". . . and we're expected to take it as it is given." A former pacifist, Saperstein warily accepted his new responsibilities. The course introduced him to a fresh set of peers, men who had previously had little personal contact with Jews. In a discussion on "our relationship to our allies," specifically Russia, "the Catholics were right on their toes" he wrote. Their remarks impressed Saperstein with "how deeply they have been indoctrinated with the anti-Communist virus. They don't trust the teacher," he reported, "because he started off the course by saying that truth is relative." Saperstein continued, "it's official army doctrine not to criticize our allies." The Catholics, he explained, "say they must differentiate between what is going on in Russia and the philosophy of Communism. It is the latter to which they object."[21] Religious perspectives diverged on the political ideologies of the era, both communism and fascism. But chaplains could not ignore the way religion and politics were necessarily intertwined in the armed forces. For Jews and Christians to worship together, as Saperstein suggested, would require finding an acceptable path through this complex thicket.

Commitment to separation of church and state offered Saperstein some guidelines for negotiating his political differences with his fellow chaplains, but it also challenged him within the hierarchy of the armed forces. He bore responsibility to his military superiors, representatives of the state, as well as to Judaism. He had to decide early in his chaplaincy career whether he would support his "commanding officer and justify all his actions," or "offer constructive if uninvited suggestions concerning ways to improve the physical, mental, and spiritual lot of the common soldier."[22] The military had no room for prophets, as he quickly learned. His role required that he minister to men of all faiths without compromising his own religious convictions. As part of the evolving SOP, the Army requested monthly reports that included a question regarding his personal efforts on behalf of men not of his religious tradition. Saperstein rarely fo-

cused on tensions that arose between the demands of Judaism
and military expectations; he preferred to emphasize those moments when his responsibilities as rabbi and chaplain, as Jew
and American, harmonized.[23] He worked hard to create a Judeo-
Christian SOP even as he did his best to guide all types of Jewish
soldiers, from the most observant to the highly secular. But the
needs of enlisted men and the wishes of their chaplains did not
necessarily coincide. Their differences reflected not only military distinctions between officers and men, but also attitudes toward Judaism as a religion and a culture.

Six months after the *Dorchester* catastrophe, Victor Geller
left his mother's Bronx apartment and his Talmud studies at Yeshiva to begin his Army service and the new experience of worshipping together with gentiles. Sent to Cornell University in
Ithaca, New York, Geller readied himself to explain to his two
Catholic roommates in the Army Specialized Training Program
(A.S.T.P.) how he prayed every morning. His previous experience with Catholics had been largely limited to Irish streetcar
conductors on the 167th Street trolley. As eager as he had been
to leave the security of Yeshiva to do his duty as a soldier, he
"understood that the transition from an orthodox Jewish environment to military life would be a big challenge."

When he arrived at Cornell, Geller was eighteen years old,
five feet four inches tall, weighed only 115 pounds, and had
lived all his life in the Bronx. His world had been framed by the
Sabbath and Jewish holidays. "Each morning began with prayers
and was followed by hours of religious studies." But Geller was
determined to transform himself from a *yeshiva bochur* into an
American soldier. He recognized that he "was leaving an inten-
sive, sharply defined milieu" of Jewish values for the "vast, dimly
outlined world of gentile America." So he tried to prepare his
roommates by explaining that in addition to his prayer shawl, he

donned *tefillin*, "small black boxes containing parchment strips of scripture," to pray. He even did a show-and-tell for them, demonstrating how he wound the leather straps seven times around his left forearm and three times around his fingers, and wore the *tefillin* on his arm and head. One of his roommates, a New Yorker, took Geller's practices in stride. The other, from Ohio, "had some trouble" with the ritual. Even for Catholics accustomed to rosaries and scapulars, *tefillin* seemed odd. Eventually both men adjusted and joked about how "Geller takes his religious blood pressure every day."[24] The metaphor worked.[25] Geller's success with his roommates encouraged and emboldened him.

But worshipping together involved not only Christians and Jews; it also included different types of Jews. The Jewish holidays in particular attracted a wide array, from traditionally observant men like Geller to liberal Reform rabbis like Saperstein. The Jewish New Year arrived before Geller had adjusted to his new routine. Reading the holy days schedule posted on the bulletin boards, he was stunned to see services planned for only one day of Rosh Hashana instead of the two days to which he was accustomed. To make matters worse, services "were to be limited to the first evening and an abbreviated two hour period the next morning." A period of two hours was utterly inadequate to encompass the long New Year's liturgy. Unwilling to accept such an abrogation of tradition, Geller promptly sought out the rabbi in his office on the Cornell campus. "From his neatly clipped moustache to his highly polished loafers, this urbane, good looking man was the perfectly groomed Ivy Leaguer." He was a Reform rabbi. Geller's "nondescript uniform testified to the difference" between them. Their religious practices were inscribed in their physical demeanor. "One other contrast topped it off": every hair of the rabbi's "carefully combed head was clearly visi-

Victor Geller and Jewish soldiers at a service in Europe, 1944. Geller prayed daily and took his tefillin with him into combat. He also accepted responsibility for leading services when no chaplain was available. Opportunities for public prayer affirmed the military's commitment to respect Judaism, symbolized by the rifle and prayerbook in the photograph.

ble," whereas Geller's "messy head was covered by a yarmulke." Most Reform Jews wore neither a hat nor a *tallis*, a prayer shawl, even during worship. Reform Judaism rejected these artifacts of Jewish ritual observance as inappropriate for the modern era. Orthodox Jews did their best to keep their head covered at all times, and always during prayer. The rabbi listened courteously to Geller's complaints about the reduced one-day schedule.

Then he explained that this "was all that the commanding officer of the Cornell ASTP had approved."[26] New to the Army, Geller couldn't imagine that the CO might determine the length of Jewish worship. He saw the question far more starkly, as a deliberate effort by a Reform rabbi to subvert Jewish tradition.

Geller's "unsatisfactory interview," his "first experience" with a Reform rabbi, confirmed his prejudices against Reform Jews. He thought it "proved" that they were trying "to hide" their Jewishness by "acting like gentiles." He determined to speak with the company sergeant, a regular Army man, who gave him permission to observe the second day of Rosh Hashana in his room. By the time Yom Kippur arrived ten days later, Geller had requested permission not only to pray privately, but also to post notices to recruit a minyan of ten men to join him in his room for the sacred fast day.[27] With the help of his company's sergeant, Geller's aggressive pursuit of his religious rights as an American Jewish soldier was rapidly upstaging the campus rabbi.

Chaplains recognized that abbreviated services often irritated Orthodox Jews. Chaplain Morris Kertzer, a Conservative rabbi, recalled how occasionally, as he was delivering his sermon, "perhaps reaching the dramatic point, a pious young worshipper would rise in the midst of the congregation and perform the *Amidah* (silent devotion), with genuflections and bowing of the head." As Kertzer's language suggests, such practice irritated him because it "would distract every eye" away from the chaplain.[28] Sermons seemed irrelevant to Orthodox Jews like Geller. Far more important were the required prayers that had been eliminated in efforts to shorten the service. Eventually Kertzer mellowed and learned not to bristle at these efforts to challenge his rabbinic authority. Worshipping together, even as Jews, required tolerance and a measure of ecumenical understanding.

Conflict with enlisted men dogged many Jewish chaplains because the chaplaincy recruited more Reform rabbis than Conservative or Orthodox ones.[29] One thousand and forty-five rabbis, over half of American rabbis, volunteered for military service, but only 311 received commissions.[30] Among those commissioned, almost half (147) came from the Reform movement, not quite a third (96) from Conservatism, and a fifth (68) from modern Orthodoxy.[31] Men like the Orthodox rabbi Herschel Schacter, featured in the chaplaincy movie that had inspired Geller to enlist, actually represented a minority of Jewish chaplains. The denominational distribution of the 311 rabbis on active duty reflected the guidelines and recruitment process. The Jewish agencies set the educational bar for the chaplaincy higher than the Army did.[32] When the Jewish Welfare Board's (JWB) reorganized Committee on Army and Navy Religious Activities (CANRA) took responsibility for recruitment and supervision, it insisted that applicants be graduates of both a seminary and a college. The war department accepted a degree from either one.[33] Rabbis who had received ordination abroad, most of whom were Orthodox, lacked a collegiate degree and protested its requirement. But CANRA refused to budge. It would not consider examinations in lieu of a college degree. It also screened prospective candidates for their appearance, speech, religious integrity and flexibility, and psychological approach. CANRA rejected men with accents and those who would be unable to serve diverse types of Jews.[34]

The Commmittee wanted chaplains like Saperstein and Kertzer who were culturally American as well as Jewish. Chaplains entered the military as visible Jews. Rabbis literally wore their Jewish identity on their sleeves and lapels. Although not all officers recognized the Jewish insignia of two tablets of the law topped by a Magen David, Jewish GIs and Jewish civilians did.[35]

CANRA insisted that Jewish chaplains be American men, although many of the soldiers who formed Jewish GI congregations came, like Geller, from observant homes.[36]

Chaplains had to bridge a spectrum of Jewish observance to make worshipping together for Jews an experience of fellowship. Artie Gorenstein's interest in Zionism and in meeting other Jews represented another point on the complex compass of Jewish experience. The chance to socialize with other Jews drew Gorenstein to chapel during basic training. Yet even here, chaplains and enlisted men often held opposing views. "The men were likely to be in a compromising mood since they were often as not lonely," wrote one chaplain, "and a Friday night at chapel filled a void in their social life and provided good fellowship."[37] Propelled by loneliness, Gorenstein found his first visit to the chapel at Keesler Field disappointing. The handful of men in the standard military chapel built to accommodate several hundred exaggerated the feeling of being a tiny minority, despite the welcome presence of a Jewish flag with its blue Magen David. Although Gorenstein appreciated the absence of Christian symbols in the Army's nondenominational chapel, the service hardly lifted his spirits.[38] At its conclusion he suggested to the chaplain that an *oneg shabbat* (Sabbath celebration) following services would allow the men to discuss issues and socialize. When Gorenstein returned a couple of weeks later for Sabbath services, "the Chaplain was absent and the Assistant conducted a discussion after the services that finally resolved into a Zionist speech by your son," he wrote home.[39] This was definitely more satisfying for such a committed Zionist.

Yet the spiritual dimensions of public worship could inspire Gorenstein as well as the experience of fellowship. "I came back from Yom Kippur Services about [a] half hour ago," he wrote his parents. It was 10:00 P.M., "Erev Yom Kippur," the eve of the

Day of Atonement when the fast began. Gorenstein had been reading *The World of Sholem Aleichem* in the Service Club. Then he got the urge to write. "Since this is really taking the place of a conversation in the parlor or kitchen at [home] I'm sure the 'Rabainu Shalailom' [Our God of the World] won't consider my writing a transgression. After all, talking to one's family is a natural thing." Giving a rationale for writing indicated Gorenstein's awareness of the day's holiness and the restrictions on behavior normally in force for observant Jews. He described the Kol Nidre services he had just attended. "The chazan [cantor] was excellent and there were over 1500 in attendence [*sic*]. The chaplain's Sermon was outstanding."[40] Since he was excused from work the next day, he planned to fast. The following evening he confessed that fasting had made him "groggy." But "now that I have food in me I feel full of life," he wrote his folks. "Then there is that spiritual cleaness [*sic*] — a 'high' phrase but the only one I can think of — that one feels after Yom Kippur. As yet I haven't been brought down to earth by the daily hum-drum of Army routine. So at this moment I am really soaring."[41] Praying in public among hundreds of other Jews in uniform conveyed more than the Jewish message of the holy day, the sense of being cleansed of one's sins and written in the book of life for another year. It affirmed the military's commitment to respect Judaism and Jews who observed its requisites. Gorenstein treasured both, the fellowship with other Jews and the validation of his American identity.

While Yom Kippur drew all those three-day-a-year Jews ready to proclaim their Jewish identity in public, along with Jews of varying political persuasions willing to worship on this holiest day of the Jewish calendar, prayer occurred every day for observant Jews like Geller, as he had explained to his Catholic bunkmates. His religious responsibilities were personal as well as collective. So his initial negotiations with his roommates and the Reform rabbi would have to be repeated each time the Army sent him someplace new. The process forced Geller to recognize not only how others saw his religious behavior but also where he might find allies. Differences among Jews along with demands for fraternity and sensitivity to others' opinions assumed ever more significant proportions. How did a man affirm his Jewish religious commitment without alienating both his fellow Jews and his American comrades? Where did a Jew draw a line between the demands of religious observance and military requirements of uniformity? The idea of a Judeo-Christian tradition made sense as a common denominator, but it resolved neither the particulars of Jewish differences nor the persistence of prejudice.

By the time Geller arrived at Fort Benning for basic training, he thought that he could handle both daily prayers with his *tefillin* and the Jewish holidays. He was unprepared for the sharp criticism he received from the only Jewish non-com on their barracks floor. A few days into basic training, he joined Geller as he was leaving the mess hall. Striding beside him, the Corporal delivered a warning. "Kid," he said, "I wanna talk to you. I've been watching you puttin' on tefillin ever since you got here. I didn't say anything the first few days 'cause I figured you had some special reason, a holiday I dunno' about or something." But now it looked as if Geller was planning to make praying with *tefillin* a regular habit every morning. Hence the Corporal's warning: "This business of puttin' on your tefillin gotta stop. Ye're not in Brooklyn any more, ye're in the army. If you wanna be religious at home, that's your business," he acknowledged. But "in the army it's different." He pointed out that Geller was attracting attention and making a spectacle of himself "in front of goyim [gentiles]." It was embarrassing. The non-com tried to explain how the men were talking behind Geller's back, not only about him "but about all Jews." Geller's daily prayers were creating problems that "we don' need." The Corporal felt strongly that distinctive Jewish religious practices needed to be set aside for the duration. "Send your tefillin home," he urged. "Tefillin don't belong in the army."[42]

The Corporal's advice rendered Geller speechless. Surprised and confused, he admitted that he had "no sense" that "putting on tefillin was making such a terrible impression on the non-Jews in the barracks, that it was having a negative impact on the other Jewish GIs." He certainly didn't aim to provoke antisemitism. But Geller also was furious. "To be denied the right to pray was wrong," he believed. It didn't interfere with his duties, and he felt strongly that he "wasn't imposing on anyone."[43] To the non-com, attuned to the endemic antisemitism at Fort Benning and bent on fitting in, Geller seemed to be waving a red flag before a bull. He couldn't fathom how Geller could be so naive or foolish or egotistical as to imagine that praying with *tefillin* was accepted by the other men. Stunned by the encounter with such a radically different Jewish view of his world, Geller appealed to the Master Sergeant, the senior non-com of the 346th infantry. "A tall, pale man with sparse, blond hair," he wore rimless glasses that made him look scholarly. He was, however, a lean North Dakota farmer whose thin build belied his strength. The Master Sergeant confronted the Corporal. "You know that I'm a Roman Catholic. You know that I go to Mass every Sunday morning. Many of the Protestant fellows get to chapel some time during the week," he continued. "I don't know what the Jewish fellows do, but I know that you never go. If this kid wants to pray, it's none of your business," he rebuked the Corporal. "He's going to continue to pray," the Sergeant said, "and I don't ever want to hear a word out of you telling him to stop, or cut out his religious services. And that's an order!" The Corporal followed orders. He never mentioned *tefillin* after that. Geller continued to pray daily and took his *tefillin* with him into combat in Europe. And he never forgot the Sergeant's defense of his right to put on *tefillin*, "and of my tefillin's right to serve in the army with me."[44] Jews would have to adjust to each other as well as to Christians. However, orders took precedence over personal preferences.

Orders often forced Jews to observe holidays even when they didn't care to signal their difference from their fellow soldiers. On Passover in 1945, David Jacobs "was aboard a troopship headed for the Marianas." While they were anchored in Pearl Harbor waiting to join a convoy, the commanding officer called him and another Jew, Sgt. Abe Farber, to his stateroom. "I don't know much about this Seder thing," said the Colonel, "but I'm sure you two do. Just before we shipped out, the Seattle Jewish Welfare Board delivered crates of things to be used at what you call Seder time. Get that stuff up from the hold and carry out a Seder." Singled out because they were Jews, Farber and Jacobs were ordered to enact a religious ritual which their commanding officer knew nothing about but which was part of the SOP. The CO was implementing the "Judeo-Christian tradition." Yet his command embarrassed the two enlisted men. Still, they reluctantly followed orders. With great discomfort, they roped off tables in the mess hall for a seder that would interfere with the nightly poker games. After improvising a seder plate, they wondered who would lead the seder. Neither felt "quite up to the mission." Their ideal candidate, "a child of the yeshiva," was "in sickbay."[45]

Farber and Jacobs knew what a seder was, but they associated it with Orthodox practice. Neither of them was observant. In all likelihood, the seders they remembered were orchestrated

Ecumenical observance of a Passover seder under military auspices trans-formed an intimate Jewish home ritual into a public performance. The Jewish Welfare Board attempted to fill the void of absent parents with do-it-yourself seder kits, including special food and wine, whose success re-lied upon young Jews willing to assume often unfamiliar religious roles.

by their mothers or grandmothers. Women cleaned the house and prepared the elaborate meal that occupied the center of the seder ritual, especially for less observant Jewish families. A fa-ther or grandfather would lead whatever liturgy was followed, but often this would fly by in Hebrew, which the younger gener-ation had not mastered. No matter what fond memories Jacobs and Farber had of their seders, as men they could not replicate it on a troop ship before other, mostly Christian soldiers. Wor-shipping together had its limits. Their associations of a seder in-volved the intimacy of family, not a public gathering. To make matters worse, most of the Jews on board preferred watching the evening's entertainment on deck.[46]

After advertising the wine and salami, Jacobs ran below to find the ship's chaplain. "Would you please attend our Seder?" he asked. "And sir, I know you're Episcopalian, but since there's no Jewish chaplain aboard, would you consider presiding?" "Of course," he said, observing that "the Last Supper was also a Seder." Jacobs was thrilled. The chaplain was superb. "He put on a JWB yarmulke, walked over to the ropes, untied them, invited one and all to join the party, and then conducted the ceremony in flawless Hebrew, translating as he went."[47] Without the chaplain's leadership, the seder undoubtedly would have faltered, despite the Colonel's orders. With his support, it became a memorable event.

The Jewish Welfare Board (JWB) attempted to compensate for the absence of Jewish mothers and grandmothers with do-it-yourself seder kits, including special food and wine. Chaplains recognized the appeal of kosher salami and gefilte fish.[48] Nonetheless, if these kits were to succeed, Jews would have to be willing to assume often unfamiliar religious roles. Or, as in this case, an Episcopalian chaplain would have to do so. His performance rescued Jacobs and Farber and fulfilled the CO's orders. The chaplain could enact the "Judeo-Christian" SOP because a critical part of his ecumenical behavior involved his perception that he was enacting the Last Supper of Jesus Christ. So he untied the ropes dividing insiders from outsiders and invited participation of one and all, Jew and Christian, in an ecumenical observance that raised an intimate Jewish home ritual to the status of a public event. His knowledge of Hebrew, a sign of his own advanced learning, assured the seder's authenticity.

Jacobs and Farber were lucky because some chaplains declined to worship together with Jews. Even when ordered by his superior, a chaplain could refuse a command that violated his conscience. In April 1945 a Catholic chaplain, Thomas Byrant, disobeyed orders to provide volunteers for a Passover seder. When reprimanded by his CO, Bryant appealed to the Army Chief of Chaplains. "Since the Colonel did not agree with our attitude and considered it uncharitable and being exclusive on our part," he wrote, "I had to explain that since we Catholics considered our religion true, we could not take part in religious services of a religion we considered false."[49] Bryant's letter went to the heart of the dilemma of an Army policy that encouraged chaplains to be guided by their conscience even as they followed military orders. If that conscience denied the truths of a Judeo-Christian tradition that embraced differences, then it enfeebled the Army's emerging SOP for religion.

For Jews, implementing the Army's SOP for religion required demonstrating their commitment to brotherhood, a core value of the Judeo-Christian tradition, by helping Christians celebrate Christmas. Urged on by Jewish chaplains and the JWB as an interfaith gesture of goodwill, Jewish GIs volunteered for service details and gave up their weekend passes over the Christmas holidays so that Christian soldiers could celebrate either at home or on or off the base.[50] An orthodox German Jewish refugee who became a GI fourteen months after arriving in the United States remarked that "Jews taking over duties of Gentiles on Christmas, for the privilege of getting leave on their holidays, almost became an institution."[51] He described the exchange as a quid pro quo, and undoubtedly many considered it one. The Army regularly assigned Jews to "guard and kitchen patrol (KP) duties on Christmas and Easter." Arthur Zirul "used to tell people" that he "volunteered," but admitted he "really did not."[52]

On Christmas Eve in 1943, "that policy resulted in having

Jews staffing the guard complement at Fort Lewis' eastern gate
—from the officer of the guard right down to the bottom-line
private." Fort Lewis in Washington, Zirul's first assignment, was
a highly restricted camp where guards received live ammunition. That situation produced an amusing Jewish-Christian encounter that occurred around midnight. A "car full of very drunk
and very lost war-plant workers went barreling through the eastern gate without so much as a pause." Zirul's friend Irwin was
manning the post at that gate. When the car shot past him, Irwin
shouted "HALT!!" three times. Then he "unlimbered his .45 re-
volver (1898 issue) and emptied all six chambers at the fast dis-
appearing vehicle. The shots sounded like cannon fire in the
nearly deserted camp. Irwin screamed for the corporal of the
guard." Zirul was the corporal of the guard. When he heard
the shots and the alarm, he "immediately alerted the sergeant of
the guard, Sgt. Weinbaum, who in turn awakened the officer
of the guard, Capt. Goodman." All four Jewish soldiers "rushed
to the site of the incident and helped to round up the six tres-
passers. They had fled the car in an understandably disorganized
rout. The car itself was up on the curb, all four doors were open
and there was not a mark on it." No one was hurt. To everyone's
relief, Irwin was not a good shot.[53]

The Jewish non-commissioned officers herded the intruders
in front of Capt. Goodman and awaited his orders. Goodman
looked at his watch and sighed. "It's Christmas Day," he said.
"Put them back in the car and let them go." As the car drove
slowly out of sight, Capt. Goodman eyed Irwin. "Please," he
said, "don't shoot any more *goyim* today."[54] Here the Army's implementation of the "Judeo-Christian" SOP confirmed among
Jews a sense of their own separateness. The experience of Jewishness cut across military hierarchy, and in this case Jewish
identity proved more powerful than rank.

However, more often rank did matter, especially a chaplain's status as an officer. Harold Ribalow, a Zionist who had grown up in the Bronx in a home where Hebrew and Yiddish were spoken, thought that "to the GI who saw the chaplain as just another officer, who saw that the chaplain cannot act as a friend in a case where the Army and GI clash, who saw that chaplains never spoke out against discrimination against the enlisted man, the chaplain and his church was not taken seriously."[55] Morris Kertzer agreed. "The men sometimes accused us of being 'rank-conscious,'" he wrote after the war, ". . . and often they were right." He recognized how difficult it was "to overcome the barriers set up by the army to separate officers from enlisted men. Many chaplains would have preferred to hold no rank whatever."[56] Kertzer initially tried to socialize at recreation centers with the men but quickly discovered that his presence made them uncomfortable. They saw him as an officer first. On an Army transport, military police barred his entrance to the enlisted men's deck. Rank took precedence over religious role.

Jewish soldiers and sailors occasionally turned to chaplains for help. Often this involved some sort of favor: a pass or furlough to get home, a transfer to another unit, some kosher food, reclassification, a hardship or physical disability discharge. Sometimes the request was for permission to marry, and even, on occasion, for conversion of a future spouse. Then there were more difficult issues, such as those involving a confession of homosexuality or adultery, or problems with an antisemitic officer. GIs hoped that the common bond of Jewishness would sway a chaplain to sympathy and his rank might produce results. Chaplains, on the other hand, worried about military procedures and how far they could go beyond them. Some chaplains may have identified more strongly with their fellow officers. Some may have feared that a clever GI was trying to manipulate them.

Such encounters could leave unpleasant memories for both chaplain and soldier.[57]

Yet officer rank could also produce respect and admiration, as Harry Gersh discovered to his surprise. After never finding a chaplain he liked in the Army, Gersh, who had worked as a union organizer and grown up in a militantly secular and antireligious New York City home, experienced a change of heart in the Navy. It happened at an indoctrination session for the entire battalion, given by the chaplain, a lieutenant. "The lieutenant rose, walked forward, and said, 'I am a rabbi.'" His bluntness and pride dumbfounded Gersh. Like "every boot in the battalion," he sucked in his "breath and sat forward." Then he "listened hard" to what the chaplain had to say. Gersh concluded that the speech, a standard one, was unimportant. "But the man was smart. His first sentence proved it." Rabbis recognized how unusual they were in uniform. Unlike many Jewish GIs, chaplains anticipated that they would be representing an entire people and its religious tradition. "Most of the boys had never seen a real, live rabbi before," Gersh observed. "Most of them had never even thought of one. If they had run across the word it had evoked a mental picture of some anti-Semitic stereotype." What a contrast that was to the chaplain in an officer's uniform standing before them. Here "was a man, an officer, the senior officer present, the man whom the chief and jay gees made way for and said 'sir' to, a man who calmly walked forward and said, 'I am a rabbi.'" The respect and rank accorded a Jew bowled him over. Gersh couldn't resist. "I loved him," he confessed.[58]

Once they headed overseas, chaplains and the services they conducted acquired more emotional dimensions. There were no furloughs home or passes to nearby Jewish communities. The foreign setting changed the character of worship. Feelings of isolation often drew Jewish soldiers to religious services. Some left-wing Jewish soldiers and sailors, like Gersh, unexpectedly found themselves attending services in order to stand up to antisemites. Declaring oneself a Jew in public made a dramatic statement.[59] Jewish soldiers discovered contemporary relevance in public worship. In France in 1944, one medic who felt ambivalent about his Jewish identity decided to observe Rosh Hashana. After landing at Cherbourg and moving into the town of St. George, he went into the fields with other Jews in his regiment "and used a German 88 as a pulpit to conduct the holy services commemerating [*sic*] the New Year." Without a rabbi, "on a battle-scarred field," they prayed "using the equipment of the persecutors of their faith." The service marked a change in the medic's self-understanding. "In that small bombed Catholic town," he affirmed, "I became a Jew in faith."[60] At Yom Kippur services in the European Theater, one GI marveled, "Headgear were the steel helmets, and every soldier carried his rifle, which he placed between his feet when sitting, and slung to his shoulder when certain prayers required him to stand."[61] The rustling of the GI hardware reverberated through the air and brought home to the soldiers their assembled might. Judaism appeared to be "an imposing and powerful force."[62]

When celebrated overseas, the traditional round of festivals resonated with Jewish reasons for fighting the war. In a "clearing in the woods" in Germany where the 346th Infantry "had been shunted" temporarily, Victor Geller held a makeshift seder in the morning, two days late. "There were no chairs, benches or tables." Some fifty Jewish GIs "sat on the ground" and formed "a double circle" with Geller in the middle, reading from the lone Haggadah he had brought from the States, "like a tribal story teller." The menu was limited to two hundred pounds of British matzo and some "liberated" wine. The assembled GIs had paused, briefly, in their pursuit of "the soldiers of this latest,

Yom Kippur services on New Georgia Island in the South Pacific, 1943. Once they headed overseas, chaplains and the services they conducted took on different dimensions. There were no more furloughs home or visits to nearby Jewish communities. Here Chaplain Elliot David leads worship in a foreign setting. Jewish soldiers often attended religious services to find fellowship, and on occasion they discovered contemporary relevance in public prayer.

most malevolent 'Pharaoh.'"[63] It was easy to see analogies between the present and the ancient past.

Jewish servicemen at times experienced a fellowship that united them not only with other Jews but also with their fellow Christian GIs.[64] At these moments, they worshipped together in unexpected ways. Harold Ribalow, eager to visit Casablanca when he arrived in December 1943, joined "a group of soldiers who were going to attend a Jewish religious service on Friday night." A special truck would take them to the chapel in Casablanca and bring them back. Ribalow had come with Tony Rogliano, an Italian Catholic. As Ribalow admitted, both of them appreciated "a free pass to town" even if it came with the requirement to attend Sabbath services. Both men waited patiently through the services for the opportunity afterward to sneak out to see Casablanca. The assembled group of around one hundred included "mostly soldiers, a sprinkling of officers, a few sailors and one native Moroccan woman, with wonderful black eyes." Despite their eagerness to explore the foreign city, they sensed a mood of spirituality. It was Ribalow's first religious service since leaving the United States. Rogliano sat next to him. A first lieutenant, a flier, young-faced and nervous, turned to Rogliano and whispered, "Will you show me the place?" Cued in a moment before by his buddy, a poker-faced Rogliano showed the Jewish lieutenant the proper page of the liturgy. The Italian Catholic blended effortlessly into the Jewish congregation.[65]

Ribalow thought "the usual prayers sounded more meaningful. When we recited, in English, a prayer for our country, we read with perhaps more feeling than ever before." Now that he was across the ocean, he realized how "organized religion was suddenly closely connected with home."[66] In a medical unit in Italy, Morris Kertzer recalled how he never dared to "overlook page 320 of the Jewish Welfare Board Prayer Book, containing the Prayer for Home." Many regulars at services knew it by heart. "Far from home and those I love," it went, "I find my thoughts turning to them with affectionate longing."[67] Ribalow thought that even "the ordinary prayers . . . expressed well what most of us were thinking." A gray-haired Lieutenant Colonel sat among them. Ribalow was not alone in noting how Jewish unity transcended rank. "A corporal near me," he observed, "nudged his companion and pointed to the silver oak leaf." Perhaps, Ribalow speculated, "it made him feel good."[68] Gathering for the Sabbath service reinforced Jewish fraternity across the military's hierarchy.

The naval chaplain who gave the sermon that evening was Selwyn Ruslander, a thirty-three-year-old Reform rabbi who had entered the service in July 1942. "Ruslander not only impressed" Ribalow, but "he completely won" Rogliano's admiration as well. Rogliano had never before been in a synagogue, and Ribalow "desperately wanted no mistakes made to alienate someone who was completely unaware of Judaism." Ruslander did not disappoint. He "spoke with measured words." His diction and style mattered almost as much as the sermon's substance. He told the men "how he had been forced down in a plane somewhere in the Dutch East Indies and discovered, in the wilds of the island, a lost Jewish community." Although Ribalow couldn't recall the details, Ruslander's tale of intermarriage and assimilation led him to conclude that a Jew should preserve his faith. This message of endogamy and pride in Jewishness inspired Ribalow.[69] Undoubtedly his buddy's enthusiasm for the chaplain also carried weight. As Ribalow had hoped, Rogliano learned that Jews were fellow Americans, similar enough to their comrades-in-arms to be worthy of respect.

When Harold Saperstein was in southern France, he glimpsed the new meaning prayer had for Jewish GIs. Each time a group of men moved out for the front from a replace-ment depot, he would meet with them "for a few moments just before they board the trucks." Rabbi Saperstein wrote to his wife, Marcia, that "the prayers we say take only a few minutes but invariably they come from the heart." Although he usually felt moved, he admitted that by late 1944 it had come "to be a routine job, day after day." The relentless pressure of the war's unceasing demand for replacements hardened him. Then, one time, it was different. A relatively small shipment was leaving. Saperstein barely gathered a minyan of ten Jewish GIs around him. He explained his standard procedure to his wife: "At one point in the service, I usually say — 'And now let's turn from the prayerbooks and let each of us pray in the depths of his own heart.'" This was his introduction to silent prayer. As "every one became hushed," they heard a young soldier's voice strained with sincerity and emotion. "O God, watch over me and bring me back safe to my father and mother." The heartfelt prayer ex-pressed what the other GIs were thinking. Then the soldier's "voice broke and he started to weep." Saperstein knew that "the others struggled to keep control of themselves but whether their tears were inside or outside every one of them was crying." He confessed that he "was no exception."[70] Questions of life and death transcended any particular religious faith. Soldiers in uni-form might plead for divine protection without denigrating their manhood.

The GI's prayer reminded Saperstein of what was at stake. So did saying kaddish, the memorial prayer for the dead. He spent a lot of his time burying the dead. The course he had taken in the registration of graves was far from superfluous. In this con-text, memorial services inevitably led to reflections upon the war and its meaning. Military protocol at such occasions elaborated the ritual dimensions of the Judeo-Christian tradition. Saper-

Chaplain Harold Saperstein. Saying kaddish, the Jewish prayer for the dead, constantly reminded Rabbi Saperstein of what was at stake. Military protocol at memorial services elaborated the ritual dimensions of the Judeo-Christian tradition as standard operating procedure.

stein participated in the observance of Memorial Day in Italy in May 1944. The local mayor declared a general holiday, and hundreds of residents from the villages streamed toward the newly consecrated American cemetery. "The setting was one of almost unbelievable beauty. The regular rows of gleaming white grave markers stood beside a little country church," he wrote to his wife. "It was spotlessly clean, the rows were strewn with flowers, and each grave was covered with red poppy petals." The altar, draped in crimson and adorned with flowers, was set with gleaming brass and silver candlesticks. Before it stood a casket containing the remains of an unknown American soldier, similarly draped in crimson and covered with an American flag. The local bishop "came forward, clad in his purple robes, surrounded by priestly attendants and took his seat in the special episcopal chair set up for him." The exercises began with "the

Catholic requiem mass, conducted by the Catholic Chaplain." The band softly played "Ave Maria." Then the bishop gave his blessing. The mayor spoke. But the service was not yet completed. "This was an American cemetery and although the natives [sic] gathered were almost exclusively Catholic, among the boys buried were Protestants and Jews as well. The Protestant chaplain arose and conducted a brief Memorial."[71] Then Saperstein stood up.

"Certainly it must have been a unique experience for the bishop to attend a Jewish memorial service," Saperstein thought. He understood his role in enacting the Army's version of the Judeo-Christian tradition as "training for democracy" for the Italian dignitaries who had gathered. Here was "a concrete example of what America means," he affirmed. Unfamiliar with this newly invented American ritual, the Italian guests stood "not knowing what to expect as the crucifexes [sic] were removed." Then came the rich, full notes of the cantor as he sang, "O Lord, what is man that thou takest account of him?" After Saperstein read the 90th and 23rd psalms, the cantor chanted the *El mole rachamim,* the memorial prayer. The service had moved flawlessly from Latin to English to Hebrew. A common democratic faith affirmed the equality and brotherhood of all men under God. The religious service concluded, the honor guard lifted their rifles and the shots rang out. Then the bugler played taps. Finally, "the American band struck up the Garibaldi hymn. The crowd went wild with delight, shouting and cheering."[72]

Saperstein was thrilled by the moving ecumenism of the Memorial Day service. His experience of religious equality as an American soldier left an indelible impression. Here was a "Judeo-Christian" pageant performed as standard operating procedure in the military. Its assembled components produced a coherent religious ceremony. The military entourage, the band, the color bearers, and the three chaplains represented the United States, the liberators of the Italian countryside. The altar draped in crimson, the brass and silver candlesticks and crucifixes, and the red poppy petals strewn on the graves provided a visually rich accompaniment to the Catholic requiem mass. But Saperstein saw the mass as a prelude to the main event: the removal of the crucifixes for the Jewish chaplain's memorial service. The entire ceremony was an object lesson in American democracy that demonstrated how three religions could share the same sacred space. The Judeo-Christian tradition demanded respect and equality for each faith as it combined its particular ways of honoring the dead into a single and singular tripartite service. Saperstein recognized the uniqueness of the service. Few had ever participated in such a ceremony. Although such joint memorial services would become increasingly standardized throughout the armed forces, they were not without controversy.

Perhaps the most significant example of the hurdles faced by those attempting to implement the Judeo-Christian tradition in the military can be found in the situation surrounding one of the illustrious sermons invoking that tradition: the sermon given by Reform rabbi Roland Gittelsohn at the dedication of the Fifth Marine Division Cemetery on Iwo Jima. Chaplain Gittelsohn articulated the dreams and ideals of a new religion of democracy. But the conditions under which he spoke contradicted his words. The circumstances of the sermon's story underscored the difficulties of translating vision into reality.

The sermon itself was powerful, commensurate with the tragic occasion. "This is perhaps the grimmest, and surely the holiest task we have faced since D-Day," he began. The battle for Iwo Jima took thirty-six days and resulted in more than 6,000

American deaths and 17,000 additional casualties. This was five times the number of American dead on either Guadalcanal or Tarawa.[73] The Fifth Marine Division suffered the most, with 2,265 dead and 1,640 wounded.[74] Burying the dead had been extraordinarily difficult during the battle. The dedication of the cemetery was a solemn and disturbing event. "Here before us lie the bodies of comrades and friends. Men who until yesterday or last week laughed with us, joked with us, trained with us. Men who were on the same ships with us, and went over the sides with us as we prepared to hit the beaches of this island. Men who fought with us and feared with us." Gittelsohn's opening invoked what any chaplain might have said.

But he soon veered from what might have been expected. "They have paid the ghastly price of freedom," he proclaimed. "If that freedom be once again lost, as it was after the last war, the unforgivable blame will be ours, not theirs. So it is we, the living, who are here to be dedicated and consecrated," Gittelsohn said, echoing Abraham Lincoln's Gettysburg Address. But appropriately for World War II, he delivered a message that spoke to the liberal ideals of the Judeo-Christian tradition. "We dedicate ourselves, first, to live together in peace the way they fought and are buried in this war." Then Gittelsohn named the soldiers. "Here lie men who loved America because their ancestors generations ago helped in her founding, and other men who loved her with equal passion because they themselves or their own fathers escaped from oppression to her blessed shores." He celebrated a land of immigrants, whether they came recently or several centuries ago. But he also acclaimed America's egalitarian military. "Here lie officers and men, Negroes and Whites, rich men and poor — together. Here are Protestants, Catholics and Jews — together." Well aware of segregation in the military, not to mention religious prejudice of all kinds, Gittelsohn strove to imagine a pristine equality in death. "Here no man prefers another because of his faith or despises him because of his color. Here there are no quotas of how many from each group are admitted or allowed. Among these men there is no discrimination, no prejudice, no hatred." For Gittelsohn, "theirs is the highest and purest democracy."

Gittelsohn articulated themes central to his vision of America. He imagined a country of equals, despite its racial and religious diversity. These were Jewish dreams of America. He summoned an ideal democracy and gave it the moral force of religious vision. "Any man among us, the living, who fails to understand that," he warned, "will thereby betray those who lie here dead." He even suggested retribution against those who would violate this perfect fellowship. "Whoever of us lifts his hand in hate against a brother or thinks himself superior to those who happen to be in the minority, makes of this ceremony and of the bloody sacrifice it commemorates an empty, hollow mockery." Harsh words, indeed. But so much was at risk: all the possibilities for a more just world and for a United States that lived up to its own best aspirations.

So Gittelsohn addressed the root causes of war: economic oppression and inequality. Although not directly an attack on capitalism, his sermon vigorously condemned imperialism that sustained a false peace in order to reap unholy profits. His social democratic sentiments that peace could not be achieved without eradicating poverty and exploitation were woven into his notion of Judaism and shared by many Jews. "When the last shot has been fired there will still be those whose eyes are turned backward, not forward, who will be satisfied with those wide extremes of poverty and wealth in which the seeds of another war can breed. We promise you, our departed comrades: This too we will not permit!" His sentiments reflected some of the antiwar passions of liberals, condemning those who sought to make money from the sales of armaments and oil to Japan.[75]

Gittelsohn endowed his politics with rhetorical and spiritual force, describing an egalitarian democratic ideal that overcame differences in rank, wealth, heritage, religion, and, most important, race. Here Gittelsohn challenged the position of the United States military, which enforced segregation of African Americans and restricted most black enlisted men to non-combat units until the last year of the war. But he also distinguished between the troops and the wealthy oil and steel magnates. He did not seek to include all members of the nation in a patriotism that overlooked differences. In describing a progressive vision of one world to emerge from the carnage of war, he did not mince words. His articulation of the Judeo-Christian tradition harked back to its intellectual origins as an antifascist alternative to "Christian." Gittelsohn's understanding of the war and its meaning incorporated a universalist vision of one world rooted in a radical reading of the prophetic tradition and the social democratic thrust of the New Deal. His sermon explicitly embraced not only all American soldiers, but also all varieties of Jews, religious and secular.

But Gittelsohn did not preach his powerful sermon at the joint interdenominational service planned by the Division Chaplain, a Protestant. As he described it later, "As an eloquent expression of his own devotion to the teachings of Christianity and the high truths of democracy," the Division Chaplain "invited me, as spokesman for the smallest religious minority in the Division, to preach." Two Protestant chaplains immediately protested the idea of a Jewish chaplain "preaching over graves which were predominantly those of Christians." Taken aback, the Division Chaplain responded that "the right of the Jewish chaplain to preach such a sermon was precisely one of the things for which we were fighting the war." Then six Catholic padres "on Iwo sent their senior representative to the Division Chaplain to speak for all of them. They were opposed in general to any joint Service of Memorial, and they were opposed in particular to a sermon preached by the Jewish chaplain." They warned that if the Division Chaplain "insisted on carrying out his original intention they would refuse to participate or attend!" Faced with such intransigence, he yielded to the "objection of an entire church." Gittelsohn gave his sermon written for the ecumenical memorial observance "at our own little Jewish Service."[76] But his anguish endured.

Reflecting on the affair two years later, Gittelsohn admitted that he could not remember "anything in my life that made me so painfully heartsick. We had just come through nearly five weeks of miserable hell. Some of us had tried to serve men of all faiths and of no faith, . . . Protestants, Catholics and Jews had lived together, fought together, died together, and now lay buried together. But we the living could not unite to pray together!"[77] Gittelsohn wondered if it was more than a case of antisemitism. Many chaplains may have disliked him not just as a Jew but because of his liberal politics, particularly his support for African-American soldiers.[78] Ironically, his sermon received attention because three Protestant chaplains were so incensed at what had happened that they boycotted their own service and came to the Jewish one instead. One of them circulated the sermon throughout the island.

The conflict surrounding Gittelsohn and the invitation to deliver the sermon at a joint service consecrating the cemetery on Iwo Jima revealed the deep difficulties of worshipping together during the war. Military practice preceded theological accommodation. What would later be called ecumenism gradually became SOP in the armed forces — cooperation, joint services, ministering to men of all faiths and of no faith, as Gittelsohn put it. Learning to work across religious lines, not only those separating Christians and Jews but also the divisions between Catholics and Protestants, produced a mode of ecumenical behavior, if not belief. The vast Marine division cemetery on Iwo Jima contained rows upon rows of crosses, only occasionally broken by a Magen David. To privilege the minority by inviting Gittelsohn to speak at this moment of grief, as the Division Chaplain wanted to do, required shared convictions about the religious and political meaning of the war.

Gittelsohn's experience suggests that it was not always possible to translate behavior required by military standards into religious conviction. Profound theological differences separated chaplains and colored their understanding of one of the war's most brutal battles. One Protestant chaplain called Iwo Jima "an awful experience. My two closest buddies are now dead, as well as other close friends among the officers and men. But despite the loathsomeness and tragedy of it all," he concluded, "I can see how God has already begun to use even this battle for his glory."[79] God's glory was not on Gittelsohn's mind as he contemplated the cost of combat. He pondered the human burden of completing the task of securing democracy, and did his best to inspire his listeners to continue the moral, political, and religious struggle.

Although there were notable tensions, the experience of serving as chaplains stimulated a spirit of cooperation among Reform, Conservative, and Orthodox rabbis that endured for decades after the war ended. At a time when boundaries between Orthodoxy and Conservatism were fluid, the Committee on Army and Navy Religious Activities (CANRA) institutionalized both Jewish denominationalism and cooperation among rabbis. A special committee of three rabbis representing Reform, Or-

thodoxy, and Conservatism answered religious questions posed
by chaplains, including what to do about sabbath and holiday
observance, marriage and divorce, conversion, and finally, death
and burial.[80] The tripartite division of Orthodox, Conservative,
and Reform soon became standardized. This allowed the JWB
to develop consensus on a wide range of religious matters.
CANRA's director considered its abridged Jewish prayerbook
to be one of its most important accomplishments. "In its final
war-time revision it represents a remarkable achievement," he
wrote, "namely the agreement of the responsible Reform, Conservative and Orthodox rabbinate on a common prayerbook."[81]
Such cooperation existed on the ground as well. "For a brief
period at one time there were three Jewish Chaplains at this depot," Harold Saperstein observed in his Jewish New Year's letter
to his congregants back home. "We joined in our services and
though in civilian life one had served an orthodox congregation,
the second a conservative, and the third a reform, we were
aware not of differing interpretations but only of our common
Jewishness."[82] Emanuel Rackman, an Orthodox rabbi who led a
neighboring congregation in Lynbrook, agreed with Saperstein.
"Jewish unity was an ideal that we not only espoused but lived,"
he recalled. Rackman credited his years in service for teaching
him how to live in harmony with other Jews. "We learned this
together in our military experience," he affirmed, "and never
forgot it."[83]

World War II provided an arena not only for implementing
in pragmatic terms the Judeo-Christian tradition as America's
faith, but also for translating that religious vision into a commitment by such influential American military leaders as Dwight D.
Eisenhower.[84] Over the course of the conflict, worshipping together in uniform gradually came to be accepted by soldiers and
sailors as the American military norm. The armed forces prac-

ticed ecumenism on the battlefield, in hospitals and camps, and at thousands of memorial services honoring the dead. In its efforts to integrate Jews and Christians as equal partners in uniform, the military enabled chaplains to move from cooperative behavior to common belief in a religious worldview that sustained American democracy. Aware of pervasive antisemitism among their fellow Americans, rabbis in uniform tended to emphasize those moments — and there were many — when Jews were accepted as equals and were given unprecedented measures of power and respect. They used those times to advocate a vision of democratic equality and Jewish pride. "Every Jewish soldier knew that prejudices did exist in the army," wrote Chaplain Morris Kertzer, "that racial and religious discrimination could not be eradicated by military fiat." Although prejudice and bias endured, worshipping together left an ineradicable imprint.[85] Christians and Jews alike would remember these moments. By 1945, the symbolism of the four chaplains represented a living reality.

6

UNDER FIRE

1.

Hate Hitler? No, I spared him hardly a thought.
But Corporal Irmin, first, and later on
The O.C. (Flying), Wing Commander Briggs,
And the station C.O. Group Captain Ormery —
Now there were men were objects fit to hate,
. . . bastards in your daily life,
With Power in their pleasure, smile or frown.

2.

Not to forget my navigator Bert,
Who shyly explained to me that the Jews
Were ruining England and Hitler might be wrong
But he had the right idea. . . . We were a crew,
And went on so, the one pair left alive . . .

3.

All the above were friends. And then the foe.

—HOWARD NEMEROV,
"IFF [Identification Friend or Foe]"[1]

NOVEMBER 9, 1944. The moon shone brightly, illuminating
the fields around the formidable fortress city of Metz. Crouched
in a foxhole on the perimeter of a ravine around a hundred yards
from where his buddies were sleeping, Paul Steinfeld shivered.
The cold, damp air in the Moselles Valley felt as if it had worked
its way into his bones. The enemy was on the other side of the

hill, close enough that occasionally he could catch fragments of German conversation. If the Germans moved up the ravine, they would first encounter the riflemen on the perimeter. Tonight, that meant him, Paul Steinfeld. Guard duty with the 379th Infantry Regiment, part of the 95th Infantry Division at the top-most point of a ravine outside Metz, was a long way from his first face-off with a pork chop that had been his introduction to life in the Army. Steinfeld's thoughts turned to his wife, Lillian. He looked up at the brilliant moon and vowed not to live just for himself if he survived the war. He would like to have children. His partner on watch nudged him. A Southerner, he hated the cold and his two hours were up. But the next relief was "Hog Trough Charlie," who "cottoned up to the lowest element in the unit," including a bunch of antisemites from the Milwaukee area. Charlie and Steinfeld had clashed in the past. Charlie once called him "a kike." Steinfeld had grabbed him and said, "Charlie, you call me a kike again, you're gonna be a sorry boy." Steinfeld felt that he could take on Charlie; they were evenly matched in strength. But Steinfeld's threat did not settle the matter. "Steiney, be careful," warned his guard partner. "But get 'im out here. I'm shivering. I can't take it."[2]

Steinfeld ran back to the foxholes to wake up Charlie. "Charlie," he said, "your turn for guard duty." A rant of antisemitic profanities greeted him. Steinfeld exploded. He forgot about the Germans. All he could think of were the insults. Furious, he reached down, grabbed Charlie, and pulled him out of the hole. Steinfeld's helmet went clattering on the rocks. The men in the surrounding holes heard the noise. "Steiney," they pleaded, "you're gonna get us all killed." But that didn't slow him down. "Charlie," he hissed. "I told you." Then he pummeled Charlie hard and kicked him out toward the perimeter. "Charlie," he

*Paul Steinfeld on his discharge from the Army, October 1945,
with his sergeant's stripes and one "hash mark" for more than
six months of overseas service. Fighting the Germans involved
opposing their ideology of fascism and racism. Yet antisemitism
among his comrades in arms forced Steinfeld to fight two battles
simultaneously to secure the respect of his fellow GIs.*

said, "get the hell outta here and go over and join Hitler's Army."
He pressed him. "If that's the way you feel, why don't you go
over?" he taunted. "It's only a short distance over there."[3]

Steinfeld wanted to "teach Charlie a lesson." He had learned
as a teenager that antisemitism was the essence of Nazism, but
this was less obvious to his fellow GIs. For him, fighting the
Germans meant opposing their ideology. The American ideals of
freedom and democracy represented polar opposites to the German values of fascism and racism. Steinfeld thought it utterly
bizarre that he had to fight two battles at once among his fellow Americans and against the Germans. Recalling comments
"about our cowardice and Jewish unwillingness to fight," one
Jewish GI exclaimed: "Here we were fighting the Nazis, and
then this madness in the United States Army!"[4] Steinfeld was a
soldier and a man who demanded respect. Jews were the equals
of other GIs and not to be insulted with impunity. Soon word
got around about the altercation; the men knew that all Steinfeld had done was to wake Charlie to stand watch. "Steiney,"
the Sergeant queried, "the Lieutenant wants to know if you'll
press charges." Steinfeld demurred. "No, I'll take care of Charlie in my own way," he replied. "I'm not pressing charges." Like
Reines, Steinfeld preferred not to lodge a formal complaint. He
didn't want to escalate the conflict. But Steinfeld believed that
he finally had won the psychological battle because "the sympathy of the men was all for this Jew."[5] That was crucial — to be
trusted and accepted by his comrades.

The anger that fueled his attack on Charlie may have made
Steinfeld a better soldier. On night patrol outside Metz, he saw
a faint light flickering through some blanket holes. Steinfeld
barked for the Germans to come out. He brought them back.
His Lieutenant cited him for a silver star, but it came back
bronze. One of the other Jewish men in the outfit, a cook's

helper, told Steinfeld, "I know why you didn't get a silver star — because you're Jewish." This he claimed he had overheard at the officer's mess. It was not easy for a Jew to win recognition for bravery; it went against an ingrained notion of Jewish cowardice. Steinfeld's bravery under fire won him promotion to sergeant, but prejudice in his own ranks remained.

Steinfeld's vindication came not quite a month later, when a replacement platoon leader arrived. His name was Berger. He was Jewish. Steinfeld overheard some men say, "Oh, Berger. What kind'a name is Berger? Who's he?" One of the men replied: "Berger," he said. "I think he's a lousy kike." This time Charlie, "Hog Trough Charlie," reprimanded him. "Ay, ay, ay. Don't say that," he urged. "Steiney doesn't like it." So Steinfeld had won a measure of respect after all, not only for himself but also for other Jewish soldiers.[6]

While Steinfeld fought his way to respect as a Jew and an American infantryman outside of Metz, Jeremiah Gutman was engaged in a similar battle near the Belgian border. He confronted deep-seated doubt about whether Jews could be military leaders.[7] A corporal in the 2nd platoon, Company G of the 273rd Infantry Regiment, Gutman itched to prove his worth. His failure to win a commission at Fort Benning, despite his R.O.T.C. training at City College, continued to rankle. Young, cocky, and aggressive, he was the only Jew in his officer group when he washed out. To his fellow officer candidates, who were required to rank one another, he didn't seem likely to inspire confidence in the men as a leader. Gutman was passionate about the war. He had grown up hating Nazism and Hitler. Before he left Camp Shelby in Mississippi, he told his parents that he "was gonna stop" Hitler. Gutman was determined to get to Germany and get Hitler "somewhere in a corner" and kill him. The Army obliged Gutman and assigned him to the 69th Infantry Division.

Part of General Hodges' First Army, the 69th entered the fighting in Europe after the breakout from Normandy and the Allies' successful pursuit of the German armies in France. But Gutman wasn't thrown into the line until the fall. His first taste of combat was terrifying. Men were wounded and killed. In the midst of it all, Gutman felt that the men resented him. They regarded him as "a kind of a tag-along." "Well, he came in with these stripes," went the common assessment. "He didn't earn 'em." They muttered, "Who the hell is he to be commanding us?" Gutman knew they thought he was not "as good as, as smart as, as lithe as" the other non-commissioned officers.[8]

Gutman's chance to demonstrate his leadership abilities came on a patrol when his squad leader "really screwed up" and made mistakes that cost several lives. To make matters worse, the squad leader panicked and ran. As second in command, Gutman got the men together and brought them safely back. His competence won him the position of squad leader but did not erase resentment toward him. His squad "was then put into the reserve" so that they "were not on the line." Although they promoted him, his superiors apparently still didn't really trust him.[9] But the pressures of war meant that neither Gutman nor his squad could remain on reserve for long. The 69th saw action in France, Belgium, and Germany.[10] "In desperation," Gutman's commanding officer put him out "one day on a reconnaissance." Told to take four men to obtain information, Gutman successfully carried out his orders. "This little Jew from New York" surprised both his superiors and his comrades-in-arms. "From then on," respect for Gutman "went up tremendously among the guys." He became "chief reconnaissance non-com" not only for his platoon, but subsequently for the company and then the battalion. The job provided a measure of satisfaction as well as promotion to sergeant. Gutman stayed with his unit until the end of

Jeremiah Gutman, in his undershirt, with his comrades in Germany, 1945. Eager to fight the Nazis, Gutman learned that he repeatedly had to prove his competence as a soldier. But once he was accepted as a skilled fighter and non-commissioned officer, he discovered that he gained satisfaction from doing his job.

the war in Europe. He had felt he had to prove himself, but then, he admitted, he "got really to enjoy it."[11]

Combat revealed previously unknown aspects of his personality. Of average height, Gutman had never been "a physical person." Sports didn't interest him much. Now, suddenly he was crawling and sneaking around, occasionally "doing what had to be done," a euphemism for killing. The real surprise was that he felt good about doing it. Without a doubt, Gutman possessed "a sense of mission" — so much so that when he was wounded or received citations for "what they called bravery," he responded much as many other soldiers did. He was, after all, just "doing what you're supposed to do."[12] Once he was accepted, he acted like other GIs. But he never forgot his failure to win a commission, although he did earn additional stripes in recognition of his leadership.

Gutman's and Steinfeld's accounts suggest the difficulties Jewish soldiers faced under fire. Although some prejudices disappeared under the pressures of combat, others stubbornly endured. "In war, there are two kinds of battles and many times it is hard to know which is worse," wrote Theodore Draper in his history of the 84th Infantry Division. "There is the battle to kill the enemy and there is the battle with yourself to live." Draper argued that the former was "against people" and the latter against a host of other ills: mud, ice, rain, vermin, boredom, homesickness, or "imaginary terrors."[13] Although a Jew himself, Draper didn't include prejudice in his list. But Gutman's and Steinfeld's struggles to survive involved combating not merely physical and psychological forces but also the stereotypes of their fellow GIs. Soldiers brought their attitudes from civilian life to the battlefield, including prejudices that at times made Jews wonder where the battle lines were.

Infantrymen depend upon each other to survive and to fight.

The Yanks mop up on Bougainville. Fighting for the United States, Jewish GIs also fought against antisemitic stereotypes of their fellow GIs that Jews malingered or avoided military service. Eventually, Jewish soldiers earned the respect of their comrades and came to share the experience of trust on the battlefield.

"In the midst of seeming chaos it was the love of individuals, one for another, that enabled them to carry on. The fighting soldiers were sustained by a regard for others," wrote the British historian John Ellis, "in which self-respect and mutual esteem were so inextricably intertwined that courage was a commonplace, self-sacrifice the norm."[14] Jewish GIs eventually came to share that experience of trust, but not without overcoming some hurdles. First they would have to prove their presence at the front; then they would have to demonstrate their competence in bat-

tle. They would have to earn the respect that was more commonplace among other American soldiers.

But if Steinfeld and Gutman worried about whether they
could count on their comrades-in-arms, they were certain about
their reasons for fighting. That sense of purpose would help to
sustain them as they faced combat. Having grown up in homes
that idolized Franklin D. Roosevelt, they believed in his "Four
Freedoms" message to Congress. Like other Jewish soldiers,
when asked their reasons for fighting the war, they placed the
Four Freedoms at the top of their list.[15] Their education taught
them that Hitler, Nazism, and Fascism epitomized the opposite
of American values. Their parents and friends all hated Hitler
and had watched his steady victories over the past decade with
dismay. They also were aware that Nazism was only the latest
and deadliest version of an ancient antipathy against Jews. As
Harold Freeman explained to his wife Bea, "in a romantic vein,
I likened my voyage to Europe to a crusade to combat the very
forces of evil that some 40 years ago plagued my parents."[16] The
opportunity to right the wrongs of the past was at hand. An ideological antifascist, Freeman accepted the challenge.

Although Freeman knew that many of his fellow GIs disliked
Jews, he attributed such prejudice to ignorance. He assumed
that most of his rural southern "comrades-in-arms had never
met a Jew in their lives — and thought they all had long noses
and horns."[17] He figured that they had imbibed stereotypes from
childhood even if they had never encountered a Jew.[18] Still,
while Freeman shrugged off such caricatures of Jews, he did his
best to surmount calumnies of Jewish cowardice. No soldier
could afford to be considered a coward. The charge expressed a
fundamental distrust for a man and jeopardized his life. Freeman served as a buck private, a rifleman in Company C, 329th
Infantry, which started as a National Guard unit drawing mem-

Harold Freeman during the Battle of the Bulge. In the 83rd Infantry Division, Freeman had to prove his presence at the front. A committed antifascist, he knew that the prejudices of some ignorant GIs were mild compared to the antisemitism he would have faced as a Jew under the Nazis. This was one of the reasons he was fighting the war.

bers from northern Kentucky and southern Ohio. He did not write to Bea about antisemitism, in part because he was acutely aware that his lieutenant was reading his mail as censor.[19] One incident occurred in Luxembourg in October 1944, during Freeman's first few weeks at the front. "We were sitting on the edges of our fox holes on the 'reverse slope,' i.e., behind a low ridge of hills" between the GIs and the enemy. The Germans suspected that the Americans were there and lobbed occasional shells at them. "Most landed at a distance," but when the men heard one coming they would all drop into their holes. "It was unnerving." In this tense situation, Freeman confronted an unexpected attack from one of his own. "One of the men in a nearby hole kept bitching about the rear echelon boys who were enjoying the war — and at the Jews who were never even in the army at all." Malingering and manipulation to avoid military service were part of the arsenal of antisemitic stereotypes. "Between jumps" into his hole, Freeman managed to tell him he "was a Jew." The GI looked at him "in disbelief, but said nothing."[20]

As Freeman lived down such demoralizing stereotypes in the 83rd Infantry Division, so did his fellow Jewish GIs. Freeman recalled how "one of our sergeants, with a Jewish name, was wounded 3 or 4 times but always came back."[21] Freeman attributed the Jewish sergeant's persistence to a desire to disprove stereotypes that Jews were unwilling to fight and eager to get off through a slight wound. Sergeant N. Jay Jaffee, a squad leader, remembered how surprised some of the old-timers were to see him when he rejoined his company in the 415th Infantry Regiment at the front after recovering from a wound. But their prejudices lingered. "The men probably questioned my hospital stay," he mused, "figuring I was the only one who had gotten the rest they thought they were going to get after the Holland campaign."[22] Resentment and mistrust simmered near the surface.

Jaffee, Freeman, Steinfeld, and Gutman well knew that the prejudices of some ignorant GIs were mild compared to the antisemitism they would have faced as Jews under the Nazis. This was one of the reasons they were fighting the war. They recognized that being Jewish shaped their politics and their actions; they had come to their hatred and fear of Hitler and Nazism through their education and political commitments. They understood the economic, social, religious, and political roots of antisemitism, all of which they had discussed back home with friends and family. They expected the war to make a difference.

Nonetheless, knowing the sources of prejudice didn't make coping with it any easier.

For most American soldiers, "to end the war was the reason you fought it. The only reason."[23] Larger political issues, especially those focused on the dangers of Nazism to American democratic values, did not interest most GIs. The GI paper, *Stars and Stripes,* published a joke making the rounds in 1944: "The Russians are fighting for their lives, the British for their homes, the Americans for souvenirs."[24] Col. James E. Rudder, who led the D-Day assault on Pointe du Hoc, summarized such attitudes in his letter to his troops: "There is only one reason for our being here and that is to eliminate the enemy that has brought the war about. There is only one way to eliminate the enemy and that is to close with him. Let's all get on with the job we were sent here to do in order that we may return home at the earliest possible moment."[25]

Tracy Sugarman, a naval officer, found this bottom line profoundly disturbing. "For too many of the Americans, this war was not really our war. It was their war." The Americans came to Europe to help save the British. Reflecting on his men's attitudes, Sugarman blamed their immaturity and youth. "American education had ill prepared them to understand how uniquely fortunate their own country was due to geography," he thought. "Nor did most of them understand how indebted we were to those who fought alone for so many years, although the shattered homes and churches and towns around them bore dreadful testimony to the high price that the English had paid for all our freedom."[26] "What are we doing in Europe?" GIs asked a Jewish chaplain in Italy. "Our fight is with the yellow men."[27] Racist attitudes toward the Japanese coupled with a conviction that Pearl Harbor had to be avenged convinced many American soldiers that the war that mattered was in the Pacific Theater. In their eyes, Germans and Italians resembled Americans. They certainly did not see Nazi antisemitism as a reason to fight the fascists, until the liberation of the death camps made them realize its pernicious force.[28] Some American soldiers even espoused intolerance.

Run-of-the-mill prejudice grated on Jewish officers and men alike, but officer status changed relationships with enlisted men. Stern and Sugarman, two Jewish naval officers, "were censoring the mail when Stern started cutting a paragraph out of one of the letters." He handed it over to Sugarman and said, "Take a look at this." It was "a copy of that goddamn paragraph that was circulated in the States about two years back." The ditty went as follows:

> First man to sink an enemy battleship — Colin Kelly.
> First man to set foot on enemy territory — Robert O'Hara.
> First woman to lose five sons — Mrs. Sullivan. Etc.
> First son of a bitch to get four new tires — Nathan Goldstein.

Tracy Sugarman lost his temper. He told his wife June, "I was so mad I could have spit nails." He picked up the paper, walked up to the kid who was sending it out and said, "I cut this out of your letter. I don't think it's funny. My brother in France doesn't think it's funny, and my cousin in the paratroops who was killed on D-Day doesn't think it's funny." But the waves of fury that swept over him didn't subside with the confrontation. "I was so angry I came back to my room and sat down." The adrenaline wouldn't stop pumping. "I think I was shaking like a guy with palsy."[29] Antisemitism could do that. It could set the adrenaline flowing. It could color a Jewish officer's attitude toward his men.

The doggerel that so disturbed Sugarman appeared shortly after the attack on Pearl Harbor, probably initially in Boston-area naval yards and harbor defenses. It spread rapidly. It was clever, humorous, and, some would claim, harmless. Challenged to explain why they circulated the doggerel in Army or Navy publications, editors and officers often expressed surprise that it was considered offensive or divisive. It contained few vulgarities, unlike ditties focused on Jewish avarice, malingering, draft dodging, and manipulation of gentiles. Jews weren't mentioned as such. Although the Navy issued a specific directive against publishing the "First American" when it appeared in a naval base paper, Jewish organizations failed to stop its spread among civilians.[30]

Responding to the incident, Sugarman unburdened himself in a long letter home. "The inconsistency between the American fighter and the American sailor or soldier is staggering," he told his wife. "I remember so well how inadequate I felt when I tried to tell you how wonderful those guys on the beaches were last June. I wouldn't take back a word of it," he affirmed. "I feel now as I did then, but coupled with it goes a feeling of wonder. Wonder as to how such marvelous fighters can be such rotten people." Sugarman had commanded LST 491 during D-Day at Utah Beach, albeit late in the afternoon when the devastating fire had abated. Now aboard LST 357, in February 1945, he was busy ferrying men and supplies across the channel to the continent. In the months of practice and preparation in the cold waters of the English Channel prior to the D-Day assault, he had written how "you pay and pay in inconvenience, drudgery, repetition, and responsibility" for the "pride and satisfaction of being a naval officer." He admitted to his wife that "it's a debt that never gets paid. You hope for the respect of your superiors and the affection of your men."[31] Sugarman's men performed admirably, and he was full of respect for them. But eight months later his patience for his men's bigotry had worn thin. Sugarman didn't mince words: "The American GI is a source of shame and embarrassment." His vehemence reflected not just chagrin at the men's behavior on shore in England, but more specifically, their antisemitism.[32]

Sugarman remained loyal to his men, despite their prejudices. "Individually, I would do anything for any of them," he reiterated. "But as a group they are the antithesis of anything I desire." He felt he could not close his eyes "and pretend the bad and the wrong and the ignorant aren't there. . . . Those things are real, and too important to both of us." Sugarman insisted that he wanted "only to reject their standards and their values. They revolt and shock me," he confessed.[33] Later he regretted pulling rank and losing his cool. But "when the careless locker room bigotry about 'lazy niggers' or 'avaricious Jews' surfaced, it triggered a deep fury," and he "felt compelled to respond."[34]

The linkage of Jews and blacks was not accidental. Many Jews recognized that anti-black racism often accompanied antisemitism. Just as Sugarman joined the two in his reflections on prejudice, so Gutman saw a connection between his efforts to be accepted and the lot of African-American GIs. He welcomed the fifth platoon of black soldiers that was added to their company as true comrades-in-arms. Held in reserve, relegated to the rear on each chow line, they, too, had to fight to win acceptance as soldiers.[35]

Like Gutman, Ralph Jackson, one of the Dragons, did his first fighting stateside when he struggled to get sent overseas, but unlike Gutman, Jackson was rewarded even before he faced the enemy. A member of a bombing crew, he relished the acceptance by his fellow airmen. "We were very very close. All of us," Jackson enthused. "We got along well with each other which was what it should be." Jackson had always dreamed of flying, so when the opportunity came to apply for cadet training, he didn't hesitate to give up his "cushy job" as a mechanic at Lowry Field in Denver. Worrying that he might be overweight, he had fasted for twenty-four hours to make the cut. Then after completing the course, he had protested when he was told he would be kept stateside as an instructor. He was full of enthusiasm. Even his Commanding Officer's final blessing, "I hope you get killed," had not deterred him. Jackson was confident, not a fatalist. Like Steinfeld and Gutman, he thought he was invincible. His long period of air crew training before heading overseas confirmed the wisdom of his decision. The bottom line was trust: "you're depending on each other."[36] That elusive element transformed strangers into team players and a Jew into a crew member in the eyes of his buddies. Jewishness became one part of Jackson's personality rather than defining his identity.

Jackson arrived in East Anglia, England, on New Year's Eve, 1943, a navigator/bombardier with two sets of wings and a member of the Eighth Air Force's 67th Bomb Squadron, 44th Bomb Group. In early 1944 almost the entire Eighth Air Force of more than forty heavy bomb groups and twenty fighter groups crowded into nearly 130 airfields in a compact area in England. Although the tide of the European war had turned in favor of the Allies by the end of 1943 with the successful campaigns in North Africa, the surrender of Italy, and the Russian offensive, Hitler's fortress Europe still stood firm. In the months preceding Jackson's arrival, the Eighth Air Force had launched a series of daylight raids into Germany that inflicted heavy damage at the cost of shocking casualties. "In one grisly week in the autumn the Eighth Air Force lost 148 bombers (1480 men)," pursuing a policy of strategic bombing aimed at military and industrial targets.[37] Few were privy to the official statistics, but Jackson was vividly aware of the dangers he faced in flight and the men who didn't return.[38] After a tragic accident involving their radio operator when he was not on board, Jackson's crew

Ralph Jackson interned at Addlebowden, Switzerland, 1944. As a navigator bombardier, Jackson had contemplated the possibility of capture. He discussed with other Jewish fliers the question of keeping his dog tag with its telltale "H." Jackson decided not to remove his dog tag, despite the risk of German persecution as a Jewish prisoner.

"never flew" without him. He was an integral, vital member of the team.³⁹

Jackson had been in England for three months when the Passover holiday rolled around. When he heard that the Jews in Norwich had invited Jewish airmen in the area to attend a seder, he expressed a desire to go. The commander announced that anyone who wanted to attend the seder would get a two-day pass. Stationed only thirty miles away, Jackson requested one. He was comfortable with his fellow crew members and felt free to express his Jewishness. But as the first night of Passover approached, he faced a dilemma. He was torn between his loyalty to his crew and his desire to join fellow Jews, both soldiers and civilians, in celebrating the holiday with its rich family associations. Not an Orthodox Jew, Jackson resolved that he would fly with his crew and forgo the seder. Loyalty to his buddies prevailed over the pleasures of Jewish companionship. So that Friday afternoon before the holiday Jackson checked the Charge of Quarters bulletin board where the lists were posted "announcing the crews" scheduled to "fly the next day." But the list, normally available by three o'clock, was not up. The truck to Norwich was leaving around five. Time was getting tight. So Jackson went down with his pilot to the operations office. He explained his situation and asked if the operations officer could tell them whether his crew was scheduled to fly. "No, they're not scheduled to fly and they're not standby." He told Jackson, "go in."⁴⁰

The seder exceeded his expectations. It took place in a tremendous hall, filled with rows of long tables placed end-to-end. As more people came in, more tables were set up. "The people in Norwich never expected the response they got. They had no idea how many" Jews were in the B-24 outfits in the vicinity. The services were not exactly memorable, but dinner was. When it came time for the meal, "they didn't have enough food." So "they started at one end of the table with the first course. When they ran out of the food, at that point they started the second course." And on through the many courses of a seder meal. Eventually, everyone had something to eat but nobody had a full dinner. It didn't matter. "Even though all of us," Jackson admitted, "were unsatisfied as far as the quantity of food — with the must-have-been hundreds of airmen there — there wasn't a single complaint." Jackson thought "it was a wonderful thing," especially "officers sitting next to enlisted men, nobody concerned with rank. We all had one thing in common: we were Jews."[41] Such socializing across ranks did not normally occur. Usually the officers stuck together, as did the enlisted men.[42] That evening Jewish fellowship cut across military hierarchy. Only the camaraderie of Jackson's crew matched the family atmosphere of the seder.

After the festivities Jackson stayed overnight in Norwich, as did most of the men. He expected to meet his crew, the officers, the following evening. So Jackson went down to await the Saturday night liberty run. His crew wasn't on it. The men getting off the bus from his group said that there had been a mission that day and it had not gone well. They had lost a lot of planes. Jackson had a premonition, but he pushed it out of his mind. "Maybe they stayed back," he thought. The next day was Easter Sunday. But by Sunday he had confirmed that his crew had gone on that mission without him. And they hadn't returned.[43]

Sunday night Jackson came back to camp from the seder with a bitter taste in his mouth. "It was kind of rough going into the empty room" which the four men had shared. On Monday he had the painful task of "separating their personal possessions into three piles, making out inventories, and packing them up." The report from the final mission of his crew "was that the plane was last seen on fire and spinning," but no parachutes had been observed. Although the men were officially considered missing in action, everyone assumed that they had been killed. That afternoon the squadron commander asked Jackson if he wanted a few days off to recuperate from the loss. The commander knew how difficult it was for a survivor. Or would Jackson want to fly? "I'm ready to fly," Jackson replied. There was a crew in the squadron that needed a navigator. "Fine," he said, "I'll fly with them." He didn't even ask who they were. It didn't matter any more. His intimate comradeship had been shattered. Recalling his state of mind, Jackson knew that he "would have been a good subject for a psychiatrist then." His guilty conscience plagued him.

So Jackson flew Tuesday and Wednesday. On Thursday, April 13, on a mission to Litchfield Airdrome, near Augsburg, they were hit by flak and lost an engine. Since "this was one of the deepest penetrations from England," Jackson recognized that they probably wouldn't have been able to return running on three engines. Then there was the danger of "being alone and up in the sky." Still, when the pilot requested "a course to Switzerland," Jackson wasn't happy. They landed at the little town of Dubbendorf, near Zurich. "As the plane was rolling along, the trucks with armed guards were keeping pace." By the time the men got out of the plane, they were completely surrounded by armed guards and "had to surrender." They "had come into a neutral country under arms, and under the Geneva Convention" they were categorized as internees. This was a more desirable category than prisoners of war and sufficiently comfortable to sit out the war, something Jackson did not want to do. The Passover seder a week before had initiated a train of events that Jackson could not have anticipated. Preferring the close-knit comradeship of his crew over the more diffuse fellowship of other Jews, Jackson was ambushed by events.

Jackson did his best to adjust. Every morning around ten o'clock, the other interned fliers listened to the radio. They particularly enjoyed "Axis Sally," who played their favorite swing music as enticement for her propaganda. At the end of her broadcast she always named two or three airmen who had been captured. Since the men never knew whether they would hear a name they would recognize, everybody listened intently for the macabre roll call. One day one of the enlisted men shouted out: "That man was with your crew the day they went down." Jackson didn't recognize the name because his crew usually had another sergeant who was Jewish. But he had gone to the seder with Jackson.

Armed with this promising information, Jackson wrote to the international Red Cross, trying to learn if any of his fellow officers had been captured. He gave their names and even remembered their serial numbers, a sign of how close he felt to them. He received an answer informing him that his fellow officers "were all alive," prisoners of war in Stalag group number one. As soon as he got word from the Red Cross, he cabled his wife, Rita. She spread the news that the crew had survived. Her tidings cheered their families. Like many fliers' relatives, the officers' wives and sisters corresponded during the war, often becoming friends. Jackson's luck in hearing that his crew might have survived and his ingenuity in contacting the Red Cross assuaged some of his remorse about the flight and revived his sense of connection with his old crew. It relieved him of a fraction of the guilt he felt for leaving them for the Passover seder, and it helped restore his own sense of responsibility toward them.[44]

Jackson had known ahead of time about the possibility of capture, including the risks of bailing out over enemy territory. Foremost among these risks was the question of keeping his dog tag with its telltale H. He discussed with other Jewish fliers whether the Germans would persecute them as Jewish prisoners. They debated whether, if they went down and were captured, they would be identified as Jews by the dog tags and separated from their American comrades. Jackson "decided never to remove the dog tags."[45] He affirmed his dual identity as a Jew and an American. But he never had to test his decision. Interned in Switzerland, he did not fear being singled out as a Jew. He even attended Jewish New Year Services off the base at Koor.[46]

Robert Kotlowitz, an infantryman, also thought about the H and its potential to mark him as a Jew rather than an American. Crouched in his foxhole on the line outside Lunéville, with artillery barrages flying overhead, he began to worry about his dog tags. "Should I wear them? Should I get rid of them?" His uncertainty touches on many of the issues Jewish soldiers faced. "They bore an 'H,' for Hebrew, along with my blood type and other essential information. Hebrew was what the US Army had decided to call Jews. I had never been called a Hebrew before. Not even by Hebrews. To the world I had always been a Jew. To myself, as well. Why, then, was a 'J' not good enough for the US Army?" he asked himself. "But I wasn't really worrying about the US Army. I was worrying about the Germans," he admitted. "What would they do with me if I became a prisoner when they saw the 'H' on my dog tags? What had happened to other 'H's when they were captured? POW camps, as an American GI, like any other? Or a German concentration camp, as an 'H'. *Juden* [Jews], as we were known beyond the Rhine—*Juden,* scum of the earth, a phrase I had learned during the thirties from news reports from Germany." Kotlowitz recognized with hindsight that "these questions were hypothetical, all the worry mere inner bombast. I couldn't imagine myself without my dog tags, whatever they read," he confessed. "My dog tags were the sole material proof of my identity, so important that they were stamped out of metal to resist destruction, the only external objects I carried that set me apart from everyone else. Without them, who was I?" he queried. He decided to "keep them, however threatening the situation. I would be an 'H,' as the Army insisted."[47]

In contrast to Jackson, the ordeal of imprisonment took Harold Radish by surprise. Questions of life and death had preoccupied him, not the possibility of capture. As a replacement reconnaissance sergeant, he had joined the 90th Infantry Division outside of Metz, a long way from Brownsville, Brooklyn. It had taken a while for the unit to trust him, and he didn't get into the thick of things until they were fighting in the Ardennes forest. By the time of the Battle of the Bulge, he had become seasoned, hardened, and accepted. Then he crossed the Saar River. His platoon had to attack the pillboxes that made up the West Wall, an important part of the German defenses. One night his unit reached what they thought was a pillbox, blew the door in, went inside, and discovered forty enemy soldiers. Taking them by surprise, the GIs disarmed the Germans and made them prisoners. Radish set up his machine guns outside because there were no openings to fire out of. Then it dawned on him that they had come upon a gigantic underground bedroom. It wasn't a pillbox. They had made a mistake. Later that night more German troops returned and blew the machine guns away. The GIs retreated into the fortified room. They pressed the door back into place and waited. Depressed and disoriented, the first lieutenant

The ordeal of imprisonment took Harold Radish by surprise. He did not know if the Nazis would single him out or if his American uniform would shield his Jewishness. But Radish found partners in suffering with his fellow GIs.

stopped giving commands. Soon the K-rations ran out. After three days, "things got rough." They lacked water. So the men started to drink urine.[48]

In this stalemated situation early one morning a voice in a German accent inquired, "Do you have vounded there?" Radish asked the lieutenant, "What do we do?" He answered, "Tell him we have wounded." Radish knew a little German, mixed with Yiddish, which he knew quite well. He had gone to a Yiddish *shule* (school) in Brooklyn and studied the language. The similarities between German and Yiddish, literally "Jewish," made for an uncomfortable intimacy between enemies. Jewish GIs who knew Yiddish often found themselves serving as translators. At times, Yiddish could save a soldier's life.[49] At other times, it could endanger him. Radish yelled: "Yes, we have wounded

here." Back came the German-accented English: "We will declare a truce for an hour, two hours. One of you, or two, no matter how many of you want to, can come up here unarmed." "I'll
go," the lieutenant said. A couple of other soldiers accompanied
him. When he came back he announced, "It's all over fellas." He
explained, "The Germans are here. They're all around us. There
are no American troops anywhere near here. They pulled out
because it didn't pay for them to fight this hard to go through."
Then he concluded, "We're gonna have to give up." One guy argued in favor of fighting, but he replied, "No, we can't. It's sui-
cide."[50]

When he heard that the German soldiers were coming in,
Radish got rid of his dog tags. "I was afraid," he admitted. He
didn't know what to expect, but he did know about "the Hitler
mentality" that Jews "were not good." Many other men also dis-
posed of their dog tags in sympathy. Such comradeship cheered
Radish. Although there were only a couple of Jews in the group,
the GIs closed ranks around them. They would not let the Germans make distinctions among American soldiers. Then the
Germans trooped in. "Some were kids, smiling, not vicious."
They were not as Radish, only nineteen himself, had imagined.
They exchanged photographs. One guy showed Radish pictures
of his wife and children. Then he asked, "Do you have anything
to trade?" Radish had some powdered juice. "I'll give you some
cigarettes," the German soldier offered. They made the trade.
As a prelude to becoming a prisoner of war, "it was a little un-
real." The Germans marched the GIs back behind the lines and
temporarily put them in jail, but also gave them "good, heavy
soup." Soon elderly German guards accompanied them to a railroad depot. The guards were so old that they tired of holding
their rifles, and the prisoners, in a gesture of respect, "carried
their rifles for them."[51]

Radish's small group joined a larger number of GIs and crowded into boxcars. "The doors were shut. There was one little opening." A can in the corner served as a toilet. When American planes bombed and strafed the train, some of the prisoners started singing "God Bless America." Radish "thought they were out of their minds." Their flamboyant patriotism made him uncomfortable. Finally the train entered a regular prison camp: Stalag 12A. Although the trip had taken seven or eight days, they were in western Germany, not far from where they had been captured. Weakened by the trip, Radish climbed the stairs of a building that resembled a castle for his interrogation.[52] Interrogations were dangerous moments because, alone and vulnerable, a Jewish prisoner faced the possibility of being asked if he were Jewish.[53]

Radish did not know what to expect. What would be the consequences if he confessed his Jewishness to a German officer? The officer requested his name, and Radish gave his name, rank, and serial number as POW protocol required. Then the officer asked, "What group were you with?" "Well, I can't tell you that." So the German queried, "What'd you do in America?" "I was training to be a teacher." He said, "I was a teacher too. I taught social studies." The two bantered back and forth until the officer gave up. "Well, you don't have to tell me." He pulled down a screen, like a window shade. Radish saw his whole division: name, rank, serial number, the last guy who was shot, and even the most recent replacements. The Germans had pieced together a lot of details. Then came the moment he had been dreading. The interrogator looked at him and asked, "Radish, Radish. What kind'a name is that?" This was not an unfamiliar question. Radish knew what he was getting at. The problem was how to respond without revealing either that he was a Jew or that he was disguising his identity. The answer came to him in a flash. "It's English, like Pepper." A clever retort. The German officer smiled and looked at him. Then he said, "Yah, yah, OK." Radish wasn't sure why he let it pass, but was relieved that he had survived the interrogation. Now his daily ordeal as a POW began.

Radish did not know if the Nazis would single him out or if his American uniform would shield his Jewishness. Nor could he anticipate if his imprisonment would bring him an added measure of comradeship with his fellow GIs or stimulate antagonisms. Radish received a loaf of bread. He went down to the barracks where he met another sergeant. The two men "palled together." They slept "in the same little wooden slotted bed." They shared bread. They picked lice together. They woke each other up every morning. Without his buddy, Radish doubted that he could have "made it." The food was watery soup and a hunk of black bread, divided among thirteen men. They all had dysentery. They never washed. As a non-commissioned officer, Radish couldn't work, so he had relatively few opportunities to trade for food. But at least he didn't suffer from back-breaking labor. Occasionally, the prisoners received a Red Cross package, two men to a package. Radish shared with his pal. The two American POWs suffered and survived together.

Radish's knowledge of Yiddish allowed him to query prison guards on behalf of his fellow GIs. He felt good translating for his buddies. But as the war neared its end, conditions worsened. The Germans moved the prisoners deeper into Germany to avoid the approaching British troops. This time the freight car ride resulted in many deaths. Radish lay "next to dead people" without realizing it. When the Germans opened the doors, the stiffened corpses tumbled out. The troops guarding them were younger and aggressive. Standing for inspection in a new camp, Radish asked a question in Yiddish, though he tried to accent it to resemble German. The SS soldier patrolling the prisoners looked at him and screamed, "Du verfluchter Mensch!" (you damned bastard!). Then he started cursing Radish in German. "You started the War!" Radish didn't understand all the German curses, but when the SS uttered the word "Juden" (Jews), Radish paled and fainted. He knew that word all too well. Some GIs gathered around him and asked, "Radish, what happened? I never saw you look like this." And he answered, "Look fellas, I don't know any German. I don't speak German any more." The brief encounter terrified him. He sensed how vulnerable he was as a Jew.[54]

Unlike the 350 POWs in Stalag 9B who were sent to Berga, a slave work camp, Radish was not singled out as a Jew for special treatment. The GIs shipped to Berga were chosen because the Germans thought they had Jewish-sounding names.[55] Other American Jewish POWs denied that they were Jews when asked. When a German officer in Stalag 12A asked David Schenk, "Sind Sie ein Jude?" (Are you a Jew?), Schenk replied, "Nein. Ich bin Catholique" (No. I am Catholic). The officer sneered but dismissed him. Captured during the Battle of the Bulge, Schenk still wore his dog tags with the H "but no one ever looked at them." Later, in the barracks, he agonized over his "cowardly reply." Not admitting his Jewish identity bothered him. A combat soldier, Schenk was disturbed that he had succumbed to his fears of being recognized as a Jew. He "decided to atone for it." He borrowed a pocket-size Jewish Welfare Board *siddur* (prayerbook) from another Jewish POW, and once a day he "stood up amidst hundreds of non-Jewish POWs and recited the Kaddish prayer" for his father, who had died eight months earlier. His fellow POWs protected him. The experience restored his confidence in his American GI identity. As a GI among other GIs, he could be a visible Jew. But on March 23,

1945, when he was packed into a crowded boxcar and evacuated, a fellow POW pushed him, saying, "Get away from me, you dirty Jew. It's your fault that we are in this war and I am in this boxcar."[56] A big Irish man intervened. A stranger to Schenk, he warned the other man not to touch him.

Radish and Schenk found partners in suffering. What had once been a badge of Jewishness — fear, suffering, humiliation — now characterized all of the POWs. Although on rare occasions Germans segregated Jewish POWs, as happened in Stalag Luft I, imprisonment as a POW usually erased ethnic and religious differences among American Army and Air Corps men.[57] The struggle to survive dominated all else. Fear for the future preoccupied them. Approximately 94,000 American servicemen were interned in more than fifty POW camps in Europe and the Mediterranean.[58] Almost all survived, but most suffered grievously from the harsh conditions that bred disease and malnutrition. By the time the British liberated him, Radish had lost a lot of weight. Starved and hungry upon liberation, the men shot a cow and immediately carved it up to eat. But Radish remembered being cautioned not to eat too much or too quickly or he would die.[59] Reflecting on his experiences in Berga concentration camp, a Jewish GI compared it to the Nazi policies against Jews. For most, death came within a couple of months through exhausting labor, debilitation, starvation, and finally a death march. Still, this GI's identity as an American medic saved him from the fate of the other Jewish slave laborers. Climbing a steep hill on the fourth day of the final forced march, he staggered past hundreds of crumpled figures clad in striped prison garb, their skulls blown apart by bullets.[60]

Although Radish had few chances to escape as a POW, Ralph Jackson recognized that opportunities existed as an internee. Jackson could depend on his comrades to collaborate with him and to keep his planning secret. He was ready to take the risk under the right conditions. He knew that his old crew had survived, but nevertheless he was sitting out the war in the relative comfort of a Swiss internment camp while his crew "was rotting in a German prisoner of war camp." He felt he owed it to his crew to get back into the fight. He yearned to see his wife Rita. And he "wanted to test" his own courage. Though the crew never held it against him, nagging in the back of his mind was someone saying "that Jew took off at the holidays." So he plotted the progress of Allied victories on a wall map in his room. As the Germans retreated from much of France after the Normandy invasion, Jackson glimpsed the possibility of escape. By early September, the Germans had been pushed back from the Swiss border with France. "Getting out of the camp was not the most difficult thing." But crossing the Swiss border "was the problem. The penalty if you got caught, and many many did," was severe. Neverthless, Jackson and three others took the risk. The four men trusted each other. They devised an ingenious scheme that depended on the help of underground contacts as well as four internees who did not want to escape. Using forged identification cards to get them paroled out of camp and railroad tickets to get out of town, the men made their way to Zurich. Their accomplices slept in the escaped men's beds each night until a fifth man returned the cards to them and they could surface. In Zurich, Jackson and his three buddies received civilian clothes and hooked up with members of the underground.

Jackson and his partners understood that escape required an elaborate network of implicit confidence and commitment. They were taken to a ramshackle, deserted hotel. They "found a room in the back, on an upper floor, with a mattress." Then they drew straws to see who would be in the middle, the warmest spot. They found some newspapers to serve as blankets at night.

Across the debris-strewn backyards a light beckoned: the back door to a café. The men went there after dark. Sitting at a table together, afraid to speak English, they realized that they stood out. The determined gaze of a woman made them nervous. As soon as she left, the men made a hasty exit. That was the last time they ate together. They would now take turns, trusting each man to go alone and return.

Their contact chose the evening of Christmas day to head for the border. Under a brilliant moon, they started across a hay field. They had almost reached the middle when they saw a glint at one end. Jackson knew that "there's no glint from a haystack." Somebody was there. They started to run. A patrol fired shots. Jackson was not sure whether the Swiss aimed to hit them or not, but the guards did not pursue them in their headlong flight into a woods. After several hours the men made another attempt. This time their guide took them to a deep, icy stream. On the French side people helped them cross, one at a time, in a rubber dinghy. Then Jackson tramped through a swamp, his feet cracking through the veneer of ice, until he reached a road and a farmhouse. Cold and wet, the four men spent the rest of the night in a barn. The next morning a truck drove them to an American mission in Annecy. Usually, escapees got a change of clothes and were shipped out. But since Jackson's group included a captain, the men were allowed to rest for several days before going to Lyons, and from there the Americans flew them back to England. Jackson landed, coincidentally, on New Year's Eve of 1944, "exactly one year from the date" when he had arrived with his crew. After returning to his base, he was flown to the States for debriefing at the Pentagon. Only then could he come home to New York to see his wife Rita and enjoy some rest and relaxation before receiving additional training on the new B-25s.[61]

The need to prove oneself as a Jew undoubtedly influenced not only Jackson but also Steinfeld, Jaffee, Gutman, Freeman, and many others who fought on the front lines. Jewish men took risks, at times, to win acceptance. They struggled to overcome their fears and to set a positive example. They accepted responsibility for their Jewishness and used it as an incentive to strengthen their own resolve. When they won respect as a Jew, the victory was less personal than collective. It was the squad's or the platoon's victory. It affirmed core American values that refused to distinguish between Jew and gentile, accepting both as equals. At those times, whether they were Jews or Christians no longer mattered. Then they were just American soldiers, although the meaning of that term now embraced all men, as Roland Gittelsohn had so powerfully preached at Iwo Jima.

The experience of acceptance that seemed to come more easily to Jewish fliers took some effort to achieve for infantrymen. But when it arrived, it bound Jewish soldiers up in an intimate comradeship that affirmed their manhood. Paul Steinfeld's moment occurred when his lieutenant ordered him: "Steiney, take six men and go take the next building."[62] Knowing the risks of the assault, Steinfeld didn't pick one of his friends, a fellow New Yorker in his squad. He understood the dangers and wanted to protect his friend. The 95th Infantry Division was one of the first to cross the Saar River into Germany. G Company was at the point, in the eastern-most position to which the United States Army had penetrated in Saar Lautern. And Steinfeld and half a squad were at the point of G Company.[63]

Steinfeld and his men were flushing buildings, combing them, working their way from one house to the next, the only way to do it in street fighting. They never knew what they'd encounter. Their standard procedure was to have one or two men go down to the bottom floor and two up and then meet in the middle. Steinfeld went down to the basement with his man who carried the Browning Automatic Rifle (BAR). He ran into seven German soldiers, who surrendered because they were cornered. Steinfeld took them up to the kitchen. He had heard that the Germans had tanks, and he wanted information. So he lined the captured soldiers up next to the kitchen sink in this suburban home to interrogate them.

Suddenly, his machine gunner burst into the room. He held the light machine gun used in street fighting in his asbestos glove. Breathless, he said, "Steiney, stand aside! I'm gonna let 'em have it." Steinfeld paused. "Why?" he asked. "They just shot our medic." Steinfeld knew that. The company medic had been entering the doorway from the backyard where Steinfeld was posted, and a sniper shot him. All the men were angry. A special, highly visible white cross signaled a medic's status as a noncombatant. The conventions of war dictated that one didn't shoot medics, who were supposed to be unarmed. The machine gunner wanted to retaliate. "Oh no!" Steinfeld objected. "Ya know, we, we don't. You can't do that." American soldiers did not kill prisoners, at least not on Steinfeld's watch. He was in charge; he shoved the machine gunner aside. Then Steinfeld noticed a silver skull and crossbone insignia on the prisoners' shoulders. "What is that?" he asked. "Oh, that's our star unit insignia," they replied. Despite some unease, he didn't think too much of it. After all, he had just spared their lives.[64]

Steinfeld moved on, concerned about the tanks. Soon, one of them rumbled down the street. He watched from a living room window with a good view. His bazooka man, a Southerner from Virginia with a pink face, was in the basement. As the tank approached, Steinfeld yelled down: "Get up here with that bazooka! We got a tank!" But the Southerner called up, "Steiney, I's a'feared." So Steinfeld ran down. He grabbed the bazooka

and one of the new replacements who was willing to load.[65]
Steinfeld waited with the bazooka on the windowsill until the
German tank rolled into view. Then he fired. The explosion
bounced him backwards. As he picked up the remaining cartridges, he thought: "There's my day's work. I'm going down
with this stuff." He heard the tank's engine start up. "My God!"
he exclaimed. If the tank had swung around and manned its 88-
millimeter gun, he would have been finished.[66] Instead, the engine stopped, turned over, and the tank reversed direction. As it
was backing out, he remembered something he had learned in
training: one way to disable a tank was to knock off its tread. So
Steinfeld pointed the bazooka and aimed right at the tank, dis-
lodging the tread. The tank started spinning in its tracks. But
since the far tread was operating, the tank went around in a wide
arc before it stopped about two hundred yards from the building. This time, the German gun faced the building; the barrel almost touched his nose. He faltered. Then he heard one of the
Milwaukee boys say, "Did you see Steiney go after that tank? It
was like David and Goliath."[67] To be likened spontaneously to
the mightiest Jewish hero — for Saul had killed in the thousands, but David in the tens of thousands — and this "from one
of the leading anti-Semites" in the unit, was true justification.

Steinfeld turned to his replacement bazooka man. "Let's get
off another shot. We can try again," he said. "I'll tell you what.
You fire. Maybe something's wrong. I'll load for you." So he did.
As he wound the coil, a friend called from down in the basement: "Steiney, get outta there. He's . . . elevating the gun." The
replacement hesitated and looked at him. "Get it off!" Steinfeld
ordered. The third one hit the tank. But a moment later the tank
let off a round. By that time, Steinfeld and his partner had
rounded the corner from the living room to the basement. They
actually dove headfirst down the steps. Steinfeld knew he "was

hard as a rock." He could have bounced off the walls. As he made for the stairwell, he experienced a sucking feeling at his back from the vacuum following the explosion. The German tank got off one shot that went right through the living room where he had been standing. It didn't take long for the Germans to fire again, this time into the basement.

A series of sensations ran through Steinfeld's head. "One: 'You're hit.' Two: intense surprise. 'How could this happen to me?'" He had seen many men killed by then, but he was astonished that he could be hit. Then he thought, "You idiot!" The 88 punctured his illusion of invincibility. Then he imagined: "Your head is off." Images of men he had seen beheaded flashed before him. Immediately after: "Impossible. How could you think this?" Then, "You're blind." He "saw a tremendous bright light," and then he couldn't see anything. He thought he had lost his head; in fact he had received a concussion. But on the heels of the concussion came the reassuring thought, "Lillian will love you anyhow." He was convinced that his wife, Lillian, had saved his life. "Many men died of concussion," he explained. "That whollop is enough to make you think you're dead and sometimes you fulfill that thought." Soon, one of the company medics came up to him. "It's not that bad Steiney," he said. "It's your shoulder." Steinfeld hadn't even noticed his shoulder. Later he felt it. But the wound mattered less than the victory he had achieved not only over the German tank but also over his other foe, antisemitism.

Months later, recuperating in the hospital, Steinfeld found out that the seven men with the scull and crossbone insignia "were Waffen SS, some of the worst murderers of the Jews. This Jew-boy saved the lives of seven SS," he mused. Given the opportunity to avenge the slaughter of European Jews, Steinfeld had chosen to follow the rules of war. He let his Nazi prisoners live, upholding what he considered to be American norms. But he "used to have nightmares about this." What had, at the time, appeared to be an act of rectitude, in hindsight became clouded with moral ambiguity. At one point he turned to "a dear friend" from his days as an undergraduate student at the Jewish Theological Seminary's College, Rabbi Jack Cohen. "Jack," he said, "I've had torments about this, that I saved the lives of seven SS." And Jack told him, "You had to, Paul. *Weil du bist a yid.* Because you're a Jew." Steinfeld added, "It's not in spite of being Jewish." He meant that somehow he didn't have the nerve to kill them, "the audacity to let 'em be casualties." Or the guts. Or the manhood. But Cohen reassured him. The Jewish, manly, courageous thing to do was to let them live. Steinfeld never forgot the conversation and its lessons of manhood. It confirmed that he had acted as a *mensch,* a man or human being in the Jewish understanding of the word.[68] The Jewish term *menschlichkeyt* or humaneness possessed moral dimensions that suggested responsible, mature behavior. A *mensch* did the right thing no matter what the circumstances. Steinfeld's decision not to take revenge thus reflected not only American rules of war but also Jewish ethical thinking about how to act toward his and his people's ruthless enemies.

Steinfeld's decision — and his anguish — could have gone the other way. Rabbi Cohen's interpretation reflected Jewish attitudes toward military conflict. A Reconstructionist and a Zionist, Cohen strongly supported the establishment of a Jewish state where Jews could wield arms to defend themselves as a nation. But there were limits in warfare. The SS exceeded those limits and acted as criminals. Still, that didn't give Jewish soldiers license to treat them any differently from other prisoners of war. Responses of American Jewish GIs to German prisoners, however, fell on both sides of the divide. Often, a man could not know what he would do in the heat of battle. "Ich bin ein jude" (I am a Jew), one paratrooper with the 101st Airborne told several captured German prisoners during the grueling Battle of the Bulge. He was supposed to escort them to the rear, but his trench foot made walking painful. Those four words did his task for him. The prisoners took off "like a couple of rabbits" toward the Allied lines and were shot. It was sweet revenge, pouring salt on the bitterness of defeat and blotting out Nazi calumnies that Jews were too cowardly to fight. The Germans thought they were facing an American soldier, but he let them know that they had been bested by a Jew.[69] How to treat German prisoners was not something Jews discussed among themselves or with their comrades. The majority of Jewish GIs who were not religious relied, for the most part, on their own inner moral compass to guide their actions, although it left them open to doubt and, on occasion, guilt.

Fighting in the European Theater against the Germans, who targeted Jews for annihilation, personalized the war for American Jews in uniform and sharpened their commitment. Writing home to his family after Rosh Hashana in 1944, Samuel Klausner, a religious Jew, announced with pride: "This evening there is one less town in Germany. I dropped my own personal bomb right in the center of town." He couldn't give more military details, other than to say "we really smacked it in force," but he could express his feelings. "I took great pleasure in dropping that bomb even though I knew it would not hit any military target." Why such pleasure? He elaborated: "It was just a small part of a repayment for 5,000,000 Jews."[70] The actual squadron target was a marshalling yard, a vital link of German rail transportation. But the town crowded close to the yards, and bombs rarely landed at or near the target. As a navigator in the 489th Bomb Group of the Eighth Air Force's 2nd Bomb Division,

Samuel Klausner, front row, second from left, with his crew, England, 1944. Fighting against Germans personalized the war for American Jews in uniform. On occasion, the power Jewish soldiers acquired in military service allowed them to attack Hitler's Germany not just as Americans but as Jews. Klausner relished such moments when he could fight on behalf of Europe's defenseless Jews.

Klausner did not normally drop bombs. In this case, the bombardier let him unload. His crew understood his desire to hit the town, although they probably did not seek to avenge the deaths of five million Jews. It was enough that it was an enemy town. On occasions like this, the power that Jews acquired when they entered military service allowed them to attack Hitler's Germany both as Jews and as Americans. At such moments they could also fight on behalf of Europe's defenseless Jews.

Jews often felt like a people apart, but acceptance into a fighting unit transformed them. By the time he entered Germany, Jeremiah Gutman had grown close to his men. Battle brought them together. He understood how they risked their lives for him, as he did for them. Even more than recognition of his courage, Gutman valued comradeship in combat. So it was with particular anguish that he followed an order that he thought was stupid and dangerous. The incident occurred in the notoriously treacherous "flak alley" outside of Leipzig near the end of the war. The scene from the road where Gutman stood looked different than it did from the sky, but no less formidable. "The road had a high embankment in front of it." Up on the embankment were fields that had been harrowed but not planted. In the distance, about a mile away, stood a German anti-aircraft artillery battery in place, defended by a German infantry battalion. Gutman's company of two hundred were told to cut the road. He interpreted their job as to stay put, "in case Germans came down that road because of the attack, evacuating Leipzig," Gutman explained. "We would stop them, capture them, or kill them."

Then came an order "to attack across that open field." The two hundred men with two tanks were told to assault "eight hundred entrenched men with a battalion of anti-aircraft artillery behind them." Orders were orders. But, Gutman noted, "the captain wasn't there to give the order; he sent the word up." They attacked. And they lost three-quarters of the men in half an hour. The Germans leveled the anti-aircraft artillery. Because the shells were still fused to shoot down airplanes, not people, the effect on Gutman's men was devastating. Huge pieces of metal flew across the field as the shells exploded, cutting people up like sausage. It was a disaster. Finally they took a line of dug-outs and trenches from the Germans. At that point Gutman sent a man back to give word that "unless we got immediate rein-forcements we had to withdraw and we would take casualties in withdrawing." The soldier never came back. Gutman never got any word. So he took command of what was left of his company. Of the 200 men, probably 50 or 60 remained. It was a replay on a far larger scale of his first experience on patrol.[71]

Then the fifth platoon came out. The black GIs rescued men, binding their wounds and carrying them back. "The wounded were horribly gashed. It just wasn't little holes in them. You had to take their jackets and pull their bodies together so their guts wouldn't trail out." Gutman tried to assist the badly wounded. He patched them up, crawling from one wounded soldier to an-other. The fifth platoon helped with the gruesome task. But some men were too far gone. One of his best friends begged Gutman to shoot him. Gutman could see he would die and so he did. But the misery and pain endured.

Although the black platoon salvaged as many soldiers as pos-sible, many others were left behind. After several hours of pun-ishing fire, they reached the edge of the field. Gutman jumped down onto the roadbank. While he was lying there, exhausted, the captain ran over. "Great work sergeant," he said. "How's it out there?" he asked. "Pretty rough?" Furious, Gutman an-swered, "Put your yellow face up over the top and take a look if you want to know what it's like out there."[72] The discovery of how expendable GIs were infuriated Gutman. "You would ex-pect front-line soldiers to be struck and hurt by bullets and shell fragments," wrote Paul Fussell, who served as an officer on the line in Europe, "but such is the popular insulation from the facts that you would not expect them to be hurt, sometimes killed, by

being struck by parts of their friends' bodies violently detached."
Fussell observed laconically: "If you asked a wounded soldier or
marine what hit him, you'd hardly be ready for the answer,
'My buddy's head.'"[73] Fussell's and Gutman's outrage echoes the
wrath of other front-line infantry.[74] But Gutman directed it explicitly at his captain.

Gutman's furious response to the captain provoked an accusation of insubordination. Not to be outdone, Gutman counter-
attacked. He wanted the captain's irresponsibility exposed. It
would be part of Gutman's contribution to the war effort. Such
officers should not continue to be allowed to endanger the lives
of their men. When the captain "filed charges against *me* for in-
sulting *him*, I filed charges against him. He was drunk," Gutman
asserted. "I could smell it on his breath. I filed the charges,
drunkenness on duty, unnecessary risking [of] the lives of men,
cowardice in the face of the enemy." While charges were pending, the battalion chaplain intervened. He called Gutman in and
urged him "to withdraw the charges." Gutman noticed with
some discomfort that the chaplain wore a cross. His plea for
what sounded like Christian charity grated on Gutman's ears.
In a conciliatory gesture, the chaplain explained that the captain would also withdraw his accusations. The captain was even
ready to recognize Gutman's bravery, putting him in for a Congressional Medal of Honor. "I'll take the congressional medal if
they offer it to me," Gutman replied sarcastically, but only "if
they court-martial him. Otherwise I don't want it." He wanted
Jewish justice, not forgiveness. "You're upset," the chaplain responded. "Yes, I'm upset." He seethed with anger. All of those
friends lost for nothing. The hard-won trust and respect, the
comradeship blown to pieces by German anti-artillery shells in a
foolish, dangerous, and unnecessary attack.[75]

Gutman's rage lingered in the aftermath of the clash. Though

the experience of battle united all soldiers, black and white, Jew
and gentile, the senseless bloodshed infuriated him. Recognition of his bravery did not mollify him. Too much was in jeopardy. Gutman wanted to win the war against the Germans not
only because he was an American but also because he was a Jew.
The captain's irresponsiblity threatened American victory and
cruelly wasted lives. It brought back to Gutman his old scorn for
officers that he had felt even at Fort Benning when he was trying to become one. Nor did his respect for chaplains increase.
Gutman learned that the chaplain had reported: "Sgt. Gutman is
withdrawing the charges against the captain. The captain is putting in Mr. Gutman for a citation for bravery."[76] The chaplain's
lie did not help matters. Gutman understood the stakes for himself as an American and as a Jew should the Allies not win the
war. World War II placed Jews in the eye of the storm and
threatened their American security.

In the European Theater, Jewish soldiers battled several foes.
They fought the enemy, their fellow soldiers' prejudices, and
their own anger at such hateful bias. These outer and inner
conflicts blurred together in complex ways. But the German
enemy's presence meant that their Jewishness, even if buried,
could not disappear from their consciousness. They were American Jewish soldiers fighting for respect as men, both individually and collectively. They wanted to transform Gittelsohn's vision of the ideal democracy that knows no distinctions among
men into a living reality. They also yearned to experience personal acceptance into a brotherhood of warriors. In the end,
Jews succeeded in sharing in "the abiding lesson of combat" of
World War II. "At the last extreme of the human spirit men turn
to those nearest to them for reassurance as to their own plight
and of the continued existence of common humanity," wrote
the historian John Ellis. "At the sharp end few men turned in

vain."[77] Those who survived the front lines emerged with new understanding of what was required of a man. Each Jewish soldier tried to be a *mensch,* in its private meanings, as Ellis suggests. But they also struggled to be men in the collective dimensions of the ideal. They sought to live and fight as brothers with their comrades-in-arms in a war against a racist, fascist, antisemitic foe. In this Jewish servicemen were often alone.

7

LIBERATION AND
REVELATION

It is twenty years now, Father. I have come home.
But in the camps, one can look through a huge square
Window, like an aquarium, upon a room
The size of my livingroom filled with human hair.
Others have shoes, or valises
Made mostly of cardboard, which once contained
Pills, fresh diapers. This is one of the places
Never explained.

—ANTHONY HECHT, "The Room"[1]

SEPTEMBER 11, 1944. Harold Saperstein stared in disbelief. Lining the road as far as he could see stood people with arms waving and broad smiles. Clusters of men, women, and children cheered on the Allied troops as they wound their way through the French countryside. Points of light flickered through the trees and dappled the trucks; the scene almost looked like an impressionist painting. Saperstein was sure that around the next bend the accolades would cease, but he was wrong. Hour after hour they continued. He savored the praises. He was reaping the "laurels earned by the combat forces who had slogged through two or three weeks previously."[2] Still, how could he resist this incredible welcome? It was hard not to feel "as though you yourself were the conquering hero who had won the war," he wrote home to his wife. Even the sobering sight of trucks car-

rying wounded soldiers to the rear could not dampen his enthusiasm. He knew that he was tasting victory even before it had
been fully won. "No one could have passed through that day"
riding through southern France, he declared, "without feeling
way down deep that we're fighting for something that's precious
and good."[3] Saperstein, the former pacifist, named that precious
thing: liberty. Here was justification of the bloodshed. Europe
would be free, its peoples liberated, its governments released
from the sway of fascism. American armies were coming to
throw off the yoke of Nazi oppression. As Saperstein well knew,
that meant that Jews too might finally be rescued from the horrors of antisemitic persecution.

Rabbi Saperstein could not anticipate that this final liberation
would bring revelations that would turn the sweetness of victory
bitter. Before the month had ended, he would be greeted as a
"savior and redeemer" by fellow Jews. Unlike the warm welcome on the road in France that intoxicated him, elevation to
messiah status made him uncomfortable. "You'd think that I had
singlehanded[ly] driven out the Nazis," he told his wife.[4] He
didn't want to be "the living symbol of liberation."[5] In the final
months of war, Saperstein's charged encounters with Europeans, European Jews, and finally with Germans led to unexpected
revelations that transformed his sense of himself as an American
Jew in uniform. Like so many of his co-religionists, he learned
the true scope and nature of the war he was fighting as an American and a Jew.

"Hey, there's Mont St. Michel!" Harold Freeman yelled. En
route to catch up with the 83rd Infantry as a replacement rifleman, he could not contain his excitement about his arrival in
France. He glimpsed the famous island monastery from the
back of a truck. "Behind it the sun was just beginning to sink
into the Atlantic — an exquisite, beautiful sight." His fellow GIs,

"squeezed in and exhausted," looked at him as if he were "nuts." So he "shut up" and watched until it disappeared from view.[6] Freeman was experiencing Europe, which had previously been just "geography and history" to him. Writing home, he tried to convey some sense of what it meant to "return" to the continent as part of a victorious army.

Freeman wanted to understand the French. He had given up his draft exemption to fight fascism, so he was eager to find out how the French interpreted their recent liberation. He noticed that they seemed to be equally curious about Americans. One warm Sunday in September, French men, women, and children "strolled about" his bivouac area near Tours until it "looked like Bronx Park Zoo on Easter Sunday," he told his wife. "Children ran all over the place, between the tents and over the tanks." The scene mystified him. The comparison to a zoo suggested not just familiar cordiality but also a measure of distance, voyeurism, and discomfort. These French men and women were supposed to be allies, but it was difficult to get close to them, especially since Freeman didn't speak much French. The French men stood around "envying our cigarettes, admiring our weapons and demonstrating how the manual of arms is done in the French army." It made for a pleasant day, even if the civilians did "gape while we ate chow."[7] Freeman recognized hunger in their stares and a measure of jealousy for the abundance of American food. But he could not decipher their politics.

Akiva Skidell tackled the same task of decoding French responses to American soldiers. Born in Poland, he returned to Europe with memories of the continent before the war. Like Freeman, Skidell recorded his initial encounter: trading with the local population as their convoy of trucks moved slowly through the French countryside. "We got apple cider by the gallon, apples, pears, peaches, tomatoes, bread, water, wine, onions, eggs, walnuts, and we gave in return cans of army rations, candy, sugar, coffee, gum, and above all, cigarettes," he told his wife Ettie.[8] Cigarettes were a basic item of barter and gifts. Trade was an exchange accepted even between enemies, as Harold Radish had discovered when he became a prisoner of war. The abundance of fresh fruit in France spoke to the quality of the farms, "evidence of rounded, cultivated living." Skidell was less sure about the people. The men did not impress him but the women did, "the middle-aged as well as the young. They're active, a great many work, and few look the clay pigeon type." The children were pretty and lively.[9]

Skidell was far more skeptical than Saperstein about what liberation meant to the French. He observed the "unmistakable signs of enthusiasm in the welcome" he and the other GIs received all along the road — "hands waving, stuff thrown, smiles" — but took these accolades with a measure of cynicism. He "couldn't help thinking what the reception of the German Army was like." Cosmopolitan and savvy, he sensed the self-serving and self-preserving value of such performances. "I wouldn't be surprised if a similar sight was not to be seen then," he mused. This was "pure conjecture," he admitted, but he recognized how strange it was "to see men, and mostly women, whose houses stood in ruins, welcoming those who, for whatever reasons, were the ones who caused that destruction." Skidell remembered the end of World War I in his hometown of Grodno. "The last time we all came thru the war itself," he reminded his wife. But problems arrived in the war's wake. "This time — who knows?"[10] Knowledge of the European past produced premonitions for the future. Skidell understood the etiquette of conquered and liberated alike. It disguised whatever true feelings people may have harbored toward a victorious army.[11]

Despite his halting French that forced him to speak only in

the present tense, Freeman tried to engage people in conversations about politics. He readily agreed to meet a communist journalist, a member of the French underground. They spoke in a château left untouched by the Nazis. "One wonders at this! War or not the contrast between wealth and poverty continues. The chateau dwellers live in quiet and relative plenty," Freeman observed with disgust, "while about the country-side wander refugees from many different places that have been bombed out — as well as neighborhood peasants." Their persistent stares "at every chow call" rattled him, as did the sharp contrasts between starvation and abundance. Freeman would have preferred that the communist journalist be a man of the masses rather than a "friend of the chateau dwellers." Still, the journalist was "eager to talk" and after a "bon jour" and a cigarette, he said, "When you get back to the U.S. you tell the Americans that the French people have been fighting the Nazis all the time during the occupation." The French were not merely collaborators, as it might have appeared. "Were the communists active in the underground?" Freeman asked. "They were actually the head of the entire movement." Freeman was surprised and cheered. "Do you think they will participate in the French government as in Italy?" "I think and hope so," the journalist answered.[12] Such optimism encouraged Freeman about France's political future. He hoped to see communists integrated into a new Europe. Communist participation in government spelled progressive democracy, an antidote to the fascist collaboration he despised. The friendship between the wealthy "chateau dwellers" and the communist journalist, while alarming, did not diminish his enthusiasm.

Harold Saperstein also heard about communist leadership of the French underground, but he brought different concerns to his conversations. One September morning he sat drinking ersatz coffee at the Cafe Excelsior, a favorite hangout of Jewish refugees in Grenoble. Eager to learn more details about Jewish experiences during the war, he solicited stories. It turned out that many atrocities were committed by Vichy French Police. Frenchmen apparently "acquiesced in the treatment of the Jews." Saperstein was surprised. He couldn't quite nail down French motives. Perhaps personal gain pushed people, or Nazi propaganda. Or maybe it was just basic viciousness. Were these the same people who had welcomed him as a liberator only days earlier? He discovered that only Christian organizations and communists had rescued Jews. The stories depressed him. A Jewish underground fighter was limping "from a bullet wound in the leg, recently received. In his unit there were 120 men, 26 of whom were Jews. Of these, only 5 are still alive."[13] Just as distressing, "the official records" showed "not a single one of them to have been Jewish." Saperstein immediately grasped the significance of this erasure of Jewish identity. Jewish fighters disappeared from the historical record. When France was liberated, the wounded resistance member reported to the prefecture for financial assistance. "He was received most hospitably and graciously until he stated that he was a Jew born in Roumania. Immediately the official's manner changed. 'When are you going to leave France?' he asked."[14]

The French Jewish future did not look promising to Saperstein. Jewish refugees at the Cafe Excelsior bickered over whether there were "a few good Frenchmen or only a very few." All agreed that "the French people cannot be trusted in their relationship to the Jews." But few except the Zionists drew the conclusion "frankly and squarely" that the solution was emigration to a Jewish state in Palestine. Saperstein hoped to meet some Zionists soon. In the meantime, his conversations discouraged him. The political future of Europe appeared grim. Communist participation in government didn't matter. More significant were the flourishing nationalist hatreds. "The tragedy of war won't end with the armistice," he prophesied.[15] While Saperstein contemplated the Jewish future, Freeman focused on European prospects. Optimism or pessimism depended on expectations.

Despite their varied perspectives in their role as liberators, Saperstein, Freeman, and Skidell all wanted to understand the enemy. By October 1944, Allied troops had invaded Germany. This first foray onto German soil would be repeated on a large scale, but only after American soldiers had fought bitter battles in the Huertgen forest, taken Aachen and Metz, and beaten back the last German offensive in the Ardennes.[16] Then Saperstein, Freeman, and Skidell would come face to face with enemy civilians. In October, the men's first impressions were sketchy.

Skidell hated Nazi Germany, but he had a deep curiosity about how the enemy lived. Finding himself briefly on enemy territory as part of a reconnaissance unit, he decided to find out. In the morning, after completing his turn on the radio, he "went for a little walk into a small German town." The visit gave him "a chance to look at some of the devastation from close up," he reported to his wife. "This sacred German soil is a pretty mess," he wrote with sarcasm. Then he confessed that he "couldn't help feeling completely callous." The town was deserted. Despite the destruction of many houses, he noted signs of German prosperity "and a high technological standard, as well as plenty of fancy articles — furniture, clothing and what not."[17] This evidence of German technological prowess impressed him. Technology represented civilization. Many GIs gloried in American gadgets, conveniences, and machinery, seeing them as symbols of American superiority. Discovering in Germany examples of "a high technological standard," as Skidell put it, challenged assumptions about the enemy's inferiority.

But Skidell was searching for clues to a larger and more difficult puzzle. He wanted to grasp Nazism's appeal. He didn't return to Germany until December. By then he had picked up and rummaged through books he had found on his "wanderings," as he called them, through Holland and Belgium. Fluent in German (as well as Yiddish, Hebrew, Polish, and Russian), he could comprehend Nazi publications. He said he was reading "as if in search of an answer to the question, how a seemingly enlightened people could ever fall for all that bilge." Constrained by censorship, he wrote to his wife: "I don't know whether you get the main idea, which this stuff conveyed to me, namely, what cruel instruments language and logic . . . can be; how anything, no matter how vicious, can be dressed up to sound pleasant, or at least, civil and correct." Skidell was talking about the power of propaganda to hide the murderous actions of Germans. He recognized, of course, that "it's folly to think that it was the logic of these arguments that carried the main weight. There was plenty to work on to start with," beginning with "Hitler's fanatical hatred of the Jews." That perverse antisemitism struck Skidell as "less a matter of strategic convenience . . . than of a deeply-seated persecution mania." But the disguises of language provided a glimpse "into some of the mental processes by means of which healthier people than Hitler and his gang made peace with these crazy ideas. What people won't do for convenience, and for peace of mind," he wrote bitterly.[18] Not to mention a "high technological standard."

"What all this adds up to, I don't know," he conceded. "Can't think that far. All I know is that there's something to worry about." He let the understatement stand for his deep fears for the fate of not only European Jews but also his family. "The Germans may, of course, be particularly susceptible to this kind of stuffed baloney," he mused. "So many of them are humorless and ready to accept somebody else's word, devoid of that faculty to recognize bunk when they see it. But," Skidell admitted, "it would be Nazism in reverse to say that only Germans are capable of falling for that stuff." Racial ascription, or even talk of "national character," represented dangerous thinking. It fed antisemitism and other racisms. After all, there were "plenty of humorless and mentally lazy people elsewhere," he noted. Undoubtedly, "there will always be some wrong, some grievance that they will think right to be righted."[19] Nationalism, too, could provoke willful blindness to immoral actions by the state. These far from "pleasant thoughts" preoccupied Skidell during a lull in the fighting in the Ardennes. The moral and political dilemmas of Nazism and its extraordinary appeal would grow ever more acute as he penetrated deeper into Germany.

Access to German sharpened Harold Freeman's contemplation of political tactics and rationales. While still in Luxembourg he picked up a magazine "published by the propaganda ministry for the local gauleiter," the Nazi official in charge of the occupation. Scattered throughout were "printed quotes of famous Germans." Freeman translated a few samples for Bea, his wife. Schopenhauer, Fichte, and Beethoven were all enlisted in support of Nazism. Schopenhauer's attack on religion and Beethoven's refusal to yield to fate helped sustain German morale. Freeman was astounded that "philosophers are quoted in a propaganda sheet. How meaningless culture becomes," he lamented. "All a veneer, a pitifully thin, peeling veneer over a fierce animal struggle for existence." For a man who thrilled at the sight of Mont St. Michel, this was a painful conclusion. Then he offered "another quotation, this time Goebbels." The juxtaposition of the Nazi propaganda minister with philosophers convinced Freeman that Goebbels' message "really does the rabble rousing."[20] He pondered Nazism's effective manipulation of culture.

While Skidell and Freeman were seeking to understand the enemy's appeal, another liberation was occurring in Europe — the liberation of Jews who had spent the war in hiding. The rapid retreat of German troops in the summer of 1944 brought large sections of Belgium and France into Allied hands by the fall. And September brought not just the first taste of freedom for European Jews but also the Jewish New Year, the beginning of the year 5705. This would be the first Rosh Hashana openly observed without fear since the German occupation of the continent four years earlier. It would mark the beginning of Jewish liberation — not merely the removal of the Nazi yoke but also the freedom to worship as Jews. The New Year celebrations affirmed a Jewish public presence in Europe and carried political overtones for those who participated in them. Those who attended Rosh Hashana services discovered more than they expected.[21]

The Army encouraged Jewish GIs to observe the holy day, offering passes and occasional furloughs that promised a break from routine. A circular letter from Army Chaplain's Headquarters announced that "all Jewish soldiers who could be spared from duty could receive a three-day pass to attend Rosh Hashana services in Paris."[22] The city had been liberated on August 24 by the French Second Armored Division.[23] In September it was still off-limits to most American GIs. Hearing the news from chaplain's headquarters, Fred Lennetz jumped at the opportunity. Sometimes being Jewish wasn't a bad thing. He had arrived in Normandy in June, heading south through bombed-out St. Lô. His outfit of two hundred men, an ordnance company involved in auto repair and small arms maintenance, included ten Jewish GIs (slightly higher than average). They all received permission to go to Paris. As they piled into 6-by-6 trucks, their thoughts focused less on Judaism than on "clean sheets and hot showers."[24] After three months of living in tents and foxholes, a chance to enjoy civilization exerted more appeal than an occasion to pray. There was much they could savor after the services.

What awaited them was a revelation. Their truck "pulled up in front of the Rothschild Synagogue where approximately one hundred Jews of all ages were gathered. As each truck unloaded," bringing Jewish soldiers from units throughout France, deafening cheers greeted the men along with tears, hugs, and kisses. They "could not move in the crush of the crowd." Stunned by this emotional welcome from liberated French Jews, Lennetz "just stood there with tears running down" his face. One elderly woman grabbed his hand and "held on as she reached for the yellow star with the word *Juif* [Jew] tacked to her coat. She ripped it off and handed it" to him. Then she said in Yiddish: "This is what you have done for us!"[25] The woman's gift overwhelmed Lennetz. He was her hero, though he had not seen combat. His American uniform made him a liberator. American Jewish soldiers had rescued French Jews and given them the freedom to live again in public. Lennetz had come to Paris to escape from the daily ordeals of waging war, and instead he was being swept up in a collective Jewish fellowship. Unaware of the extent of Jews' wartime suffering, he was unprepared for their gratitude. He never imagined that he had pulled the badge of humiliation and persecution from the coats of French Jews. But he kept the souvenir of war, identity, faith, and victory. That Rosh Hashana he learned not only what it meant to be an American Jewish soldier in Europe but also what it felt like to be part of world Jewry. He rejoiced with fellow Jews in their liberation from Nazism. It was a New Year to remember, unlike any other. As was Yom Kippur, the Day of Atonement, ten days later.

But a solemn day of fasting, reflection, and prayer contrasted sharply with the optimistic promise of a new year and victory over a hated foe. The liturgy of Yom Kippur raised issues of life and death, the need to account for one's past behavior. It reminded Jews of the future's uncertainty. Yom Kippur prompted contemplation of the price paid for survival as Jews emerged from hiding and living under false identities. Saperstein compared these hidden Jews to the *conversos* of Spain, "pretending to be Christians to save their lives, maintaining their loyalty to Judaism only in their hearts."[26] For S. Hillel Blondheim, a first lieutenant in the Army Medical Corps, joining French Jews for Yom Kippur allowed him to witness "the age-old miracle of Jewish survival."[27] Blondheim dwelt upon the handful of living Jews, although aware of the many dead and missing if not yet of the full extent of the Holocaust.

The men in Blondheim's unit, a group of regular participants at Friday evening services, debated whether to go to Paris when they heard the Army directive or to attend Yom Kippur services at a nearby synagogue. The building had survived the war intact, along with Torah scrolls, prayer books, chairs, and furnishings. But the congregation had disappeared. When its rabbi returned with his family, he told some soldiers that he would hold services nonetheless. So the men, most of whom were observant Jews, voted to give up Paris to become his congregation, passing up clean sheets and a chance to see the City of Light. They would honor fellow Jews who had suffered and would affirm bonds of brotherhood. Perhaps their presence would inspire hope among the handful who had survived the cruel occupation. The GIs donned their field uniforms and ties in honor of the holy day. Then they were trucked into town. As they turned down the street of the synagogue, the men saw waiting for them a congregation. "Cheers, applause, and tears" surprised and welcomed them.

Services and the meal afterward to break the twenty-four-hour fast revealed to the GIs the difference their uniform made. They belonged to the armed forces of the most powerful democracy dispatched to crush the common enemy. They did not know terror as French Jews did. Blondheim discovered how Jewish fellowship could emerge out of diversity. Conversations flourished in a babel of languages: Hebrew between a GI and a Sephardi from Turkey, Hungarian between two *landsleyt* (countrymen), Yiddish of the "strictly second-generation American, very scant and halting," a bit of French, a smattering of English. Blondheim broke the fast at the rabbi's home. Dinner reflected the blending of GI and civilian. The modest meal included canned gefilte fish — a soldier's gift — while the rabbi's wife contributed vegetable soup and fried potatoes. There was only dark bread. Peaches from a local orchard were served for dessert, accompanied by tea, hoarded for just such a special occasion. Sharing the simple fare drew Blondheim into the orbit of Jewish culture. He tasted more than food around the table. He savored a palpable bond of Jewishness, and he sampled the tales of surviving a war that aimed to annihilate Jews. Revelation of what these European Jews had experienced provoked reflection. Even before Jewish soldiers encountered the depths of Nazi savagery, they struggled to interpret the meanings of the German war against the Jews.[28]

Before Harold Freeman returned to Germany in February 1945, he reported how "the law against fraternization was again layed [*sic*] down to us — strongly. It is a court-martial offense," he explained to his wife. "A curt response to a German's 'hello' or 'good day'" was "not considered fraternization." That cheered him because he felt it "goes against the grain not to respond." But he had "nothing but bitterness for the German civilian."[29] American policy prohibited "mingling with Germans upon terms of friendliness, familiarity, or intimacy, whether individually or in groups, official or unofficial dealings." This comprehensive ruling barred American soldiers from "visiting German homes; drinking with Germans; shaking hands with them; playing games or sports with them; giving or accepting gifts; attending German dances or other social events; accompanying Germans on the street, in theaters, taverns, hotels, or elsewhere (except on official business)." Also prohibited were "discussions and arguments with Germans, especially on politics or the future of Germany."[30] There would be no repeat in Germany of Freeman's conversation with the communist journalist. Freeman thought that the German civilian was "equally, if not more, guilty than the soldier for this mess." The civilian masses "voluntarily (to a large extent) put, and kept, Hitler in power. The soldier was drafted and represents the military manifestation of Naziism," he reasoned. "As such he must be killed and defeated. The *guilt*, however, is the burden of all the German people."[31]

The question of German guilt was a harsh one. The theory of collective responsibility sounded just. Assessing German guilt broadly made citizens accountable for their nation's actions. But Freeman soon discovered that his political values did not necessarily help when he confronted German civilians. Like many GIs, he would quickly learn that no German he met would admit to being a Nazi.[32] Furthermore, all absent husbands and sons were fighting on the eastern front, against the Russians, not the Americans. It would not be easy to judge the conquered.

By late February of 1945 Freeman faced the contradictions of Nazism directly: Germany's technological prowess ran in easy harness with its political viciousness. "The big drive is on," he told his wife. In Mariadorf, Freeman was lodged in a basement that was "part of a housing development of the kind one sees in the outlying sections of New York. There are rows of connected

Harold Freeman sitting on the tank's gun, April 1945. Fighting in Europe allowed him to experience it at first hand. Writing home, he tried to convey some sense of what it meant to "return" to the continent as part of a victorious army.

houses, built of brick, with plenty of space between the rows." He admired their "good looking exteriors." He thought that "on the whole the Europeans handle bricks better than we do. The plumbing, however, is far below our standards — even primitive."[33] Living in German housing made Freeman ponder the material benefits that Nazism appeared to have brought. Did these pragmatic rewards help explain German acceptance of such vile politics? He wondered at the enemy's ongoing resolve to fight. Did the publications he had read keep them going? A week later in Neuss, American soldiers not only conquered but also liberated. "Hundreds of Russian and Polish 'slaves' worked in the factories in this area," Freeman explained to Bea. "They are a sorry looking lot and of course were overjoyed at the turn of events."[34] The contrast between slave laborers and German civilians struck Freeman. Here was living evidence of Nazi racial politics. Perhaps the prosperity he saw in Germany derived from such racist exploitation.

Despite his encounter with slave laborers, drawing a line between enemy civilians and soldiers proved more arduous than he had anticipated. The draconian rules against fraternization suggested potential difficulties, but Freeman had emphasized their abstract principles, not their pragmatic details. The civilian dress, the presence of women and children and old people, made it difficult to see anything except ordinary human beings. The similarities in physical appearance to white Americans heightened commonalities. Since Freeman spoke some German, he occasionally did the negotiating. Usually this meant evicting local people from their homes. "What a rotten job it is," he confessed to his wife. "Of course I'm in complete agreement with this procedure, but still —. Damn it, these people made their bed, now let them lie in it!" he fumed. Then he hesitated. "Still it's one thing to shoot a man in the heat of battle and another to chase a woman on crutches out into the night." Freeman's gendered distinctions made him think he was "soft."[35] The ideal was to be "hard." The issue grew more complicated as time passed. "I can't get my feelings towards the German civilians straight," he admitted.[36]

Ideology had its limitations. Before Freeman came to Germany, the issue was clear: "The German people must be made to suffer for their crimes against civilization." Freeman had been ready to uphold that standard. But he learned that it was "another matter to stand by and watch them suffer." That made him uncomfortable. He kept vacillating. "Yesterday an elderly couple came into our area. They said they wished to return to a bunker they had been living in for some food and for some clothes for themselves and their child." Freeman "had to tell them that they could not go to the bunker and that they had to leave the area immediately." He knew that civilians were banned from the section and that "military necessity" dictated "such a course, but . . . But, but, it's always 'but'!" He tried to reconcile his politics and his emotions. The reality dawned on him slowly. He could "approach the problems of 'humanity in general' quite cooly and intellectually," he decided. "However, toward 'humanity in particular'" it turned out that his "emotions predominate." Surprisingly, those "predominating emotions" were "of pity and sadness, rather than hate."[37] Freeman looked at Germans and saw people suffering from war. He did not see guilty men, women, and children who had put and kept Hitler in power.[38]

Akiva Skidell held a contrary view. His socialist Zionist politics framed issues of responsibility and guilt in a way that was similar to Freeman's antifascist ideology. But actual Germans provoked disparate sentiments. Hate came easily. So did revulsion. It was impossible to forget Nazi brutality toward Jews. Skidell, too, reentered Germany at the end of February with his unit, the Second Armored Division. He even noted the date: "Tonight is Purim." The carnivalesque holiday celebrated an unexpected victory over Haman, a royal vizier who had wanted to slaughter the Jews in ancient Persia. Skidell had hoped "to be able to go to services some time today or tomorrow," but resigned himself that it wouldn't happen. Instead, he celebrated the day "by a re-entry into the land of the modern Haman."[39] It was not hard to see Hitler with his murderous antisemitism as a "modern Haman." (Would that Hitler had been foiled in his plan as Haman had!) By early March, Skidell could write, "the end does seem to be in sight." That afternoon he listened to the news "about the Rhineland and Cologne." To his surprise, he "rejoiced to hear that the Cologne cathedral survived the ordeal. It's nothing but so much stone," he reflected, "yet it is a symbol of old and better days." He intended no irony. "Certainly better than these mad years have been," he elaborated, "and all the terrors of the Crusades and the Inquisition are as nothing compared to what that guy Hitler has done to us."[40] The "us" here signified Jews. Skidell was not writing only as a GI. He had taken the opportunity two days before to speak to some of the Polish slave laborers who had been liberated. He asked them about the conditions of Polish Jews. "They all told the same story: there are none left. Hitler's worst fury turned against them," he reported.[41] Little hope remained for his family.

Skidell's reflections on Germany, then, came amidst optimism about the imminent Allied victory and pessimism about the situation of European Jews, his own relatives among them. In addition to dealing with his emotions as conqueror and liberator, Skidell felt profoundly connected to the Jewish victims. They were his people and he was implicated in their fate, despite his American uniform. And that cruel fate dominated his emotions, blocking all feelings of "pity and sadness." He could appreciate historic German architecture, like the Cologne cathedral, but he felt little of the pity that Freeman expressed for German civilians. "There are children in these German houses, too," he told his wife, "and, like the children that they are, they play up to you and act friendly. But I for one find it impossible to take to them," he confessed, "tho I know well enough that they are not to blame." It was not a question of guilt but a matter of emotion. A father himself, he could not sympathize even with children. Bitterness against the Germans welled up inside him. That "cold feeling" he got when he faced "one of these Germans — regardless of how pleasant they try to sound," came over him. They made his skin crawl.

Skidell thought that Germans were "expert t.l.ers" (*tuchus-*

likhers, or ass-lickers). So were their children. It wasn't difficult for him to illustrate his point, especially given his multilingual abilities. "Understanding the lingo around here" had its advantages, although he made it "a point, while talking to the Poles and Russians, to say as little to the natives [i.e., Germans] as is absolutely necessary," since he lived "in one house" with them. "I need not tell you how I feel about these people," he wrote to Ettie, who did, surely, understand what was unstated. "They are worse when they begin to whine, proclaiming their innocence." Convinced of German guilt and citizens' responsibility for Nazism, Skidell had no patience for protestations of purity. "There was one woman who, unprovoked, started telling me how she always worked for peace and international cooperation, how she had relatives in Brooklyn whom she'd like me to look up some day," he wrote, "until I came across a photograph of a Nazi demonstration with some guy making a speech, and there she was, staring right into the camera."[42] Caught in her web of lies, she blanched and turned away. Her response only proved his point: all Germans were Nazis. Unlike Freeman, Skidell could not distinguish among them. Young or old, male or female, it didn't matter. His emotions condemned them all.

Skidell assumed that his anti-German sentiments extended to his fellow GIs. There wasn't "a trace of that open-handedness with candy and chewing-gum that is so characteristic of the GI in friendly territory. If only," he sighed, the GIs "could make themselves stay away from the women more than they do, there would be no sign of fraternization." On the other hand, perhaps sexual relations did not spell friendship. Some of the men "say that isn't fraternization anyway — as long as you don't talk. And talking isn't essential."[43] Though Skidell did not write to Ettie with tongue in cheek, the notion that sexual intercourse without talking didn't qualify as fraternization was a standard joke among GIs. Women understood that soldiers demanded sex as payment for food or favors. It was part of the code of the conquered.[44]

Neither Skidell nor Freeman contemplated punishing Germans, but to his surprise Ira Koplow did. A long way from Sioux Falls, he reported that by mid-April west of the Rhine there were "few cities, towns and villages that aren't feeling the fury of war. The more they burn down, the better we'll like it," he assured his mother. To his astonishment, he discovered that "the average Germans we come across still aren't regretting the misery they caused the rest of the world." This infuriated him. Koplow thought that the Americans were "being too easy on them — much too easy. Throwing them out of their homes and confiscating anything of value isn't enough. Something should be done," he urged, to put German civilians "under the suffering they caused others and keep them under it long enough so that they know they can never again get away with what they have for the last decade." He told his mother, "If only everyone in the U.S. could see some of the things we have seen (and we aren't actually on the front lines) they would know what we are fighting for over here."[45] His outrage upon seeing the misery of liberated slave laborers made him insist on a harsh occupation. He didn't want Americans sympathizing with Germans and undermining the victory the GIs were winning. He wanted to enlist all of America's might to punish the vanquished. Koplow perceived little remorse among Germans for the crimes they had committed. German pride troubled and shocked him, surviving even a crushing military defeat.

Harold Saperstein went even further: he considered revenge. "If the history of the last 15 years had been different," he wrote less than a week after arriving in Germany, "I might have been coming to Germany now as a tourist." Undoubtedly he would have enthused over "the beauty of its scenery," its historical shrines — and its people. "But more than a decade of barbarism, persecution, murder and war have made that impossible." Saperstein went on to advocate a program of action: "If the Jewish people has any self respect, Jews will never more go to Germany as tourists. To them it must ever remain a cursed land." No matter how much he and other soldiers might marvel at the autobahn or other evidences of German engineering and prosperity, the bottom line remained Nazism. Yet Saperstein found himself tempted to appropriate German property. When living in a requisitioned house, he walked into a baby's room and noticed some very attractive pictures. He took them and thought he'd send them home to decorate his son's room. Then revulsion swept over him. He put the pictures back. He didn't want his son to "grow up in a room decorated with pictures stolen from some other baby." Still, he admitted, "there are lots of things I find myself able to do for revenge that I would never have considered myself capable of."[46] This was an unexpected revelation for the chaplain. Such emotions and desires had not animated him before he entered Germany. Although Saperstein's notions of revenge — taking property that did not belong to him or urging Jews never to visit Germany — did not involve violence, Jews with weapons on occasion behaved in ways they did not imagine possible. Even the small gesture of turning the tables on Germans by allowing former prisoners to appropriate German goods reinforced a sense of the rightness of the Allied cause.[47] Such an act helped to rectify Nazi injustice. And it removed direct responsibility from a Jewish GI for acts of revenge while assuaging his fury at Nazi racism.

Bringing the war home to the enemy meant a different kind of combat. As a rifleman, Jeremiah Gutman did not relish fighting local "crazies," as he called them. He preferred the battlefield to pacifying urban residents. Near the end of the war in Leipzig Gutman's unit was "mopping up," which forced him to confront German civilians face-to-face. Sent to deal with an incident of "gunfire from the roof of an apartment building," Gutman and two soldiers "drew fire" as they approached. He "tried to get in the building to go upstairs" but found the door locked. Treating this as a civilian dwelling, Gutman took the end of his rifle and broke the pane of glass. Then without thinking he reached "through the door to open the knob from the inside." As he put his "hand on the knob," suddenly an axe came down. He pulled his hand back in the nick of time. "Somebody inside there," he realized, "wanted to cut" his arm off. So he turned the rifle around and poked it through the shattered glass. He "came across some flesh" and pulled the trigger. The axe-wielder turned out to be "a lady." Obviously she hated Americans as much as he disliked Germans.[48]

Chagrined by the surprise attack, Gutman resorted to military methods. He "blew the door open with a hand grenade hung on the doorknob." Then he took his soldiers inside. Another surprise awaited them: "a guy in the passageway back there with a pistol in his hand." He had the advantage. Gutman started to bring his rifle down but before he could, the man fired and hit him. Then he disappeared into the cellar. The wound in Gutman's arm wasn't serious, but the pistol fire caused him to "pull back out of that doorway." He and his two men hunted around the building, looking for a window to the cellar. Finding one, he kicked it out and threw in a "fire concussion grenade." A particularly nasty explosive, it burst eardrums and "whatnot of everybody" down in the basement, which turned out to be "the air raid shelter of the building." Gutman subsequently discovered "it was filled with people who lived in the house." He estimated that he "killed twenty–thirty people there that day—

residents of that apartment building." Maybe they included the guy who took a shot at him. Subsequently Gutman went up to the roof. But by the time he reached it, "the guys who had been shooting" had fled.[49] Killing twenty to thirty German civilians left Gutman with painful memories but little remorse. He learned to his surprise that he felt no pity. The incident reminded him that he needed to remain alert. It also blurred distinctions between enemy soldiers and civilians. It made Gutman wonder if there were any Germans who had not been Nazis.

Since the war was not yet over in April, Akiva Skidell puzzled over the behavior of some soldiers who were willing to risk punishment for violating non-fraternization rules.[50] When quartered in a mansion in Germany, he overheard a conversation between a wealthy resident and some GIs. "One of the young women engaged a couple of the fellows in somewhat of a discussion about the war, Germany and such." Skidell didn't know if she was a Nazi, but he thought "she certainly talked like one, tho of the respectable, semi-intellectual variety." This meant that she spoke about class differences. A socialist, Skidell had no sympathy for the suffering of the rich. He listened as she rambled on "all about the threat of communism in Europe, and what a poor country Germany is, and how hard its people have always had to work on that account, and how she can't understand why no one shows any sympathy for the German nation." Her comments turned his stomach, but when finally "the two fellows raised the question of how the Germans have treated the other peoples of Europe, and particularly the Jews," his ears pricked up. "Yes, she confessed, that was something she herself could never see either." Then the GIs dropped their bombshell: "They told her that they themselves were Jews — which they were — and that was the end." Skidell couldn't see her reaction, but the two Jewish soldiers reported later "that her face paled, and the next thing they knew she vanished into thin air."[51] Nazism had made Jewishness a crime, and Nazis hunted down Jews mercilessly to be murdered. Germans might imagine that they could find common ground with Americans. But when Americans turned into American Jews, Germans seemed stunned.

Jewish GIs who met Germans pondered the question of whether to make their Jewishness public, unless, of course, they adhered strictly to non-fraternization rules. Many Jewish soldiers considered their Jewishness a private affair. Army service taught them that it was irrelevant in dealing with enemy civilians; what mattered was their American military role and responsibilities. Yet despite forces mitigating against Jewish self-identification, Jewish soldiers often felt compelled to declare their Jewishness. It was part of their war against Nazism.[52] Self-identification as a Jewish GI forced Germans to confront a Jew who had power and authority. It was a different matter if it involved other Jews. Skidell was far from shy about announcing that he was Jewish and was eager to meet other Jews. But not until a May Day celebration did he meet his second Jew in Germany. This man came from Czechoslovakia, went to France after the Munich pact, volunteered for the French army, and was taken prisoner in 1940. "A lawyer by profession, he is now on the administrative staff of the hospital," Skidell explained. "He told me he was a Jew early in the evening. I said: me, too. He said: I know. How, I don't know." Skidell was taken aback. "Perhaps by the name," he mused. "Not unlikely, is it. Anyhow," he told Ettie, "it was good to talk to him and I did for quite a while."[53]

Irrespective of a Jewish GI's self-identification, nothing prepared him for entering the concentration and death camps. The rapid conquest of Germany in the spring of 1945 left little time to dismantle the camps. Allied armies rushing to defeat remnants of the German army did not particularly target the camps. Few were military objectives. As a result, American soldiers liberated the camps almost by accident. The discovery of the death camps changed everything. The sight and smell of a death camp exploded in soldiers' faces. Like burning phosphorus, the fact of the horror stuck to their brains and guts. Despite early news reports of atrocities, GIs could not anticipate what they found. Contemporary accounts reveal reactions of shock and horror. The camps stunned these battle-tried soldiers. Often, infantry and armored units rolled through and stayed only a couple of hours. They left the camps' manifold problems for the rear-echelon troops, who determined what to do with the barely living and recently dead.[54] As J. D. Salinger, who served in the 12th Infantry Division, later told his daughter: "You never really get the smell of burning flesh out of your nose entirely. No matter how long you live."[55] The experience of liberating the camps, no matter how brief, would endure a lifetime.

Brad Dressler, a tanker, offers an account that includes the salient features of liberating a concentration camp. It began "early one morning" when his "alleged unit was on 'patrol.'" Dressler explains: "alleged because we were reduced to three tanks and the medic jeep. 'Patrol' meant that we didn't know where we were going or where we'd been." The lead tank commander was on the radio. "We must be gettin' close to a factory area," he reported. "I can smell a jute mill up ahead." The first signs of the camps were the smells. Vile odors pervaded the countryside for miles. In this case, however, Dressler and his fellow GIs "all snickered." The lead commander "came from an industrial town in Pennsylvania and as a kid, had worked in a rope factory. He was always saying he could smell one a mile away." However, "damn few of us knew what a jute mill smelled like, but what we were smelling was familiar. Unfortunately. We'd

GIs discover bodies at Dachau. The experience of liberating the concentration camps, no matter how brief, would endure a lifetime. Despite rumors and reports, GIs could not believe what they saw when they actually entered a camp. Although the camps contained all nationalities, Jewish GIs learned to their dismay how awful was the Nazis' single-minded slaughter of Jews.

lost a lot of buddies in tanks that had taken direct hits. And there's a distinctive aroma to burnt flesh."

Suddenly, the lead tank was reporting "something moving up ahead in the woods to the right." The men slammed their hatches shut, "ready for anything." Anything turned out to be "a couple of strange-looking characters just came out on the road." Phil in the lead tank reported, "They ain't armed, and they're wearing funny uniforms." He sounded confused. But so were Dressler and his fellow tankers as they "pulled up behind him." The men looked weird. The two they saw "wore striped pants,

baggy striped jackets and skullcaps. No shoes, socks, or shirts."
Until that time, Dressler had never seen anyone "suffering from
severe malnutrition." He "couldn't believe the size of their
wrists. Their cheekbones stuck out so far they looked like
horns." The two survivors just stood there and stared. Then one
of the tankers "who spoke a smattering of German, stepped forward, trying to find out what this was all about. The apparitions
stumbled backward, their hands raised in surrender."

Nonplussed, the tanker explained that they were Americans
"and asked if there was anything" they "could do" to help.
"One shuffled forward and made hand motions from his stomach to his mouth, the universal sign for food. Someone opened a
C-ration and offered it." Dressler and the others watched as
"the two grabbed it like it was caviar and started stuffing their
mouths. As they wolfed the food down, they jabbered something." The tanker looked puzzled. "I ain't never heard that
language before," he said. Then one of the tank commanders
yelled, "That's Polish." So Sig, who knew Polish, "jumped off his
tank and started talking a mile a minute." The two men "lit up
like they'd seen a blonde," and after a bit Sig turned to the commanding officer. "They're from a camp down the road. They say
the Germans have taken off. They need food. They haven't
eaten in six days." Dressler and his buddies "passed out some
more food" and moved on. "To Hell."

Dressler's first impressions surprised him. All he could see
"was what looked like miles of barbed wire fences surrounding a
bunch of ramshackle buildings and hundreds of men in their
striped uniforms, just staring, mostly at the open gates." Understandably suspicious, the tanks "rolled through those gates, alert
for enemy action." But this "battlefield" of war brought no enemy fire. The American soldiers were ready to fight. They "were
not prepared for a hoarse shout, *Amerikanischer!*' and a horde

of screaming people waving their hands and shuffling around in a crude form of a dance while some just stood there, tears streaming down their faces." Dressler's description evokes the cognitive dissonance of the "liberation." Then came the revelation.

"To our sorrow," he continued, they found their "jute mill" smell. "Neat little brick buildings, all in a row. Each one with its own set of ovens. And further on, the ultimate horror. Dante," thought Dressler, "would have cringed at the sight. An enormous pit, filled with bodies. Stick-like arms and legs protruding at odd angles. The stench was overpowering. And before our brains could even sort out what we were seeing, there were the sounds — plaintive mews, groans — penetrating our consciousness. And then the final horror — these were people and some were still alive." Dressler invokes almost all of the senses: smell, sight, sound, taste, and the imagination. The experience strained both the imagination's and the intellect's ability to comprehend. "Most of us were in our late teens and had never even seen death until the war came along," he explained, somewhat apologetically. "But even death in combat had not prepared" them for the camps. Many "were sick right on the spot." The taste of their vomit lingered in their mouths. "We couldn't absorb that Man had done this to Man." The tankers moved on "almost immediately but the sights" endured, "burned into" their heads. "For some, the memory would return in recurrent nightmares long afterward."[56]

Dressler's account masks the identities of the inmates. The two men on the road spoke Polish, not Yiddish. Whether this camp contained Jewish inmates is left unsaid. The horror is universal. It is what "man" did to "man," not Nazi to Jew, or even German to non-combatant. Dressler assimilates his experience as much as possible into what he knows. It is hell. But in truth, for these nineteen- and twenty-year-olds, there was no way to come to terms with what they saw. "That's how we learned the real meaning of the words 'death camp,'" he concludes.[57]

As soon as the first camps were discovered, rumors spread. A number of Jewish GIs reported that their first intimation of the camps was not the smell, but the rumor. "Stories are coming out in both the newspapers and radio about the atrocities found in the prisons and concentration camps now being liberated," Ira Koplow wrote home in mid-April of 1945. "I haven't seen the worst places and I can't say I want to," he admitted honestly. Recently he had observed "a large group of French prisoners of war who were just freed. They all wore stripped [sic] suits of sackcloth and most of them were merely a bundle of bones." Koplow knew that this case "was far from the worst." Still, it was "things like that that we'll never be able to forget."[58] It was hard to believe what they were hearing. Many dismissed the stories as exaggerations. News sources had reported "the more sordid facts of mass slaughter, labor and death camps, Nazi policies of enslavement of peoples deemed inferior and extermination of Europe's Jews." Yet rarely did this information figure prominently in portrayals of the enemy.[59] The imagination set limits to Nazi terror. But seeing living skeletons gave credence to reports of death camps.

Despite the rumors and reports, when GIs actually entered a camp, they couldn't believe their eyes. Many were sick to their stomach because of what they saw and smelled. David Cohen, a radio operator with the 4th Armored Division, reached Ordruf with his unit and "saw 30–40 bodies just lying around." The SS had gunned down the prisoners before evacuating the camp. Cohen noticed "the bullet holes in their backs." Ordruf was the first concentration camp with inmates that the Americans uncovered.[60] The survivors told Cohen that "the people who had just been shot in the back were coming to meet" the 4th Armored units that had stumbled upon the camp. He "saw many buildings with bodies stacked in them." Cohen walked in, and out, three times. Three times he became ill. Cohen had a camera. He "wanted to take pictures," but he couldn't do it.[61]

The fourth time Cohen entered a building, "General Eisenhower was there." Eisenhower "was green." He looked at Cohen. "God, Sergeant, you have to have a strong stomach to take this," he said. Generals Dwight Eisenhower, Omar Bradley, and George Patton toured Ordruf on April 12, 1945, a week after units of the 4th Armored Division happened upon it. After the generals inspected the camp, Patton got up on his Jeep and started screaming: "See what these sons of bitches did, see what these bastards did. I don't want you to take a prisoner." Cohen was shocked to hear him say this in front of Eisenhower and Bradley. But he admitted that he took away from that miserable day an unexpected experience of fellowship with his comrades-in-arms. It cheered him "as a Jew to see these officers and men had the same feeling." He recalled how "the Catholic chaplain was crying. . . . He said the Kaddish in Hebrew." Cohen felt "a camaraderie in our division that didn't know from Jew or Christian."[62] Neither rank nor religion mattered in the face of Nazi atrocities. He appreciated the fact that all the American soldiers shared his anguish and horror. Their stunned responses erased differences between Jews and Christians just when he discovered the gruesome fact that Jews had been singled out for extermination. Cohen was not alone among his comrades. At this moment, he knew that they *were* his comrades.

Eisenhower had another agenda. He ordered that rear-echelon troops be brought to tour the camp. "We are told that the American soldier does not know what he is fighting for," he said. "Now, at least, he will know what he is fighting *against*."[63] Later from Third Army headquarters he cabled London and Washington to urge that delegations of officials and newsmen be sent to witness the camps. The scholar Robert Abzug called this "tour" of liberated concentration camps "a ritual of exorcism and revelation."[64] Eisenhower's concerns summoned Army reporters from the Pacific Theater. His determination to let soldiers understand why they were fighting helped to bring Sergeant Fred Friendly to Europe. Friendly left the Pacific Theater on a military mission to report on the war in Europe. His assignment was to translate what he learned into a manifesto for the troops still fighting against Japan.[65]

As part of his tour of Germany in May 1945, Friendly visited the prison camp of Mauthausen. Expecting "an orderly place," he was deeply affected by the experience of this "death factory." As he approached the gates from the bucolic German countryside, the smell of petrol and the stench of human flesh overpowered him. Entering, he saw thousands of emaciated, stinking bodies, piled in stacks that towered above him. The next twelve hours were sickening.[66] He learned how Mauthausen had been built with rocks carried by 185,000 prisoners on their backs from a quarry 800 feet below. The steep steps, 186 in all, connecting the camp to the quarry were covered with blood. The prisoners called them "the steps of death." Slave laborers in the quarry had a life expectancy of six weeks.[67]

Before returning to the Pacific in the middle of May, Friendly wrote home. "I have seen a dead Germany," he told his mother. If not dead, "certainly ruptured beyond repair." He interviewed SS troopers and heard their "heritage of hate." And, he admitted with anger, "I have learned to hate." But even more important, he "learned now and only now that this war had to be fought." Peoples of fifteen different lands were butchered at Mauthausen: Poles, Czechs, Jews, Russians, Austrians, even

Germans. Although Jews did not yet represent a land or nation, Friendly included them in his list. "I want you to know, I want you to never forget or let our disbelieving friends forget, that your flesh and blood saw this. This was no movie," he assured her. "No printed page. Your son saw this with his own eyes and in doing this aged" ten years.[68] Personal testimony went beyond Signal Corps newsreels.

Friendly toured the machinery of death: the shower room, "a chamber lined with tile and topped with sprinklers." There 120 prisoners at a time "were disrobed and ordered in for a shower which never gushed forth from the sprinklers because the chemical was gas. When they ran out of gas, they merely sucked all of the air out of the room." He "talked to the Jews who worked in the crematory, one room adjacent, where six and seven bodies at a time were burned. They gave these jobs to the Jews because they all died anyhow, and they didn't want the rest of the prisoners to know their own fate. The Jews knew theirs, you see." Friendly observed the living skeletons, some of whom would die despite American medical corps work. He wanted his mother to know that these people, these victims, were not derelicts: "Some of them were doctors, authors, some of them American citizens, a scattered few were G.I.s.[69] A Navy lieutenant still lives to tell the story." Friendly wanted to reclaim their individual dignity to help his mother comprehend the extent of their degradation. He "saw where they lived" and "where the sick died, three and four in a bed. No toilets, no nothing." The "look in their eyes" haunted him.[70]

Mauthausen was an experience so overpowering that Friendly called it his bar mitzvah, his emancipation, his baptism all rolled into one. At Mauthausen he crossed the threshold to Jewish manhood and responsibility. It was his emancipation: he would be a Jew for the rest of his life. And he was baptized there "in the blood and smell" of the prison camp.[71] "Mother, I walked thru countless cell blocks filled with sick, dying people — 300 in a room twice the size of our living room and as we walked in — there was a ripple of applause and then an inspiring burst of applause and cheers, and men who could not stand up sat and whispered — though they tried to shout it — Vive l'Americansky." He would never forget the applause, the strange sound that came from men clapping who had no flesh on their hands. Nor would he ever forget the cheers and "those faces of men with legs the size and shape of rope, with ulcerated bodies, weeping with a kind of joy." Here were accolades without ambiguity. These survivors truly welcomed the American liberators. Their gaunt faces were at last filled with hope. A younger man asked him "something in Polish," which he couldn't understand. But he detected the word "yid." So Friendly asked an interpreter what the man had said. Blushing, the interpreter replied, "He wants to know if you are a Jew." Moved by the query and not embarrassed, Friendly smiled and stuck out his hand and said "yes." It was the first time since he had been wounded in Burma six months earlier that Friendly had shaken hands. Overwhelmed, the survivor "was unable to speak or show the feeling that was in his heart."[72] Friendly resolved never to forget, a resolution he kept. He told his mother to put the letter away "and every Yom Kippur I want you to take it out and make your grandchildren read it. For," he concluded, "if there had been no America, we, all of us, might well have carried granite at Mauthausen."[73] Like Skidell's use of the pronoun, Friendly's "us" referred to Jews. Taught to believe in Jewish assimilation, Friendly rejected it at Mauthausen. Instead he strengthened his identification with his people, the Jews, and his country, the United States.

Camp inmates came from all countries in Europe, but Jews

stood out among the victims. American officers noticed the large numbers of Jews who inevitably were treated worse than other prisoners. In some cases, commanding officers ordered the Jewish men of an American unit to go into a camp because they assumed there would be a commonality of language and faith. The encounter with survivors tugged at the loyalties of Jewish GIs.[74] A prisoner came up to Robert Fleisher at Dachau. "He was about my own age, and he took my hand when we started to speak, and he started kissing my hand." Fleisher was so upset that he fumed inwardly. "How dare the world do this to two human beings!" he thought. "Who am I that he should kiss my hand because he's free?"[75] The camps revealed the shocking depths of antisemitism and the pitiable vulnerability of Jews. These were strange revelations to victorious American Jewish soldiers.

Maurice Paper, a combat engineer, drew different conclusions. A captain, he received a special dispatch to go north to Dachau, "because somebody knew that I could read, understand, and speak Yiddish." His instructions were to "speak to the survivors and tell them medical and food supplies and all other necessities of life would be arriving shortly." When he "came on the scene it was unbelievable." He had heard stories, but nothing prepared him for what he saw. "Bodies were stacked up. Bodies were everywhere." Paper started to speak in Yiddish to the survivors, but they distrusted him until he gave his Hebrew name. "They were very excited when we spoke Yiddish." Paper handled the excitement, but when "a couple of them" started to kiss his hands and feet, he felt profoundly sad. This kind of obeisance and gratitude disturbed American Jewish soldiers. It made Paper into "a very strong Zionist" because he "realized there was no other answer for the Jewish people."[76] Jews should have the right to defend themselves in their own land. Although the camps contained all nationalities, Jewish GIs learned to their dismay how terrible was the Nazis' single-minded slaughter of Jews.

Discovering the death camps at the moment of victory over Germany confounded Jewish soldiers. Their revulsion at the camps collided with their recognition that these living dead were Jews like themselves. Harvey Cohen arrived in France only in 1945. He was with the 71st Infantry Division when it "stumbled upon the Gunskirchen Concentration Camp after encountering light resistance."[77] The 71st went the farthest east of any U.S. infantry division. Gunskirchen was in Austria; thousands of Hungarian Jews were killed there.[78] The first thing the American soldiers "noticed was a horrible odor"; the closer they came, "the worse it got." Then they started to see "a few people in terrible shape trying to walk down the road. Actually you couldn't call them people." That was the problem. "They were skin and bones, just indescribable." Cohen remembers the men "emptying their K rations and C rations; when you see people eating cigarettes and whatever food there was, you know they're in trouble." Utterly taken aback, he "just did not know what to do." He only heard "a cry for 'wasser' (water)." As for the barracks, they "were impossible to enter because of the odor."[79] Cohen soon came upon Jewish survivors and told them he was Jewish. "It was a very emotional moment. They began to hug" him but he saw "the lice on their bodies" and he "couldn't handle it," he confessed.[80] Howard Sachs, a medic with the 71st, vividly recalls how green the survivors' teeth were. The scene in Gunskirschen was nightmarish. Bodies lay everywhere, with no way to distinguish between the living and the dead. Sachs stood up on a Jeep to announce to the prisoners that they were free. He tried not to dwell on what he saw that day. He couldn't fathom how anyone could have lived through Gunskirchen. Nor did he feel

that he was the hero and savior whom the grateful survivors celebrated.[81] It was one thing to accept a gift of a yellow star, torn
from a coat, in front of the magnificent Rothschild synagogue in
Paris. It was quite another matter to acknowledge the hugs,
kisses, and adulation from Jews "insane with hunger."[82]

"The gulf of experience and expectation that lay between liberator and survivor," writes Robert Abzug, "disoriented and disturbed even those most ready to embrace the victims of Nazi
terror." Jewish GIs surely were among them. "An almost un-
bearable mixture of empathy, disgust, guilt, anger, and alienation pervaded each entry into a camp, compounding the palpable horror that greeted the liberator in each barracks and on
every parade ground."[83] One GI put it this way: "What we saw at
the camp our minds could not comprehend. Even after months
of combat we could not accept the gruesome sight and stench of
the bodies." He regarded the inmates "with pity, anger, repul-
sion and awe, since they were human beings who were defenseless."[84]

Jewish chaplains too crumbled in the presence of the camps.
Eli Heimberg served as the assistant to Chaplain Eli Bohnen,
assigned to the 222nd Infantry Regiment. The two men entered
Dachau on April 29, 1945, shortly after it was liberated. Before
they crossed the moat leading into the camp, they "encountered
a stench that permeated the air." Entering the camp, they "saw
pyramids of clothing and shoes piled fifteen feet high — the victims' belongings." Then they turned the corner and came upon
the "opened railroad box cars with people who had perished."
These were victims shipped from other camps as the front
closed in upon the Germans. The men penetrated further into
the camp. They were seeking the Jewish barracks. "When we
entered, we saw emaciated people whose skin was so close to
their bones, it looked as if silk stockings were pulled over skele-

tons. Some were sitting on the ground, others lying in their wooden slatted bunks, three tiers high." In the middle of the stinking barracks, Chaplain Bohnen announced, "Ich bin ahn Americaner Rabbiner" (I am an American rabbi). The simple statement seemed to unleash "all the pent-up emotions of the years in misery." Heimberg listened to the "burst of wailing and crying." The two men stood there, "unsuccessfully trying to control" their emotions "as the victims, who were able to, surged forward" to kiss their feet and hug their hands. These demonstrations of gratitude and obeisance unsettled Heimberg. "I felt humble and uncomfortable, for it was I who should have been hugging and kissing them," he reflected. Yet he could not do that. The shock of what he saw and smelled and heard overpowered him. The two men took down names and messages to send to families who were in the United States. Then Chaplain Bohnen chanted the memorial prayer *El Mole Rachamim* (God Full of Mercy) in memory of those who had not survived.[85]

Bohnen finally left the camp, but he could neither eat nor sleep. He couldn't even muster the courage to write to his wife about what he saw. It took two days before he could put down on paper a fraction of his impressions. "Nothing you can put in words would adequately describe what I saw there," he told his wife. "The human mind refuses to believe what the eyes see. All the stories of Nazi horrors are underestimated rather than exaggerated," he assured her. "We saw freight cars with bodies in them. The people had been transported from one camp to another, and it had taken about a month for the train to make the trip. In all that time they had not been fed. They were lying in grotesque positions, just as they had died. Many were naked, others in thin clothing. But all were horrible to see." That was at the entrance to the camp. Inside the camp itself, he saw the living. Bohnen focused on the Jews. They "were the worst off.

Many of them looked worse than the dead," he thought. "They cried as they saw us. I spoke to a large group of Jews." He couldn't remember what he had said. But he did recall the tears. "Some of the people were crying all the time we were there." How to explain this to his wife? "They were emaciated, diseased, beaten, miserable caricatures of human beings." He wrote, "I don't know how they didn't all go mad." There were so many thousands upon thousands of prisoners from all over Europe, but the Jews were the most miserable. "Even the other prisoners who suffered miseries themselves couldn't get over the horrible treatment meted out to the Jews." Bohnen, a Conservative rabbi, swore that "I shall never forget what I saw, and in my nightmares the scenes recur." He concluded that "no possible punishment would ever repay the ones who were responsible."[86] He left Dachau with his regiment after two days. On May 1, Chaplain David Eichhorn arrived.

Eichhorn immediately worried about the spiritual survival of the Jewish inmates. Like the medical personnel, his job was to care for American soldiers, but he shifted his priorities in the closing weeks of the war in Europe to help survivors regain some semblance of human dignity. In the brief space of a week, Eichhorn not only gathered lists of survivors but also gave the Jews of a satellite camp a Torah scroll. A local German official had hidden the sacred scroll in November 1938, on Kristall-nacht. Eichhorn, a Reform rabbi, had retrieved it. He then held Jewish worship services, including a service in the women's barracks on May 4. Buoyed by the success of these services in boosting Jewish morale, he planned a campwide service in the main square for May 5. Polish inmates, less emaciated than the Jewish survivors, threatened to disrupt it. In Dachau's hierarchy, Jews and Gypsies had been on the bottom, and a public campwide service disturbed the old order. When word of the threats

Shavuot services at Buchenwald. Chaplains tried to provide for Jewish spiritual survival and held Jewish worship services at the concentration camps. They understood freedom of worship as one of the four freedoms and integral to American victory over Nazi barbarism.

against the Jewish service reached Hollywood director George Stevens, he was furious. A lieutenant colonel, Stevens headed the Signal Corps unit that was filming conditions in the camp for the Army. He immediately complained to the camp commander. The next day an American military honor guard stood watch as Eichhorn conducted Jewish services on the camp's parade ground and Stevens' unit filmed them.[87] It was a moment of Jewish triumph amid despair. Stevens' film recorded what America valued: American soldiers protecting the free exercise of religion. Freedom of worship, one of the four freedoms, had trumped Nazi barbarism. Public Jewish worship on Dachau's parade ground overturned the camp hierarchy and made the most despised group first among equals.

Symbolic moments, however, could hardly begin to satisfy the physical and emotional needs of Jewish survivors. Jewish chaplains recognized the enormous tasks they faced; several devoted all of their efforts to helping survivors after the war in Europe ended. They sought to reunite families and rescue Jewish children. They worked within the vast American military system to improve physical conditions. They raised money from Jewish soldiers and from their congregations in the States. They freelanced and maneuvered to secure transportation, food, supplies, religious articles, and medical aid. They cooperated with members of the Jewish Brigade to bring those survivors capable of making the illegal trip to Palestine to secret ports of embarkation. Despite bias among some officers and the venality of others, they accomplished much of the Jewish mandate they set for themselves.[88]

Ordinary Jewish soldiers who wanted to help survivors were sensitive to charges of favoritism. Why were they hanging out with these people, these fellow Jews, and not with their Army buddies? "Hey, what'a you, jewboy. You're stickin' together. You're helpin' them out."[89] The charge stung. Stationed in Styer, Austria, with the 71st Infantry, Howard Sachs remembers his embarrassment about getting involved with two teenage Jewish boys, brothers from Warsaw. Still, it didn't stop him. He didn't succumb to his own anxieties. He had met the brothers one day by a bridge in town. The other GIs didn't pay attention to survivors walking around in their prison garb. Sachs did. He told the boys he was Jewish. Then he found them jobs, one as his assistant and the other in the kitchen so they could eat.[90]

The three shared a common Jewish brotherhood that tran-

scended the distance between Warsaw and Brooklyn. One afternoon, with time on his hands, Sachs hiked up a mountain with
the two boys. At the top the three of them started to sing Hebrew songs. Sachs had learned the songs at his Jewish elementary school in Borough Park; the brothers knew the same songs
from their Warsaw school days. But Sachs brought more than
Zionist melodies with him to the mountain top. He also carried
his *tallis*. Why he took his bar mitzvah prayer shawl with him
into the Army, he didn't know. Perhaps it would bring good
luck.[91] That afternoon he carried it up the mountain because he
thought the brothers might want to pray. He was right. They
were overwhelmed. They had not seen a *tallis* in all those years
of war. Sachs gave them the *tallis*. Then they stood there and
cried. He "cried with them" because he "really couldn't hold
back."[92] All the pain and suffering, the deaths of so many loved
ones, the impossible-to-believe conditions of the camps and of
combat — all these welled up with the tears.[93]

Liberating Europe had given Jewish soldiers a glimpse into
the evils of the Third Reich that muted the joy and relief
brought by victory. Ray Groden was sitting at a kitchen table
with three of his men on May 7 at around 2:00 P.M. when the
company runner came in and yelled: "The war's over! The Germans surrendered." The four GIs "looked at each other. Not one
word was said. For about five minutes" they just sat silently.
"Then one by one the three of them quietly walked out of
the room." Groden could hear a lot of shouting down the hall,
but he sat still. "Peace was too good to be true," he thought. It
would take a while for him to get used to it, for the tension to
ease slowly out of his body. Fear, his constant companion during seven months of continuous combat, gradually departed.
Groden "walked around like a ghost." No one bothered him. His
reputation as "Groden, the Kraut Killer" preceded him. Re-

placements arrived. The new men had fistfights, but not Groden. "The combat veterans never looked for trouble," he remembered. "They had had enough."[94]

All soldiers welcomed victory, but Jewish soldiers found it hard to celebrate in the wake of the terrible realities of the camps. Many Jewish soldiers never entered a camp or met a survivor. But whether they learned of the camps through experience or through the news, the knowledge transformed the sweetness of victory into a harsh revelation. The war cost more than they had ever imagined.

Victor Geller watched the surrender of the German 11th Panzer division on May 7. It was a moment to savor. His skill in languages had led him to serve as a translator to the 346th Infantry Regiment. His daily prayers with *tefillin* no longer bothered his fellow GIs. The 11th Panzer had provided his unit with its baptism of fire at the battle of Gros Rederching in Alsace. Geller remembered that first bitter taste of combat as he viewed the defeated German soldiers. They marched as though on parade: straight columns, perfect rows, heads erect, eyes front, uniforms worn but neat. "Compared to the losers, the winners looked like slobs." Geller stood off to one side since he was only a corporal, although there were no signs of rank following his division's policy. A German officer approached and spoke to Geller in English. "You won the first inning and now you have won the second," he said. "But the game has nine innings, nicht wahr, so the game is not yet over." Then he paused and continued: "Before we are finished, you will come to us for help. You will ask us to join with you against the Russians." Geller pondered his remarks. He remembered his visit to Buchenwald and his conversation there with a former Jewish inmate. "When you go home," the man had told him, "tell the Jews to remember that, although America conquered Germany, we did not defeat Hitler, may his name be erased."[95] The parting words of Jew and German stuck with him: Europe's message to America.

But then there was America's message to Europe. Sam Fuller, a rifleman in the First United States Infantry Division, "the Big Red One," remembered an earlier German surrender at Aachen. The enemy had capitulated on October 21, 1944. A formal ceremony occurred a few days later outside the Aachen Cathedral. "A few hundred German prisoners had been herded into the main square.[96] Thousands of their fellow Nazis had died in the defense of the city." Over five hundred soldiers from the Big Red One surrounded them. The Americans had lost hundreds. General Huebner allowed the German officer, Colonel Wilck, "to speak to his men over some crackly loudspeakers. His words were translated into English." Wilck reminded them that "they were still German soldiers," and to behave as such. Wilck "wanted to give his men a *Sieg Heil* and *Heil Hitler.* But Huebner wouldn't allow it. 'I can't lead you in a salute to our Führer,' concluded Wilck. 'However, we can still salute him in our minds.'" Then General Huebner took the microphone and reassured "every man of Jewish faith in our outfit that, in response to a special request, they'd have the chance to participate in a makeshift service for Yom Kippur . . . inside the Aachen Cathedral." A GI volunteered to lead the service. "Every man of Jewish faith," announced General Huebner, "who wants to take part will immediately proceed" into the cathedral. The defeated Nazis watched. "They were waiting to see how many Jews were wearing the Big Red One." Fuller's sergeant, "who was about as Jewish as a pork chop, turned" and headed into "the cathedral, as if to say 'Stick that up your *Mein Kampf!*' Every other dogface in the square followed" him too. "On that occasion, everybody was Jewish."[97] It was an act of defiance, a bold message to Nazi

Akiva Skidell with a child survivor of the Shoah, May 1945. Liberating Europe had given Jewish soldiers a glimpse into the evils of the Third Reich. Skidell went to Shavuot services and met a young boy, a survivor of Buchenwald. The enormity of the assault on European Jews made Skidell feel "like a kid" beside the young survivor.

antisemites, and an extraordinary demonstration of American solidarity with Jews.

On May 18, ten days after the war ended in Europe, Akiva Skidell went to services for Shavuot, the spring harvest festival that commemorates God's revelation of the Torah at Mount Sinai. There he met several survivors of Buchenwald, including a boy of twelve. They gave him news of survivors from Grodno, his hometown. He was hoping to learn that some family members might be alive. "What they tell is not new any more. The same story with endless inhuman variations," he wrote his wife. "But the boy struck me. It is the first child to go through this hell that I have seen. And what a sight. He looks normal enough in size and otherwise until you look at his eyes. These look as if they belonged to a man of 70. And he talks like one, with the seriousness and resignation of an old man. Not a smile, not a touch of relief." Skidell pondered the pain. "He seems to know as much of all the devilish schemes as the grown-ups. One of the soldiers said to him, 'What you must have seen!' To which he said, 'I saw all they saw,' meaning the others, and that was enough." Skidell emptied his pockets but didn't have much — a little bit of chocolate, a package of lifesavers, and some chewing gum, which he gave to the boy. "It was unnatural offering those things to the boy. He wasn't like a boy at all." Skidell "felt like a kid beside him."[98] The enormity of the assault on European Jews stripped him, a seasoned Jewish GI, of his protective armor.

Not until the war ended in the Pacific on August 14 could soldiers really start to think about the future. "It's Over!! It's Over!! It's Over!!" Sy Kahn wrote exuberantly in his diary. "Yesterday morning" he awoke on Luzon in the Philippines to find that the war was over. "It happened at 8:05 A.M.," he noted precisely. The men didn't celebrate much because everyone had been anticipating the news. Still, "it was quite plain how happy we all were. Every man's thoughts immediately turned from the news to thoughts of home and how long it will be before we see it again."[99] "The whole thing is hard to believe," Ira Koplow confessed. "It came like a bombshell to us and must have come the same way to you," he confided in a letter to the gang. "We are just getting used to the whole idea." The end of the war meant one thing. "As if you didn't know, the first thing that comes to our mind is — WHEN ARE WE GOING HOME?"[100]

All GIs shared his sentiments, but many, like Howard Sachs, had not yet accumulated enough points to leave Europe. Sachs was in Augsburg, Germany, when Rosh Hashana rolled around. It was the first Rosh Hashana since the defeat of Nazi Germany. So he decided to go to synagogue to welcome the New Year on German soil. The synagogue had weathered the war as a German soldiers' club. Although the Germans had ripped up the seats, the central platform remained. The rabbi, blind but alive, "walked down the aisle" as the small congregation wept.[101]

Just going into the synagogue turned out to be probably "the most thrilling experience" of his life, although "there were only about fifteen people in the whole place." Standing among the vestigial congregation, Sachs felt the full force of what he had come through. He glanced up. "On the ceiling, over what had been the ark, on top, the words endured in Hebrew." Neither the Germans nor the American bombs had touched them. *Da lifne mi ata omed!* "Remember before whom you stand," he translated.[102] And he complied with the command. Sachs knew who he was, an American Jewish soldier, and "before whom" he stood. Despite all of his fears about entering the service, he had managed to come out alive. When he heard the basic training lecture at Camp Blanding — "one of you is not coming back" —

he hadn't been sure of his fate. But he had survived and triumphed. He had defeated the enemy. And he had liberated his fellow Jews. He did his job well, and the Army had made him a Master Sergeant. With all the stripes on his arm, he stood "erect and straight" before the central platform. He felt the gaze of the European Jews upon him — a strong, handsome young man. They looked up at him standing in the synagogue "with more than just respect," Sachs thought. "This is an American soldier," he imagined them thinking. This is a soldier in the victorious army that defeated the powerful Nazis. Here is a soldier who represents the Jewish future: vigorous, upright, unafraid, American.[103]

Like other Jewish GIs, Sachs peered into a strange looking glass. He saw in the remnants of the congregation what might have been his own fate had his grandparents stayed in Europe. He saw himself in their eyes, as had Paul Steinfeld the moment before he was wounded, as a Jewish fighter of biblical stature. In the fractured synagogue building Sachs read the Hebrew words calling him to account for himself. And like many Jewish GIs, he was ready to take his own measure. American Jewish soldiers acquitted themselves well in military service. They fulfilled their responsibilities to their country, to their comrades-in-arms, and to their families. More than that, they discovered that they fought on behalf of those defenseless European Jews who could not strike back. Those painful receptions as saviors revealed to Jewish GIs other dimensions of their historic role. They brought to the survivors a liberation bordering on redemption. American Jewish soldiers glimpsed in that heartrending fellowship the complex meaning of their victory over Nazi Germany. The hardfought integration they achieved in military service taught Jewish soldiers how to fight not just as Americans, but as Jews. They would come home to the United States ready to complete the unfinished battles, to dedicate themselves to Roland Gittelsohn's vision "to live together in peace" as they had fought together in war. In this struggle for "the highest and purest democracy" that countenanced "no discrimination, no prejudice, no hatred," they would be able to count not only on themselves, but also on many of their fellow GIs.

8

COMING HOME

I shall go back to my mother's grave after this war
Because there are those who still speak of loyalty
In the outskirts of Baltimore
Or wherever Jews are not the right sort of people,
And say to her one of the dead I speak to —
There are less Jews left in the world,
While they were killed
I did not see you in a dream to tell you,
And that I now have a wife and son.

—LOUIS ZUKOVSKY, "A Song for the Year's End"[1]

JUNE 22, 1945. Victor Geller was finally getting to see Paris. A veteran of hard fighting as an infantryman, he had accumulated more than enough points to return to the United States, although the war had not yet ended in the Pacific. Now there was a chance for some fun. Stationed at Camp Lucky Strike in northern France, he received a one-day pass and happily joined three friends to explore the city. As they strolled along the Boulevard des Italiens, taking in the sights, they heard loud voices. Curious, they rounded the corner near the Place de l'Opéra in time to see a procession of more than a hundred people chanting slogans. Geller couldn't make out what they were saying, but he could read the placards they carried: "A Bas Les Juifs" (Down with the Jews). Geller was stunned. How could such a "demonstration be allowed?" Why were people just watching

and not protesting? "Less than seven weeks ago the long struggle to defeat Germany ended. With it, the disease of anti-Semitism was also supposed to have been erased," he thought. "Yet
here it was in all its ugliness, on one of the grand boulevards of
Paris." The demonstrators turned out to be protesting the efforts of Jews who had returned to reclaim their property in
Paris. The incident ruined Paris for Geller and made him wonder about the war he had just fought.[2]

In Geller's view, he "had just waged a war at frightful cost in
the hopes of changing things."[3] He had seen Buchenwald and
helped as a translator for Hungarian Jewish women liberated
from the Rentzemuhle concentration camp, thus hearing their
sordid and tragic tales. And through it all he had served as a volunteer Jewish chaplain, leading services and comforting griev-
ing soldiers. He had done his best to apply Hillel's teaching in
Ethics of the Fathers: "Where there is no man, strive to be a
man." A return to the status quo ante would not be acceptable.
Geller saw these grown men and women in Paris sliding back
into moral adolescence. He would be a man. He had already
changed himself from the *yeshiva bochur* (studious youth) he
had been. He was a Sergeant in the 346th Infantry. Now, after
more than two years in uniform, he was ready to go home. On
July 9, he boarded the S.S. *Frederick Lykes* for the trip back
across the Atlantic. Nine months had passed since he sailed out
of New York Harbor. As eager as he had been to enlist, he didn't
want to serve any longer than necessary. His war, the war against
Nazi Germany, had ended. The war against antisemitism would
last a much longer time.

Geller headed home with both anticipation and trepidation.
His mother and brother no longer lived in the Bronx. They had
moved to Manhattan. He could not go back to the old neighborhood, his favorite hangouts and comfortable synagogue. As

Victor Geller with "Yank" magazine in Germany, May 1945. Nine months after Geller had sailed out of New York Harbor, his war against Nazi Germany had ended. He expected the war to change the world, but he did not yet fully realize how his military service had changed him.

much as he might yearn for the familiar, he recognized that the future would be different. In fact he expected the war to redirect, in fundamental yet unknowable ways, the lives of both Americans and Jews. Geller, still a teenager, could not himself fully realize how his years in uniform had altered him.[4]

As anxious as he was to put the war behind him, Geller had gained from his military service a confidence in his own ability to overcome obstacles. He was far less ready to tolerate discrimination and injustice than he had been before he entered the armed forces. He retained a lively sense of his rights as an American. He had responded to the call to arms; he had risked his life for his country and his comrades. In the process, he had learned that his Jewishness accompanied him into the barracks and into battle. Although he kept his Jewishness to himself for the most part, he knew that his uniform did not obliterate it. He accepted the responsibilities required of a Jew as he understood them. Recognition and implementation of the Judeo-Christian tradition by the military assured Judaism a place in the religious life of American democracy. As an American soldier, Geller had fought the Germans to preserve European autonomy and democracy. But he had also fought as an American Jewish soldier to liberate European Jewry from Nazi racism and bestiality.[5]

Jeremiah Gutman returned six months later, and like Geller, he entered a strange Manhattan apartment where his parents had moved from Brooklyn during the war. His folks didn't give him much time to get used to his new home or civilian status. "What a fantastically lucky thing!" his father exclaimed as he entered the apartment. "Tomorrow is the last day for registration in graduate school. You're just in time to make it!" A bit nonplussed by his father's unsolicited advice that he immediately return to his studies, Gutman, a loyal son, raced up to City College the next morning to obtain a copy of his transcript from the registrar. Then he hopped back on the subway and went down to Columbia University. After speaking to the chair of graduate studies in English literature about the program, he went to register. "Where's a certified copy?" the registrar inquired. "Well, I just got out of the army yesterday," Gutman explained, "and went to City this morning and copied these." He promised a certified copy of his grades in a few days. But Columbia wouldn't accept his uncertified transcript, the best City College could do on short notice. So Gutman got back on the subway and went downtown to New York University, where he met the chair of the English department. This time Gutman explained that he'd have his grades certified next week. "They're accurate?" queried the chairman. "Yes," Gutman replied. So the chairman signed the page: "I certify as correct," and the registrar enrolled Gutman in graduate school. The following week he started classes at NYU. But he didn't last long. He quickly changed course and enrolled in NYU's School of Law.[6] Finding his path would take time.

Picking up the threads of an interrupted life and returning to civilian status as a different person required effort, but it did not mean that Gutman put aside his concern for the unfinished business of European Jewish suffering. To his surprise, he found himself deeply enmeshed in the Zionist cause. Unlike Zionist activist Artie Gorenstein, who raced off to a Habonim convention as soon as he received his discharge papers in December 1945, Gutman did not anticipate a struggle over the prewar British White Paper that limited Jewish immigration to Palestine. Gorenstein, however, knew that trouble was coming. By the fall of 1945 Zionists had begun sending shiploads of Jews from Europe through the British naval blockade to Palestine. As protests escalated over mistreatment of Jewish Displaced Persons (DPs), so did demands to allow Jewish survivors to leave the refugee camps for Palestine, the only place they could call home.[7] No longer viewed as a sectarian enterprise, Zionism addressed the war's remaining injustices in need of solution. DPs required a place to go, a country of their own, since so few in the world community were willing to accept Jews on their shores. Zionist sentiment spread rapidly among veterans.[8] Gutman discovered that the war had changed his attitudes. He accepted the Zionist premise. Zionism, a Jewish liberation movement, championed a state as the solution to Jewish suffering. The existence of a Jewish state and an Arab one, as proposed by the United Nations' partition of Palestine in November 1947, would integrate Jews as equals into the family of nations.[9] Gutman was not alone. In the early postwar years, liberal democrats and popular-front radicals alike agreed.[10]

As Gutman watched others struggle to establish a Jewish state, he couldn't sit on the sidelines.[11] He heard the Arabs announce, "We're going to push you into the sea." Unwilling to ignore such threats, Gutman felt, "I'll push back." His opinions shifted so radically that he began collecting arms and military optical goods to smuggle to the Hagana (Jewish Defense Forces). He stored the guns in his closet in NYU's law review office when he was editor-in-chief until he could deliver them to a Bronx warehouse. It was a risky business; getting caught was a felony that would threaten his professional future. He considered his brief career gathering weapons "a fallout from the aggressiveness that had been" indoctrinated into him in the military. Of course, he had been anxious to get into the war. He had been determined to fight Hitler. His experiences in combat did not dampen his willingness to fight, but now he was ready to take risks explicitly for a Jewish cause. Collecting guns and military supplies seemed to be the best way to "push back" while still in school. He wanted to see Jews treated equally as a nation among nations.[12]

While Gutman and Geller expressed anger at Great Britain for its policies in Palestine, they harbored their deepest resentments against Germany. They shunned and despised Germans, whom they considered guilty of Nazi crimes. Thousands of Jewish veterans swore never to visit Germany as tourists, viewing it, as Harold Saperstein had suggested, as a "cursed land." These values characterized not just returning veterans but their wives and families. The proposal of Henry Morgenthau, Roosevelt's Secretary of the Treasury, to demilitarize and de-industrialize a partitioned Germany and to prosecute and punish Nazi leaders found partisans among Jewish veterans. They didn't care if some members of the administration called it "Jewish vengeance."[13] After the discovery of the death camps, gut-level reactions supplanted the theorizing that had animated Akiva Skidell and Harold Freeman as they marched on Germany. Jewish veterans would boycott German products. No German cars or knives, no kitchen utensils, no silverware or dishes from Jewish firms expropriated by the Nazis would enter their households. An informal boycott spread among American Jews to include Japanese items as well. "Even years later," wrote a son of his father, "to suggest buying a Japanese (or German) product was to risk a terrifying explosion of anger."[14]

Military service transformed Geller and Gutman. Secure in their American identity, they accepted their new position as leaders of the most powerful community of the Jewish diaspora. As they extended their hands in support of Palestinian Jews who continued to struggle for a Jewish state, they also turned to address the unfinished business of rectifying the injustices of American democracy through fair employment practices and

Caper Cutters. Pvt. Howie Gerhartz (left) and Pvt. Tony Martelloni give out with a bit of fast stepping. They were among 6,520 members of the 97th Infantry Division who returned to the United States in June 1945, en route to the Pacific. Despite their eagerness to become civilians, American Jews committed themselves to relieve the suffering of European Jewish survivors. Irrespective of where they landed, Jewish veterans took from their years in service new understandings of their place in America.

civil rights legislation. They recognized that the fight against antisemitism involved preserving and defending democracy. As one GI confessed, the Army "made a radical out of me. And that, believe me, was not an easy thing to do."[15] University and medical school quotas, restrictive covenants, the want ads listing "Christian only" would all be challenged as un-American practices.[16] Although Geller and Gutman would not acquiesce in discriminatory practices against African Americans, which they had ignored before the war, a broadly construed struggle for civil rights required collective action, and this would take a while to mobilize. The formidable array of American Jewish organizations would have to regroup.

The creation of the Commission on Law and Social Action by the American Jewish Congress in August 1945 expressed this commitment to a broad-based civil rights struggle with remarkable clarity. The lawyer Alexander Pekelis set forth its rationale. "A decent respect for the opinions of Jews and non-Jews alike requires that we should declare at the outset," he began, "the ideological fundamentals that underlie this program of ours." Pekelis echoed the language of the Declaration of Independence. The ambitious program aimed for "full equality in a free society." This goal did not mean "painless integration of individuals of Jewish faith" into society; freedom required both individual and collective self-expression. Pekelis stressed that "Jewish equality and Jewish distinctiveness, the integrity of the Jews as a people and their dignity as individuals, comprise the twofold but indivisible aim." Thus Zionism, the recognition of Jews as a people, became central to American Jewish freedom. Individual equality could not be purchased at the price of collective individuality. To do so "would betray our place in human history and our duty to mankind."[17] World War II had altered the fundamental temperament of American Jewish life.[18] Pekelis proposed to make what Jewish veterans had learned in uniform the basis of communal policy. Integration in the armed forces had strengthened Jewish individual and collective consciousness, making Jews both more American and more Jewish.

Although the start of the Cold War and domestic attacks on American Communists sidetracked many of the left-wing programs of Jewish action designed to change the United States and secure Jewish life, their animating impulses and vision endured.[19] American Jews maintained a commitment to the ideals of full equality in a free society even as they participated in postwar prosperity. They juggled the individual demands of adjusting to civilian status with their collective awareness of an unfinished postwar agenda. Despite the rapid decline of antisemitism from its wartime highs, American Jews sought to expand their understanding of its significance.[20] While they savored the novel experience of integration into new neighborhoods, their anger at prejudice survived. Some paid attention to enlarging the realm of integration to include African Americans, supporting the NAACP's program to challenge segregation. Their willingness to take political risks to pursue their dream of a liberal society persisted even in an era of political quietism under the former Supreme Allied Commander, now President Dwight D. Eisenhower.[21] The establishment of the Judeo-Christian tradition as integral to the nation's democratic credo helped to sustain Jewish efforts to champion civil rights and racial integration.

Although military practices did not translate easily into civilian behavior, many Americans accepted the central concept of the three religions of democracy. Pundits quoted Eisenhower's famous remark to his Soviet counterpart, Marshal Zhukov: "In other words, our Government has no sense unless it is founded in a deeply felt religious faith and I don't care what it is." Less often did they comment on the sentence that followed: "With us of course it is the Judeo-Christian concept, but it must be a religion that all men are created equal."[22] Eisenhower's words, often quoted out of context to suggest the vacuousness of the religion of democracy, actually addressed a larger moral and political universe. The precept of equality belonged to all American religions. Indeed, the experience of worshipping together in uniform in World War II transformed religion in the United States in the postwar period. Judaism became a "fighting faith," and Jews were defined as one of America's three main religious groups. In 1955 Will Herberg wrote a book entitled *Protestant, Catholic, Jew* that simultaneously enshrined and criticized the Judeo-Christian tradition as American religion. By this time most Americans remembered neither the wartime origins of the Judeo-Christian tradition nor its performance as part of military standard operating procedure.[23]

Some Jews recognized that the acceptance of Judaism as one of America's three faiths would require changes in Jewish religious beliefs. In 1945 the indigenous American Jewish Reconstructionist movement published its first Sabbath prayer book *(siddur)*. The Reconstructionists, a small but influential minority among American Jews, confronted the radical implications of living in a democratic United States. In their introduction the editors justified their decision to publish a *siddur* that deviated from the "time-honored text." Seeking to balance a desire for the continuity of Judaism even as they addressed the "spiritual demands of our day," they decided to eliminate those beliefs that were in conflict with what they regarded as true. As the editors explained, "modern-minded Jews can no longer believe, as did their fathers, that the Jews constitute a divinely chosen nation."[24] Democratic nationalism, separation of church and state, and equal citizenship for Jews all required this fundamental shift. Orthodox, Conservative, and Reform rabbis who had served as chaplains supported a spirit of cooperation and consensus among Jewish denominations in the postwar era.[25]

There would be other changes in Jewish life as well. "America, insensible to the existence of a Jewish nation," wrote a leading Labor Zionist, insisted on classifying Jews "with the religious communities." Although the prospect didn't please him, he argued that Jews "have no other alternative but to constitute themselves as a community operating in a religious framework." This was "the price a secularist Jew will have to pay for his voluntary sharing in a minority status."[26] Religion would provide the required sacred canopy protecting non-believing Jews who desired to identify as Jews and to maintain their difference from the majority Christian society.

Military service had empowered Jews as Americans and as Jews, and secured their future. When European Jews welcomed them as saviors, Jewish soldiers understood their own good fortune to be wearing the uniform of the armed forces of the United States. Notwithstanding the enduring evidences of racial and religious discrimination, they believed in the commitment of the United States to move toward equality. Although they sympathized with their European co-religionists, American Jewish veterans recognized when they came home that despite the enduring antisemitism in the United States, the nation's democratic premises promised Jews a decent future if they were ready to fight for it. The United States was not like Europe, and American Jews were different from European Jews.[27]

Jewish veterans' attitudes toward Jewish identity had changed.[28] American Jews felt they held more in common with Zionists in Palestine than with DPs in Europe. Activists and fighters, they both had the will and means to build secure lives for themselves and for Jews who came after them. American Jewish veterans knew that, like their Israeli cousins, they were willing to risk their lives for their country. They shared as well a common duty to collective action and cooperation. Once Zionists established the State of Israel in May 1948, American Jews defended the partnership.[29] Most veterans saw their own experience as American soldiers validated in the heroism of Jewish fighters for Israel. As they cheered the battle that brought a Jewish state into existence after almost two thousand years, they could not realize how quickly the extraordinary accomplishments of Israelis would overshadow their own military service in World War II.

In 1951 Artie Gorenstein made *aliya* (immigrated) to Israel to fulfill his youthful Zionist dreams. Those ideals also included fighting "with like-minded people everywhere for the emergence of a better society."[30] After completing a B.A. in Bible and Jewish history at the Hebrew University, he returned for doctoral studies in American history at Columbia University. Just before he graduated, he hebraized his name. He was now simply Goren. Looking back on the postwar period as a historian of American Jews, he dubbed it "the golden decade." He observed that "one could confidently point to a baseline that demarcated American Jewry from what had existed prior to 1945 and that would hold, for the most part, during the decades ahead."[31] Although he did not use the term, Goren implied that the war marked a watershed.

The war had changed everything, although it would take time for American Jews to assimilate the breadth of the transformation. Those changes most immediately visible occurred on an individual level. The GI Bill helped Jewish veterans fulfill their dreams of attending college, especially those who could not otherwise have afforded post-secondary studies.[32] Military training convinced some that they were smart enough to benefit from college. Others, like Gutman, used the bill to finance professional studies. The GI Bill gave veterans tuition plus a living stipend. There were no geographic restrictions. Committed Zionists, like David Macarov and Artie Gorenstein, chose to attend the Hebrew University in Jerusalem on the GI Bill.[33] As the historian Gary Gerstle observes, the GI Bill "made World War II soldiers the most lavishly rewarded group of veterans in American history." Not only did it ratify the importance of their efforts on behalf of their country, but it also "gave veterans opportunities to rise in American society."[34] And Jews were ready to seize those opportunities.

Raymond Groden didn't go back to school on the GI Bill, but he did something that would have been unthinkable for his parents' generation: he took out a mortgage at the beginning of his married life. He used a veteran's mortgage from the GI Bill, twenty years at 3.5 percent, to purchase a house in Queens. The GI Bill made it easier to risk such indebtedness so early in life, before he had accumulated any substantial savings.[35] Moving next door to Christians in the burgeoning suburbs, Jewish veterans possessed sufficient confidence to build synagogues as appropriate sacred spaces. Although they were more comfortable mixing with Christians than their parents had been, Jewish veterans knew where they differed from others. For the most part they observed the "five o'clock shadow" that descended in many suburban subdivisions when men returned from work. Then Jews and Christians separated, socializing with like-minded friends and family. Divisive feelings between Jews and Christians still existed, but veterans had learned in the service how to negotiate the unspoken boundaries of friendship.[36]

Few Jewish veterans spoke about the events of the war, its psychic toll, and how they had changed. Sy Kahn came home in November 1945 intent on continuing his college studies and immediately "closed the book on the war." But he "never forgot.

For both better and worse," he reflected, he "was changed by the war, haunted in dreams and memory, rendered restless, and sometimes alienated, sometimes more at home abroad than in the United States, sometimes a stranger everywhere, and in mysterious ways beyond my knowing, perhaps a casualty." Kahn spoke metaphorically of the living whose unseen wounds kept splitting open. A veteran of "over three hundred bombings," he did not realize at the war's end what two years unloading ships on remote Pacific islands would mean for his own future. He did not know that he "would never be able to hear silence again" or that faces and events from those years would continue to fill his dreams. But Kahn did understand how he had matured. The ordeal he had undertaken took him on an inner quest that uncovered new dimensions of his identity. In this "womanless world," he became a man. He had fulfilled his goal of serving in the war, "the most important event" of his century. He did not regret memorizing the eye charts. He lived to reach his twenty-first birthday after all.[37]

World War II injured many who wore a uniform, not only those who received a Purple Heart. The war brought death to millions of civilians as well as thousands of soldiers. All GIs knew that no question marks surrounded the other casualties of war. The dead never came home, except to be reburied. For many of the lucky men, like Kahn, normalcy remained fragile and provisional.

Not every Jewish veteran who survived the war came home and stayed. Even some of the Dragons perceived Brooklyn in a new light. Once satisfying and comfortable, it now appeared narrow and drab. All of the Dragons had seen other parts of the United States; several were restless and viewed their prewar life with distaste. As soon as they could they packed their bags and headed west, joining what would become a huge migration of Jews to cities such as Los Angeles.[38] Several Dragons enrolled in the 52/20 club, the GI Bill's weekly $20 unemployment stipend that lasted a year. Unlike welfare, veterans' benefits came without strings or onus, giving veterans a year's grace period to figure out what they wanted to do. After the dislocation of military service, they needed some time to chart their course.

Irrespective of where they landed, Jewish veterans took from their years in service new understandings of their place in America. First, the establishment of the Judeo-Christian tradition promulgated equality for Jews and Judaism as one of the three pillars sustaining American democracy. American equality was now officially celebrated on the basis of policy that could be construed as consistent with a principle of group identity. Second, veterans had earned respect as American Jewish men, in their own eyes and in those of other servicemen. Though Jewish soldiers often felt that their knapsack carried extra weight, that they were judged by a discounted standard, many thought that by the war's end they had won their comrades' trust. As men, as Americans, and as Jews, they had learned to handle complex physical and psychological situations. These were vital skills and attitudes to build upon when they came home. Finally, they had confronted the horror of the death camps with their evidence of murderous inhumanity toward Jews. Jewish GIs remembered the weeping eyes that stared at them with a love that seemed to carry an unnerving weight of expectation. Without exception, eyewitness reports by Jewish soldiers emphasized the disorienting emotions that tore at them: feelings of Jewish bonds, of physical disgust, cultural distance, pride, inadequacy, anger, confusion, and pity. Some Jewish GIs resolved to do something about this in the future. They were not alone. As the historian

Leonard Dinnerstein observed about the postwar period, "Many Americans resolved to do something about bigotry in America."[39]

Their resolve took diverse forms. Many Jewish veterans championed a Jewish state. Some committed themselves to Jewish organizations dedicated to combating antisemitism and expanding civil rights. Others strengthened their dedication to Judaism. But many would find that they could not weather the transition to the demands of civilian life — parents, housing, jobs, schooling, wives, and children — and still maintain their focus on doing something. The rush of events, both domestic and international, would take its toll. Nonetheless, the transformation would not be undone.

Peering at the Virginia shore as his troop ship approached, a Jewish soldier pondered his immediate past. "I felt that I had spent a lifetime away," he mused, "but it would soon be over."[40] Jewish GIs had participated in one of the most important events of their century. They had crammed a lifetime of experiences into a couple of years. Now they were returning to start a new life even as they resumed their old activities. Raymond Groden arrived in the fall of 1945 at a New Jersey pier. It was night. The darkness enveloped him as he climbed down the gangplank with his gear onto the dock. Then he entered the pier and walked into a blaze of lights. Before him stretched tables loaded with doughnuts, hot coffee, and fresh cold milk, "courtesy of the Salvation Army." Groden ignored the coffee. He had had plenty of that in Europe. But he couldn't stop drinking the milk. Milk with its nourishment and innocence proclaimed America. "How sweet it was to be home!"[41]

Notes
Bibliography
Acknowledgments
Illustration Credits
Index

NOTES

✪ ✪ ✪

1. War and Identity

1. Epigraph: Max Kozloff, *New York: Capital of Photography* (New York: The Jewish Museum; New Haven: Yale University Press, 2002), p. 75.

2. *Danzig 1939, Treasures of a Destroyed Community,* catalog of an exhibit at The Jewish Museum, New York, ed. Sheila Schwartz (Detroit: Wayne State University Press, 1980). The synagogue was torn down in June 1939. E-mail communication from Vivian Mann to Rachel Weinstein, June 5, 2003.

3. Frederick C. Voss, *Reporting the War: Journalistic Coverage of World War II* (Washington, D.C.: Smithsonian Institution Press for the National Portrait Gallery, 1994), p. 1.

4. "Its secret clauses effectively permitted the Soviet Union, in the event of a German-Polish war, to annex eastern Poland up to the line of the Vistula and the Baltic states of Latvia, Lithuania and Estonia." John Keegan, *The Second World War* (New York: Penguin Books, 1990), p. 43.

5. The *Athenia* was sunk with loss of life and spurred Americans to attempt to evacuate Europe. *New York Times,* September 4, 1939, p. 1; September 5, 1939, p. 4.

6. Harold I. Saperstein, "Can Jews Afford to be Pacifists?" (December 1937), p. 61, and "Unconquered" (September 14, 1939), in *Witness from the Pulpit* (Lanham: Lexington Books, 2000), p. 69. See also "Undying Fires," ibid., pp. 83–84, 87.

7. See Gerald L. Sittser, *A Cautious Patriotism: The American Churches and The Second World War* (Chapel Hill: University of North Carolina Press, 1997), p. 6.

8. The best account of antisemitism in the United States is Leonard Dinnerstein, *Antisemitism in America* (New York: Oxford University Press, 1994).

9. *New York Times*, September 2, 1939, pp. 8, 12.

10. On Jews at the World's Fair, see Barbara Kirshenblatt-Gimblett, "A Place in the World: Jews and the Holy Land at World's Fairs," in *Encounters with the "Holy Land": Place, Past and Future in American Jewish Culture*, ed. Jeffrey Shandler and Beth S. Wenger (Philadelphia: National Museum of American Jewish History, 1997), pp. 77–79.

11. Interview with Martin Dash, August 19, 1995. Unless otherwise specified, interviews were conducted by the author.

12. Estimates suggest that as many as two-thirds of American Jewish families kept kosher homes. See I. Steinbaum, "A Study of the Jewishness of Twenty New York Families," *YIVO Annual of Jewish Social Sciences*, 5 (1950), pp. 234–235, and his methodological critique, pp. 236–239.

13. For a good discussion of immigrant Jewish food choices, see Hasia R. Diner, *Hungering for America* (Cambridge, Mass.: Harvard University Press, 2002), chaps. 4–5.

14. Interview with Martin Dash, August 19, 1995.

15. In 1938, "at least 50 percent of Americans had a low opinion of Jews," writes Leonard Dinnerstein; "45 percent thought that they were less honest than Gentiles in business." Dinnerstein, *Antisemitism in America*, p. 127.

16. See Dan Oren, *Joining the Club: A History of Jews and Yale* (New Haven: Yale University Press, 1985).

17. "Akiva's Autobiography and Scrapbook" by Akiva Skidell, typescript in the author's possession, n.d., pp. 6–24.

18. Gulie Ne'eman Arad, *America, Its Jews, and the Rise of Nazism* (Bloomington: Indiana University Press, 2000), pp. 197–202; Haskel Lookstein, *Were We Our Brothers' Keepers? The Public Response of American Jews to the Holocaust, 1938–1944* (New York: Hartmore, 1986), pp. 35–80. For a good discussion of press coverage see Deborah Lipstadt, *Beyond Belief: The American Press and the Coming of the Holocaust* (New York: Free Press, 1986), pp. 98–109.

19. Robert Rosenstone estimates that 30 percent of the volunteers in the Abraham Lincoln brigades were Jews. New York State provided the largest number, 499 out of 1,337 or almost 40 percent. Given

the concentration of Jews in New York, this data would support his estimate. Robert A. Rosenstone, *Crusade of the Left: The Lincoln Battalion in the Spanish Civil War* (New York: Pegasus, 1969), pp. 370–371.

20. Skidell, "Akiva's Autobiography and Scrapbook," pp. 21–23.

21. "Japanese soldiers of all ranks tortured, raped, mutilated, and murdered tens of thousands of Chinese of all ages and both sexes." Williamson Murray and Allan R. Millett, *A War to be Won: Fighting the Second World War* (Cambridge, Mass.: The Belknap Press of Harvard University Press, 2000), p. 160.

22. I thank Irene Golden Dash for remembering these lyrics and melody.

23. "The idea of pacifism as a means of securing world peace was widespread in the 1930's. Tens of thousands of students had signed the Oxford Pledge, which stated that they would never bear arms, even in defense of their own countries. Many of these youngsters were then drawn into the orbits of various left-wing organizations that espoused pacifism." Rosenstone, *Crusade of the Left,* p. 215; Skidell, "Akiva's Autobiography and Scrapbook," pp. 21–23.

24. The socialist Jewish Labor Committee on September 11 as reported in *American Jewish Year Book,* "Review of the Year 5700," 42 (1940), p. 271.

25. "Is it good for the Jews that the Fascist alliance has been shattered?" queried a leaflet entitled "Is the Treaty Good for the Jews?" published by the New York Committee of the National Council of Jewish Communists in 1939. "LISTEN TO WHAT THE SOVIET SIDE HAS TO SAY," it urged. Quoted in *Jewish Workers in the Modern Diaspora,* ed. Nancy Green (Berkeley: University of California Press, 1998), p. 127.

26. Henry L. Feingold, *A Time for Searching: Entering the Mainstream, 1920–1945* (Baltimore and London: Johns Hopkins University Press, 1992), pp. 222–223.

27. Up in the Catskills, at a Habonim camp in Accord, New York, Lakey Kahn remembers how the youth leaders "gathered around a car radio to listen to the news reports of the Nazi march into Poland. It got pretty crowded bunching up around the car, but this was our

only link to the outside world. Suddenly, as we listened, the world seemed a much more real and familiar place than we had ever known. We, the 'intellectuals' of Habonim, had seen it coming." Kahn thought that Habonim made them "more sensitive to the coming cataclysm" than their counterparts in Chicago's Jewish neighborhood and more informed "than most insular American adults." Lakey Kahn, "From Chicago to Accord, Autumn 1939: 'That Night, We Learned to See the World Another Way,'" in *Dreamers and Builders: Habonim Labor Zionist Youth in North America,* ed. J. J. Goldberg and Elliot King (New York: Cornwall Books, 1993), p. 79.

28. Telephone interview with Akiva Skidell by Arthur A. Goren, November 17, 1990.

29. For statistics on Jewish participation in military service collected by the Jewish Welfare Board, see Isidore Kaufman, "The Story the Figures Tell," *American Jews in World War II* (New York: Dial Press, 1947), vol. I, pp. 348–356, and Louis I. Dublin and Samuel C. Kohs, *American Jews in World War II* (New York: Dial Press, 1947), vol. II, pp. 7–31.

30. This change does not appear to have occurred among all Americans, according to some historians of World War II. Paul Fussell quotes John Keegan, who argues that the war "'exposed over 12 million of them,' [Americans] says Keegan, 'to a system of subordination and autocracy entirely alien to American values.'" Quoted in Paul Fussell, *Wartime: Understanding and Behavior in the Second World War* (New York: Oxford University Press, 1989), p. 83.

31. "To be a fighter," Irving Howe has written, ". . . testified to the forging of collective selfhood." Irving Howe and Kenneth Libo, *World of Our Fathers* (New York: Harcourt Brace Jovanovich, 1976), pp. 306–307.

32. Some had proposed such a model. See Louis Finkelstein, J. Elliot Ross, and William Adams Brown, *The Religions of Democracy: Judaism, Catholicism, Protestantism in Creed and Life* (New York: Devin-Adair, 1941).

33. Deborah Dash Moore, "Jewish GIs and the Creation of the Judeo-

Christian Tradition," *Religion and American Culture: A Journal of Interpretation,* 8:1 (Winter 1998), pp. 31–53.

34. This formidable shift in official attitudes was one of the reasons why historians could argue that Jews and Catholics became "white." In religious terms Jews and Catholics became respectable Americans, but that did not mean that their ethnicity disappeared.

35. Harold I. Saperstein, "A Jewish Veteran Returns," in *Witness from the Pulpit,* p. 120.

36. Ibid., pp. 118–122; quotation on p. 121.

37. Chaplain Albert S. Goldstein took a poll of all the Jews who showed up at the chapel or JWB office at Sheppard Field in Texas or participated in any activity that got their names on a mailing list. His survey found that 46 percent of the men came from New York City. "Faith in the Army," *The Jewish Layman,* 18:1 (October 1943), p. 12.

38. See Deborah Dash Moore, *At Home in America: Second Generation New York Jews* (New York: Columbia University Press, 1981), chaps. 2–3.

39. See *American Jewish Year Book* (1940) for population estimates.

40. William L. O'Neill begins his discussion of America in 1941 with a description of urban life that emphasizes its immigrant and ethnic character. *A Democracy at War* (New York: Free Press, 1993), p. 7.

41. "By providing students with just enough leeway to exercise choices and with enough room for 'social cooperation,'" argues the historian Paula Fass, "the extracurricular activities became a significant arena for the continuing expression of ethnic association among the second and third generations." Paula S. Fass, *Outside In: Minorities and the Transformation of American Education* (New York: Oxford University Press, 1989), p. 79. See also p. 75 on high schools as ethnic enclaves during the Depression.

42. Nettie Pauline McGill and Ellen Nathalie Matthews, *The Youth of New York City* (New York: Macmillan, 1940), p. 84.

43. On New York Jewish life during the Depression see Beth S. Wenger, *New York Jews and the Great Depression* (New Haven: Yale University Press, 1995).

44. Ronald Bayor demonstrates how conflicts on city streets often reflected struggles not merely over turf but also over international politics. Ronald H. Bayor, *Neighbors in Conflict: The Irish, Germans, Jews, and Italians of New York City, 1929–1941* (Baltimore: Johns Hopkins University Press, 1978).

45. Rachel Weinstein and Deborah Dash Moore, "GI Jew," paper presented at the Third Biennial Scholars Conference of the American Jewish Historical Society in Denver, Colorado, 2000.

46. Alfred Kazin's postwar memoir, *A Walker in the City* (New York: Harcourt, 1951), beautifully evokes these tensions.

47. McGill and Matthews, *The Youth of New York City,* chap. 12.

48. On the religious provincialism of urban Catholics, see John McGreevy, *Parish Boundaries: The Catholic Encounter with Race in the Twentieth-Century Urban North* (Chicago: University of Chicago Press, 1996), pp. 15–25.

49. On the commercial activity around Rosh Hashana in the immigrant era, see Andrew R. Heinze, *Adapting to Abundance* (New York: Columbia University Press, 1989).

50. Ruth Gay's memoir evokes the spirit of these domestic changes. Ruth Gay, *Unfinished People* (New York: W. W. Norton, 1996).

51. Nowadays they are referred to as "two-day-a-year" Jews, since observance of the second day of Rosh Hashana has declined.

52. According to one survey of Jewish males, 72 percent of youth aged sixteen to twenty-four had not spent any time in religious services during the year but identified as Jews nonetheless. McGill and Matthews, *The Youth of New York City,* p. 343.

53. For a discussion of these practices see Jenna Weissman Joselit, *The Wonders of America: Reinventing Jewish Culture, 1880–1950* (New York: Hill and Wang, 1994), pp. 247–252.

54. The term means "lightning war." Keegan, *The Second World War,* p. 54.

55. He was not alone. "The war in Europe seemed far away in 1939–41," Daniel Hoffman recalled. "Over the radio and in the papers we learned of first the 'phony war,' then the blitzkrieg." Hoffman "was in high school, memorizing French irregular verbs, pushing a mower on our suburban lawn the day France fell. In college, studies

and campus life were more immediate." Daniel Hoffman, *Zone of the Interior: A Memoir, 1942–1947* (Baton Rouge: Louisiana State University Press, 2000), p. 5.

56. For example, Lend Lease, initiated in March 1941. Interview with Martin Dash, August 19, 1995.

57. In December 1939 the United Palestine Appeal's "Night of Stars" recruited the renowned violinist Jascha Heifetz as well as Hollywood stars to fill Madison Square Garden in New York City. "At the close of the five-hour cavalcade of entertainment, the audience received pledge cards in the name of the 'greatest artists of stage, screen, radio and opera to contribute to the United Palestine Appeal.'" Arthur A. Goren, "Celebrating Zion in America," *Encounters with the "Holy Land": Place, Past and Future in American Jewish Culture,* ed. Jeffrey Shandler and Beth S. Wenger (Hanover: Brandeis University Press, 1997), p. 50.

58. The phrase is Victor Geller's. Victor B. Geller, "Take It Like a Soldier," manuscript in author's possession, n.d., p. 240.

59. Skidell, "Akiva's Autobiography and Scrapbook," p. 24.

60. For a discussion of Zionist debates in this period see Aaron Berman, *Nazism, the Jews and American Zionism, 1933–1948* (Detroit: Wayne State University Press, 1990).

61. Not all Zionists agreed. Pvt. C. E. wrote in a letter published in the May 1943 issue of *Furrows,* the monthly publication of Habonim, Labor Zionist Youth, that "the denunciation of England should commence now, and should be carried on incessantly. It is England and England alone which stands in the way of rescue to Palestine" (p. 30).

62. Saperstein's anguish lasted longer than that of Judah Magnes, a Reform rabbi, Zionist, and chancellor of the Hebrew University. In October 1939 at a speech opening the new academic year, Magnes renounced his pacifism. He characterized his "agonizing change" as "virtually a change in religion." Magnes confessed that he was "transgressing" God's "word knowingly" because "Satan is abroad. The incarnation of the devil sits on the German throne. It is the principle of evil made flesh." J. L. Magnes, "War and the Remnant

of Israel," *In the Perplexity of the Times* (Jerusalem: The Hebrew University, 1946), pp. 19–21.

63. "Author, Rabbi Harold Saperstein," *Forward,* November 23, 2001.

64. Harold I. Saperstein, "The World We Make," *Witness from the Pulpit,* p. 76, note 2.

65. The Battle of Britain lasted from July 10 to October 30, but the bombing raids against London began on September 7. Keegan, *The Second World War,* p. 94.

66. Harold I. Saperstein, "Suffrance is the Badge," *Witness from the Pulpit,* pp. 76–82; quotations on pp. 76, 80.

67. Feingold, *A Time for Searching,* p. 212.

68. Franklin D. Roosevelt, "Annual Message to Congress," in *Selected Speeches, Messages, Press Conferences, and Letters,* ed. Basil Rauch (New York: Holt, Rinehart and Winston, 1957), pp. 274–275.

69. Harold I. Saperstein, "Undying Fires," *Witness from the Pulpit,* p. 84.

70. Interview with Martin Dash, August 19, 1995.

71. Keegan, *The Second World War,* pp. 182–201, 288–289; Lipstadt, *Beyond Belief,* pp. 157–158.

72. Harold I. Saperstein, "Undying Fires," *Witness from the Pulpit,* pp. 83–89. Reference to Job on p. 89.

73. Lucy S. Dawidowicz, *On Equal Terms: Jews in America, 1881–1981* (New York: Holt, Rinehart and Winston, 1982), p. 129.

74. See Deborah Dash Moore, *To the Golden Cities: Pursuing the American Jewish Dream in Miami and L.A.* (New York: Free Press, 1994), p. 154.

75. Gaines M. Foster, "A Christian Nation: Signs of a Covenant," in *Bonds of Affection: Americans Define Their Patriotism,* ed. John Bodnar (Princeton: Princeton University Press, 1996), pp. 120–138.

76. "The integration of so many new ethnic groups into the mainstream of national life was the greatest American accomplishment of this era. The greatest national failure was the continued oppression and segregation of blacks." O'Neill, *A Democracy at War,* p. 8.

77. Gary Gerstle, *American Crucible: Race and Nation in the Twentieth Century* (Princeton: Princeton University Press, 2001), pp. 138–155.

78. Several scholars argue that this transformed Jews and Catholics into Euro-Americans and made them white. See Gerstle, *American Crucible,* pp. 231–237; Matthew Frye Jacobson, *Whiteness of a Different Color: European Immigrants and the Alchemy of Race* (Cambridge, Mass.: Harvard University Press, 1998). Karen Brodkin, *How Jews Became White Folks and What That Says about Race in America* (New Brunswick, N.J.: Rutgers University Press, 1998), emphasizes the impact of the GI Bill rather than military service.

2. Joining Up

1. Epigraph: Stanley Kunitz, "Reflection by a Mailbox," in *Poets of World War II,* ed. Harvey Shapiro, American Poets Project, Library of America (2003), pp. 39–40.
2. Victor B. Geller, "Take It Like a Soldier," manuscript in the author's possession, n.d., pp. 34–59, 157–158, 238–245; quotation on p. 245.
3. Sy M. Kahn, *Between Tedium and Terror: A Soldier's World War II Diary 1943–45* (Urbana: University of Illinois Press, 1993), pp. xv–xvi, 86, 202; entry dated December 7, 1944.
4. Chaplain Albert S. Goldstein's survey of Jewish soldiers at Sheppard Field, Texas, in 1943 confirmed that "these men know why they are fighting." Their war aims were, first, the Four Freedoms, then the Atlantic Charter, followed by the Bill of Rights, followed by Henry Wallace's "Century of the Common Man," and then more general civil, personal, and religious liberties and "making the world safe for them to raise their families." "Faith and the Army," part 2, *The Jewish Layman* (November 1943), p. 22.
5. William O'Neill, *A Democracy at War: America's Fight at Home and Abroad in World War II* (New York: The Free Press, 1993), p. 138.
6. Michael C. C. Adams, *The Best War Ever: America and World War II* (Baltimore: Johns Hopkins University Press, 1994), p. 88.
7. Paul Fussell, *Wartime: Understanding and Behavior in the Second World War* (New York: Oxford University Press, 1989), pp. 127, 137.
8. Ari Lashner, "Correspondence," *Furrows* (June 1943), p. 30.

9. Jews could not serve as reserve officers in Germany, although they could, and did, serve as reserve officers in the Hapsburg army. See Marsha L. Rozenblit, *Reconstructing a National Identity: The Jews of Hapsburg Austria during World War I* (New York: Oxford University Press, 2001), pp. 92–93; Istaván Deák, "Jewish Soldiers in Austro-Hungarian Society," Leo Baeck Memorial Lecture no. 34 (New York: Leo Baeck Institute, 1990).

10. See Sander Gilman, "The Jewish Foot," in *The Jew's Body* (New York: Routledge, 1991), pp. 38–59, especially pp. 42–53.

11. Joseph W. Bendersky, *The "Jewish Threat": Anti-Semitic Politics of the U.S. Army* (New York: Basic Books, 2000), pp. 38–39, 11.

12. Quoted in ibid., p. 38.

13. ChaeRan Y. Freeze, *Jewish Marriage and Divorce in Imperial Russia* (Hanover: Brandeis University Press, 2002), p. 28. On the Jewish masculine ideal see Daniel Boyarin, *Unheroic Conduct: The Rise of Heterosexuality and the Invention of the Jewish Man* (Berkeley: University of California Press, 1997).

14. For the importance of sports for second-generation Jewish youth, see Gerald Sorin, *The Nurturing Neighborhood: The Brownsville Boys Club and Jewish Community in Urban America, 1940–1990* (New York: New York University Press, 1990), pp. 30–34, 82–85. See also Peter Levine, *Ellis Island to Ebbets Field: Sport and the American Jewish Experience* (New York : Oxford University Press, 1992).

15. Art Buchwald, *Leaving Home: A Memoir* (New York: Fawcett Columbine, 1993), pp. 118–120; quotation on p. 120.

16. They would not be as lucky as the Dragons. Sal Walken, who lived with his widower father on the corner, was killed in New Guinea. Nat Buser, who lived down in the block on 44th Street, was killed in Europe. And Oscar Beskowitz, who lived next door to Sal, joined the Marines. He survived, but suffered a bad case of shell shock.

17. Interview with Herbert Walters, September 1, 1995.

18. "Herman Kogan," in Studs Terkel, *"The Good War": An Oral History of World War II* (New York: Pantheon Books, 1984), p. 364.

19. Michael Stanislawski writes that psychic incentives and physical torture were used to convert Jews, though the exact number cannot be

determined with precision. See Stanislawski, *Tsar Nicholas I and the Jews: The Transformation of Jewish Society in Russia, 1825–1855* (Philadelphia: Jewish Publication Society, 1983), pp. 15–33.

20. The job of selecting recruits devolved to the Jewish communities, which eroded collective solidarity and the authority of traditional Jewish elites. See Stanislawski, *Tsar Nicholas I and the Jews,* pp. 127–133. John Klier, *Imperial Russia's Jewish Question, 1855–1881* (New York: Cambridge University Press, 1995), provides a slightly different interpretation.

21. Benjamin Nathans, *Beyond the Pale: The Jewish Encounter with Late Imperial Russia* (Berkeley: University of California Press, 2002), p. 28.

22. Jerold S. Auerbach, *Jacob's Voices: Reflections of a Wandering American Jew* (Carbondale: Southern Illinois University Press, 1996), pp. 2–3.

23. Interview with Wilton Hill [Hilowitz], August 21, 1996.

24. Interview with Lester Klauber, September 22, 1995.

25. Interview with Henry Baker, February 17, 1996.

26. Interview with Herbert Jawitz, August 13, 1996.

27. Interview with Ralph Jackson, February 28, 1996.

28. Interview with Artie Kolin, August 23, 1995. Merv Reines, studying at Penn State, also didn't know what Pearl Harbor was.

29. Quoted in Leonard Dinnerstein, *Antisemitism in America* (New York: Oxford University Press, 1996), p. 136.

30. See, for example, Victor Riesel's articles in the *New York Post,* "Washington Heights Vandals Desecrating Synagogues," December 29, 1943, p. 3; "Police Fail to Protect Jews Against Violence, Say Clergy," December 30, 1943, p. 5; "Attacks on Jews Spread in Bronx," December 31, 1943, p. 5.

31. Did the officer know about Jewish aversions to uniforms? The Boy Scouts did have Jewish members, even troops sponsored by synagogues, but it was far more popular among Christians than Jews.

32. Interview with Martin Dash, August 18, 1995.

33. Ibid.

34. The war did not change these practices. See, for example, Leo M.

Swaim, Jr., "Trustees Back Prexy Hopkins on Limiting Jews at Dartmouth," *New York Post,* August 9, 1945, p. 10.

35. This was the experience of Dragon member Herbert Jawitz around 1939 when he was looking for work. The job would have paid $19 per week, a good wage at the time. The interviewer asked if he was Jewish and then told him that they were tied up.

36. On antisemitism at Yale see Dan Oren, *Joining the Club* (New Haven: Yale University Press, 1985).

37. Interview with Martin Dash, August 18, 1995.

38. Ibid.

39. Interview with Herbert Walters, September 1, 1995.

40. Ibid.

41. See, for example, Daniel Hoffman, *Zone of the Interior: A Memoir, 1942–47* (Baton Rouge: Louisana State University Press, 2000).

42. Kahn, *Between Tedium and Terror,* p. 86.

43. Raymond Groden, "The Dragon's Teeth: Memoirs of Raymond Groden" (1990), typescript in author's possession, p. 29.

44. Geller, "Take It Like a Soldier," p. 248.

45. Ibid., pp. 41–59.

46. See Jeffrey S. Gurock, *The Men and Women of Yeshiva: Higher Education, Orthodoxy, and American Judaism* (New York: Columbia University Press, 1988), pp. 84–89.

47. Geller, "Take It Like a Soldier," pp. 291–298; quotation on p. 292.

48. *New York Times,* March 2, 1943, p. 1. For a discussion of the Stop Hitler Now rally organized by the American Jewish Congress and Stephen Wise at Madison Square Garden that drew over 21,000 people, see Aaron Berman, *Nazism, the Jews, and American Zionism, 1933–1948* (Detroit: Wayne State University Press, 1990), pp. 101–103.

49. Geller, "Take It Like a Soldier," p. 3.

50. See, for example, Howard Fast's comments in "Under Forty: A Symposium," *Contemporary Jewish Record* (1944), pp. 25–27. See also Joan Wallach Scott, "Preface," in Benedict S. Alper, *Love and Politics in Wartime: Letters to My Wife, 1943–45,* selected and ed-

ited by Joan Wallach Scott (Urbana: University of Illinois Press, 1992), p. x.

51. Interview with Paul Steinfeld, June 29, 1999.

52. Unpublished letters of Harold Freeman to his wife, Bea, from Europe, June 15, 1944, edited by Harold Freeman (1995).

53. The Jewish poet George Oppen, antifascist during the war years, left his job as a pattern maker at Grumman Aircraft in Hempstead, Long Island, and moved to Detroit at the end of November 1942, knowing this would provoke his induction. He served in an antitank company in the 411th Infantry in the 103rd Division in the European theater. *The Selected Letters of George Oppen,* ed. Rachel Blau DuPlessis (Durham: Duke University Press, 1990), pp. xiii–xiv.

54. Interview with Harold Freeman, June 1997.

55. On Howe's attack on Rahv and other left-wing writers who urged critical support of the Allies, see Edward Alexander, "Irving Howe and the Holocaust: Dilemmas of a Radical Jewish Intellectual," *American Jewish History,* 88:1 (March 2000), pp. 97, 103–105.

56. The socialist Paul Jacobs recalled that he and his political friends were convinced that the war "would be an imperialist one." They debated whether to support the Allies against the Nazis and Italian Fascists. Paul Jacobs, *Is Curly Jewish?* (New York: Vintage Books, 1973), pp. 127–128.

57. Quoted in James Atlas, *Delmore Schwartz: The Life of an American Poet* (New York: Farrar, Straus and Giroux, 1977), p. 202.

58. Howe was drafted into the Army and spent most of the war stationed in Alaska. Schwartz held onto his deferment. He taught grammar and composition to Navy classes as well as undergraduates at Harvard. Atlas, *Delmore Schwartz,* p. 202; Irving Howe, *A Margin of Hope: An Intellectual Autobiography* (New York: Harcourt, Brace, Jovanovich, 1982), pp. 90–103.

59. Letter to Editor from Sgt. Harry Sosewitz, December 21, 1943, in "Correspondence: Soldiers' Corner," *Furrows* (January 1944), p. 28.

60. Jeffrey Weiss and Craig Weiss, *I Am My Brother's Keeper: American Volunteers in Israel's War for Independence, 1947–49* (Atglen, Pa.: Schiffer Military History, 1998), pp. 40–41.

61. Deborah Lipstadt, *Beyond Belief: The American Press and the*

Coming of the Holocaust (New York: Free Press, 1986), pp. 135–196.

62. Yet he considered himself a fraud and didn't study hard enough to get acceptable grades to keep his student deferment. Robert Kotlowitz, *Before Their Time* (New York: Alfred A. Knopf, 1997), p. 3.

63. Interview with Artie Kolin, August 23, 1995.

64. Interview with Merv Reines, March 4, 1997.

65. Interview with Bernard Miller, March 19, 2001.

66. See Isidore Kaufman, *American Jews in World War II* (New York: Dial Press, 1947), vol. I, p. 351.

67. Jewish women joined the Army as well. Many wanted to trade dull or difficult home lives for the adventure of new experiences. Often, as a first step taken alone and without the support of their families, enlistment represented a move toward their own liberation as women. The excitement of military service enticed them. The Women's Army Auxiliary Corps, established in May 1942, offered women the opportunity to contribute to the war effort and find purpose in their lives. For one account see Rose Rosenthal, *Not All Soldiers Wore Pants: A Witty World War II WAC Tells All* (Rochelle Park, N.J.: Ryzell Books, 1993), p. 9.

68. Interview with Jerome Minkow, June 30, 1999.

69. Interview with Artie Kolin, August 23, 1995.

3. Eating Ham for Uncle Sam

1. Epigraph: Conversation with Allan York, June 21, 2002.

2. Italian Jews wore six-pointed Magen Davids around their neck, a sign of their acculturation. See unpublished letter by Harold Saperstein, "The Eternal City," July 1944, in American Jewish Archives.

3. Interview with Herbert Walters, September 1, 1995.

4. Dash does not recall ever using his Masonic membership, and after the war he deactivated it.

5. Interview with Martin Dash, August 18, 1995.

6. Quoted in Ralph G. Martin, *The GI War 1941–1945* (Boston: Little, Brown, 1967), p. 2.

7. Interview with Arthur Aryeh Goren [Gorenstein], February 6, 1996.

8. Ibid. Their names were also close in the alphabet, which would help to keep them together.

9. Some sons received gifts of *tallis* and *tefillin* (prayer shawl and phylacteries), a more traditional form of religious connection than the mezuza or Magen David. Interview with Herbert Walters, September 1, 1995.

10. Letter, Arthur Gorenstein to "Folks," n.d. [July 24, 1944], "Monday nite, 23:40."

11. Interview with Herbert Walters, September 1, 1995.

12. Akiva Skidell decided to start a Habonim monthly, *Furrows*, to maintain connections.

13. Copies of *The Dragon Weekly* are in the possession of the author.

14. Letter, Arthur Gorenstein to Saul and Lillian Gorenstein, July 25, 1944.

15. For a brief discussion of the laws of kashrut see *Encyclopedia Judaica* (Jerusalem: Keter Publishing House, 1971), vol. 6, pp. 26–45.

16. Interview with Arthur Aryeh Goren, February 6, 1996.

17. Some Orthodox Jews refrained from eating meat and relied on shipments of salami from home. Kosher supplies provided by Jewish chaplains supplemented army food. A handful of observant Jewish recruits consulted their rabbis regarding what was permissible. In general, the guidelines decreeed that what one could eat varied in proportion to the amount of stress. The greater the stress, the more lenient the rules. Under battle conditions, anything could be consumed. See, for example, the account by Gottfried Neuburger, "An Orthodox G.I. Fights a War," *Commentary* (March 1949), pp. 265–272.

18. Interview with Paul Steinfeld, June 29, 1999.

19. Interview with Herbert Walters, September 1, 1995.

20. Interview with Jerome Minkow, June 30, 1999.

21. For a discussion of circumcision in Europe see Sander Gilman,

"The Jewish Psyche," in *The Jew's Body* (New York: Routledge, 1991), pp. 90–95.

22. "A Report on National Character," Columbia University Research in Contemporary Cultures, February 1951. Prepared for Working Group on Human Behavior under Conditions of Military Service, Capt. P. E. McDonall [?] Research and Development Board, Chairman. "The Jewish Soldier" by R. Landes, p. 140. Emphasis in the original.

23. John Ellis, *The Sharp End: The Fighting Man in World War II* (1980; rev. ed. London: Pimlico, 1990), p. 12.

24. Letters, Ira Koplow to Goldie Halpern Koplow, November 22, 1942; December 9, 1942; January 30, 1943; April 30, 1944; Ft. Benning, Ga.

25. Interview with Merv Reines, March 4, 1997.

26. Paul Fussell, *Wartime: Understanding and Behavior in the Second World War* (New York: Oxford University Press, 1989), p. 190.

27. Interview with Jerome Minkow, June 30, 1999.

28. See, for example, the account of Theodore Koton in *The International Jewish Monthly*, December 1991, pp. 15–16.

29. Interview with Jerome Minkow, June 30, 1999.

30. Victor B. Geller, "Take It Like a Soldier," unpublished memoir, n.d., p. 265.

31. Interview with Jerome Minkow, June 30, 1999.

32. Ibid.

33. See, for example, Sy M. Kahn, *Between Tedium and Terror: A Soldier's World War II Diary 1943–45* (Urbana: University of Illinois Press, 1993), p. 107.

34. Interview with Jerome Minkow, June 30, 1999.

35. In *Jews and Feminism: The Ambivalent Search for Home* (New York: Routledge, 1997), Laura Levitt writes about her father: "In Army basic training in Arkansas my father insisted that despite his dog tags, no one knew that he was Jewish." Levitt doubts this. "I see no correlation between my father's sense of Jewish invisibility and how others saw him, especially at that time and in that place." Still, her father "took pains not to call attention to himself, keeping quiet

and showing no emotion. Unlike his 'kinky haired' friend stationed in Georgia, my father did not make the mistake of talking about racial politics with his fellow recruits. He is relieved, even now, that he was able to pass unnoticed as a northern Jew stationed in Arkansas in 1944" (p. 144).

36. N. Jay Jaffee gave up folk music, an integral part of his civilian life. Folk music expressed his left-wing politics, which had been shaped by Brooklyn's Jewish milieu. He discovered to his chagrin that songs he knew by Woody Guthrie and Leadbelly had other original lyrics. Disillusioned, he decided that his political versions of these songs were inauthentic. N. Jay Jaffee, "The Expendable," unpublished memoir, 1996, p. 4. Don't "turn every conversation into an intellectual discussion," one veteran soldier recommended. Pressing a point, as a new Jewish recruit had urged, needed to be foresworn while in uniform: "It will win you the argument but lose you a friend." Walter Eldat, 321st Infantry, "Soldiers' Corner," *Furrows* (September 1943), p. 24.

37. Letter, Arthur Gorenstein to "Folks," July 31, 1944.

38. Interview with Herbert Walters, September 1, 1995.

39. Art Buchwald describes a similar situation in the Marines, a painful incident he had forgotten until reminded by his drill sergeant. Art Buchwald, *Leaving Home: A Memoir* (New York: Fawcett Columbine, 1993), p. 175.

40. Interview with Herbert Walters, September 1, 1995.

41. Interview with Jerome Minkow, June 30, 1999.

42. Ibid.

43. Ibid.

44. N. Jay Jaffee arrived at Camp Adair in Oregon for infantry training, "twenty-one years old, healthy, and tough as nails!" He had "long since left the security of family life." Since age fifteen and his mother's death, he had lived alone, subsisting on the meager wages he earned. Army food and training appealed to him. N. Jay Jaffee, "The Expendable," p. 3.

45. Hyman Samuelson, an officer with the 96th Engineers, expressed enthusiasm for his superiors and fellow officers. "Last night we had a little party on the ground by lamp light," he confided to his diary

shortly after he was called up. "Colonel Pohl and Major Martin, executive officer, joined us just as if they were shave tails [second lieutenants]. They are great guys," he affirmed with conviction. Later he noted: "All college graduates and intelligent." Hyman Samuelson, *Love, War, and the 96th Engineers (Colored): The World War II New Guinea Diaries of Captain Hyman Samuelson,* ed. Gwendolyn Midlo Hall (Urbana: University of Illinois Press, 1995), pp. 3–5.

46. Letter, Arthur Gorenstein to "Folks," July 31, 1944.

47. Letter, Lillian Gorenstein to Arthur Gorenstein, July 31, 1944.

48. Interview with Arthur Aryeh Goren, February 6, 1996.

49. Letter, Ira Koplow to Goldie Halpern Koplow, January 13, 1943.

50. Bureau of the Census, *Sixteenth Census of the United States: 1940, Population,* vol. 1, Number of Inhabitants (Washington, D.C.: Government Printing Office, 1942), p. 1006.

51. Interview with Harold Radish, August 22, 1996.

52. Interview with Herbert Walters, September 1, 1995.

53. Jeremiah Gutman used to answer such questions with "I'm an American," though he knew they wanted to know if he was Jewish. Interview with Jeremiah Gutman, February 13, 1996.

54. William Manchester in his memoir of the war describes one man in his Marine unit who was Armenian. He never realized, until many years later, that he was a Jew who had adopted a more exotic but less fraught identity. See Gary Gerstle, *American Crucible: Race and Nation in the Twentieth Century* (Princeton: Princeton University Press, 2001), pp. 225–226.

55. Letter, Arthur Gorenstein to "Folks," August 6, 1944.

56. Interview with Arthur Aryeh Goren, February 6, 1996.

57. Herbie Jawitz, Bernie Miller, and Lester Klauber all had reputations as ladies' men.

58. Letter, Louis Gruhin to Sophia Gruhin, "From A.P.O. 44, Ft. Bragg, N.C., Outside Wadesboro, N.C.," October 30, 1941.

59. Interview with Howard Sachs, February 24, 1996.

60. Ibid. Sachs's story echoes Freud's well-known tale about his father, whose hat is knocked into the gutter by antisemites, only Sachs is now among the bullies who rule the sidewalks.

61. Choosing the "blank" category left an enlisted man open to proselytizing by every group, as Paul Jacobs, a committed secular socialist, discovered to his chagrin. "After being bombarded for a week by suggestions that I attend Catholic, Protestant, Hebrew, and I even think Christian Science services, I gave up." He had his "dogtags stamped with the initial 'H' for 'Hebrew,' thus at least removing myself from the anxious ministry of the other groups." Paul Jacobs, *Is Curly Jewish?* (New York: Vintage Books, 1973), p. 129.

62. The Dillingham Commission's *Dictionary of Races* classified groups largely on a linguistic basis, using Hebrew to denote Jews, irrespective of the countries of origin. See Oscar Handlin, "Old Immigrants and New," in *Race and Nationality in American Life* (Garden City, N.Y.: Doubleday, 1957), pp. 84–85. For a discussion of Jewish opposition to such classification, see Esther Panitz, "In Defense of the Jewish Immigrant (1891–1924)," *American Jewish Historical Quarterly,* 55:1 (September 1965), pp. 90–92.

63. For an interesting debate see Simon Wolf, "Report of the Board of Delegates on Civil and Religious Rights," in Union of American Hebrew Congregations, Thirtieth Annual Report (February 1904), pp. 5027–28, 5042–51. On "Hebrew" as a substitute for "Jew" in the nineteenth century, see Michael A. Meyer, *Jewish Identity in the Modern World* (Seattle: University of Washington Press, 1990), p. 21.

64. "Officers are the majority in this escapist category," wrote Edward T. Sandrow in "Jews in the Army — A Short Social Study," *The Reconstructionist* (March 17, 1944), p. 13.

65. Kahn, *Between Tedium and Terror,* p. xxiv.

66. Interview with Jerome Minkow, June 30, 1999.

67. Sgt. Harry Sosewitz, December 21, 1943, "Correspondence: Soldiers' Corner," *Furrows* (January 1944), p. 28.

68. Interview with Ralph Jackson, February 28, 1996.

69. Interview with Arthur Aryeh Goren, February 6, 1996.

70. When he was at Fort Benning, Ira Koplow saw "a notice in the daily orders about letting the Jewish boys get a furlough" for Passover. Although he planned to ask the Captain about it, he doubted he would get one "because lots of times nobody pays any attention to the daily

orders," he explained to his mother. In the end, Koplow didn't ask. Letter, Ira Koplow to Goldie Halpern Koplow, March 29, 1943.

71. Interview with Arthur Aryeh Goren, February 6, 1996.

72. Ibid.

73. She used his Hebrew name. Letter, Saul Gorenstein to Arthur Gorenstein, September 24, 1944.

74. Letter, Lillian Gorenstein to Arthur Gorenstein, October 6, 1944.

75. Representative John A. Flanagan of West Virgina fumed "on the floor of the House that he did not want 'any Ginsberg' to lead his son in battle." Leonard Dinnerstein, *Antisemitism in America* (New York: Oxford University Press, 1994), p. 136.

76. Herbert Aptheker trained as an artillery officer at Fort Sill, Oklahoma. He requested black troops, and he received the 350th artillery. Shortly before leaving Fort Bragg for overseas, he was called in by the commanding officer of the camp. A general was there. "'Why did you leave Camp Maxey in Texas so quickly?' I said, 'The commanding officer over there was an antisemitic fanatic. And I'm Jewish. I was about to go to Command and General Staff School and be promoted. He knew that, so he had me transferred.' He said, 'We're investigating this Buell Smith. Do you have evidence of this?' I said, 'Well, it was notorious.' He said, 'No, do you have *evidence?*' And then I thought to myself, yes. I said, 'When I was transferred, Col. Theodore Parker sent me a letter referring to the "unfortunate prejudices of Col. Smith," and that's why I was transferred, and regrets, and that kind of thing.' And the general said, 'Do you have that letter?' I said, 'Yes, but it's a personal letter. I'll get Parker's permission.' He responded at once and we used it."

After the war Aptheker learned from a rabbi that Parker's letter had helped in the court-martial of Smith and that Smith had been reprimanded, confined in grade, and confined to noncombat. "Interview of Herbert Aptheker" by Robin D. G. Kelley, *Journal of American History,* 87:1 (June 2000), pp. 156–157.

77. Rowland Berthoff, a Christian American, recalls an incident that confirms some bias. "In the last four months of 1944 I had a pretty cushy job at the Infantry School at Fort Benning, as what they called a 'bird dog,' a second lieutenant overseeing a platoon of officer can-

didates. Four of the fifty-two were Jews," a higher percentage than average. "One, whose record was marginal, had to appear before a panel, although I thought he was quite a good candidate. He happened to be a very Jewish-looking person, very Jewish-looking indeed to the colonel in charge of the panel." When the candidate had withdrawn from the room, the colonel asked Berthoff, "Well, you wouldn't want someone like that as an officer, would you? Who would follow a person who looks like that?" This was a tough question but Berthoff "did try to stand up for him." Berthoff continued his story: The colonel said, "He was a good sergeant; we need sergeants like that; leave him there; he's a sergeant. Wouldn't you do that?" Berthoff replied, "If I were his commanding officer, I would consider it my duty to send him to OCS to become an officer." Berthoff concludes in retrospect that the incident was "very trivial." It went on behind the scenes, as it were, "where nobody would ever hear of it; it was nothing of record, nothing." He then reports that the candidate was turned down. Roland Berthoff, "A Rejoinder on Wartime Antisemitism," in "A Round Table: The Living and Reliving of World War II," *Journal of American History,* 77: 2 (September 1990), p. 590.

78. Jaffee, "The Expendable," p. 3.

79. Jews who came from small towns might have already gained a lot of experience dealing with antisemitism. Anne Polland recalls that her grandfather used to tell her proudly about beating up antisemites when he was in the first grade in Wisconsin. Comments of Anne Polland, Pew Spring Fellows Conference, Yale University, May 3, 2002.

80. Interview with Howard Sachs, February 24, 1996.

81. Ibid.

82. Comments of Mary Ellen Koneiczny, Pew Spring Fellows Conference, Yale University, May 3, 2002.

83. Albert Isaac Slomovitz argues that during World War I, "organizationally and individually, the mood of American soldiers during the war reflected themes of brotherhood and self-respect." *The Fighting Rabbis: Jewish Military Chaplains and American History* (New York: New York University Press, 1999), p. 51.

84. "Once you were called a dirty Jew," Art Buchwald thought, "you had no choice but to fight, or risk being considered a Jewish coward." Cowardice was not a label any soldier wanted, especially a Marine. "Since I was young and cocky, I wasn't sure whether my fights with other Marines were because they thought I was a little shit, or because I was Jewish. Like most Jews I have always assumed that the only reason anyone picked on me was that they were anti-Semitic." Buchwald, *Leaving Home,* p. 174.

85. Interview with Paul Steinfeld, June 29, 1999.

86. Interview with Artie Kolin, August 23, 1995.

87. Interview with Howard Sachs, February 24, 1996.

4. Crossing Over

1. Epigraph: *The Forward,* January 30, 2003, p. 13, excerpted from Kenneth Koch, "To Jewishness," in *New Addresses.*

2. Sy M. Kahn, *Between Tedium and Terror: A Soldier's World War II Diary 1943–45* (Urbana: University of Illinois Press, 1993), pp. 1–9. Diary entries dated September 15, 1943, September 23, 1943, September 26, 1943, September 27, 1943, October 2, 1943.

3. Hyman Samuelson interview with Susan Perez, Austin, Texas, November 18, 2000; Museum of Jewish Heritage.

4. Hyman Samuelson, *Love, War, and the 96th Engineers (Colored): The World War II New Guinea Diaries of Captain Hyman Samuelson,* ed. Gwendolyn Midlo Hall (Urbana: University of Illinois Press, 1995), pp. xv, 20–21, 25, 27, 30, diary entries dated November 10, 1941, November 13, 1941, November 15, 1941, December 8, 1941, December 14, 1941, December 15, 1941, February 13, 1942.

5. Samuelson interview with Perez, November 18, 2000.

6. Samuelson, *Love, War, and the 96th Engineers,* p. 40. Diary entry dated April 5, 1942, Easter morning.

7. Kahn, *Between Tedium and Terror,* pp. xv–xvi.

8. Samuelson interview with Perez, November 18, 2000.

9. John Ellis, *The Sharp End: The Fighting Man in World War II* (London: Pimlico, 1980; rev. ed., 1990), p. 156.

10. Interview with Herbert Walters, September 1, 1995.

11. Kahn, *Between Tedium and Terror*, p. xv.

12. Other Jews thought of their return to Europe as Americans "first and foremost." Such was the attitude of Laura Levitt's father. "Although relieved not to have been sent to a more foreign place in the Pacific," she writes, "he refused to consider the complications of his Jewishness in making this journey back across the Atlantic." Laura Levitt, *Jews and Feminism* (New York: Routledge, 1997), p. 142.

13. Letter, Harold Freeman to Bea Freeman, June 30, 1944, Tilshead, England.

14. Even those who made the trip in winter when dark seas and skies prevailed expressed amazement. "I'm sharing the general air of holiday spirit that's prevalent aboard — casual, unconcerned, remote," Tracy Sugarman, a Navy ensign, observed. "You have to pinch yourself to realize that you are actually going overseas," he explained to his wife, June, "that you are actually in danger of attack — that all these guys who you are sleeping, eating, playing poker with are actually going to war!" Sugarman made the "surreal" trip in February 1944 on board the speedy *Queen Mary*. Letter, Tracy Sugarman to June Sugarman, n.d., in Tracy Sugarman, *My War* (New York: Random House, 2000), p. 22.

15. Letter, Harold Freeman to Bea Freeman, July 1, 1944, Tilshead, England.

16. Ibid; emphasis in the original. Other second-generation ethnics, including Irish, Italian, and Polish men, also experienced the voyage to Europe as a "return" to their parents' homelands.

17. Chaplain Morris Kertzer learned the difference between the front lines and the rear at Anzio. "First, I woke up every morning to find that I was still listed on Morning Report as alive and intact. Next, I learned that most of a battlefield was made up of empty space, with isolated pockets of activity. Then I discovered that we who were back in the regimental area were not even considered in the battle zone. The rifleman, the machine gunner — *they* were fighting. To them, company headquarters was rear-echelon, battalion headquar-

ters was practically a picnic-area, and the regimental command post was somewhere this side of Chicago." Morris N. Kertzer, *With an H on My Dog Tag* (New York: Behrman House, 1947), p. 5; emphasis in the original.

18. Interview with Jeremiah Gutman, February 13, 1996.

19. Letters of Harold Freeman to his wife, Bea, from Europe, June 15, 1944, edited by Harold Freeman.

20. Ira Koplow worked in the battalion supply office of the service battery of the 420th armored field artillery, 10th Armored Division. His office followed on the heels of the 420th. When the 420th was caught in the Battle of the Bulge, Koplow was trapped with them. His invariably cheerful letters home to his folks in Sioux Falls offer a glimpse into life behind the lines for a non-commissioned supply officer. On December 3, 1944, he admits, "we have had some pretty harrowing experiences." Then he notes that he is "billeted in houses here in Germany" and observes that "they live much better here than they do in France. The houses are modern and the insides are really furnished nice. Our platoon has one house for ourselves with a toilet and running water and even a bathtub and shower with hot water. We sleep in beds or on mattresses and it really doesn't seem like war until the 88s come over." Letter, Ira Koplow to Goldie Halprin Koplow, December 3, 1944, "Somewhere in Germany."

21. Samuelson, *Love, War, and the 96th Engineers*, p. 60. Diary entry dated June 17, 1942.

22. Ibid., p. 258. Letter to Dora Samuelson, April 9, 1944.

23. Ibid., p. 265. Diary entry dated May 7, 1944.

24. Samuelson interview with Perez, November 18, 2000.

25. Samuelson, *Love, War, and the 96th Engineers*, p. 290. Diary entry dated September 23, 1944.

26. Ibid., p. 290. Diary entry dated September 27, 1944.

27. Samuelson interview with Perez, November 18, 2000.

28. Sol Dubner served two years with a medical unit in the Pacific. He seemed to be the only Jew there. A group of Christian missionaries offered him companionship, and he underwent baptism. Back home in New York City in 1944 on a furlough, he sought out a priest. When Dubner returned to Hawaii, he pursued conversion. His

mother's death when he was in high school had left no intermediary between him and his rigorously orthodox father. While stationed in the Pacific he read a book, *Rebuilding a Lost Faith*. The book's last chapter included a discussion of Mary and the power of Marianic devotion for those who had lost their earthly mothers. Wartime pressures pushed Dubner to hunt for answers. He found them in Catholicism, especially its Marianic faith. Stephen J. Dubner, "Choosing My Religion," *New York Times Magazine,* March 31, 1996, section 6, p. 41.

29. Interview with Merv Reines, March 4, 1997.

30. Irving Howe similarly struggled with antisemitic slurs for two years at Fort Richardson outside Anchorage, Alaska. Once, he protested the slurs of a southern barracks mate. The GI was shocked. Howe was his buddy. "The Jews" loved money. He didn't see the connection between "the Jews" and his buddy. Embarrassed and frustrated, Howe retreated into silence. Irving Howe, *A Margin of Hope: An Intellectual Autobiography* (New York: Harcourt, Brace, Jovanovich, 1982), pp. 90–103.

31. Kahn, *Between Tedium and Terror,* Introduction, p. xxv.

32. Ibid.

33. Kahn, *Between Tedium and Terror,* pp. 69–75. Diary entries dated February 6, 1944, February 14, 1944.

34. Ibid., diary entries dated July 14, 1944, p. 153; May 3, 1944, p. 111. Quotation on p. 111.

35. Ibid., diary entry dated October 17, 1944, p. 184.

36. Ibid., diary entry dated December 16, 1943, p. 37.

37. Ibid., diary entry dated January 24, 1944, p. 62.

38. Ibid., diary entry dated October 17, 1944, p. 184.

39. Gerald F. Linderman, *The World Within War: America's Combat Experience in World War II* (Cambridge, Mass.: Harvard University Press, 1997), distinguishes between fighting the Germans and fighting the Japanese. He calls the former "the war of rules" and the latter "war unrestrained." But for Jews, "the war of rules" possessed dark and unrestrained dimensions.

40. For one such account see Sidney Rochelson, "Feeling Fine: The

Adventures of Sidney Rochelson as Told by Himself," ed. Susan and Rachel Gross, typescript in the author's possession.

41. Interview with Irving Fishman, February 24, 1997.

42. Letter, Herman Hellerstein to Mary Leah Feil, February 7, 1945. Quoted in Herman K. Hellerstein, *A Matter of Heart* (Caldwell, Idaho, 1994), pp. 65–66.

43. Hellerstein, *A Matter of Heart*, pp. 69, 89.

44. Interview with Irving Fishman, February 24, 1997.

45. Thomas Childers, *Wings of Morning: The Story of the Last American Bomber Shot Down over Germany in World War II* (New York: Addison-Wesley, 1995), p. 123.

46. Interview with Irving Fishman, February 24, 1997.

47. Letter, Kieve Skidell to Ettie Skidell, October 31, 1944. Akiva Skidell Papers, O.75/139, Yad Vashem Central Archives, Jerusalem, Israel.

48. Letter, Kieve Skidell to Ettie Skidell, January 28, 1945.

49. Writing to his wife from Algiers, Ben Alper described a meal that included "the local superintendent of education in town, very black hair, eyebrows, and rimmed glasses." To Alper's surprise, "half-way through he asked everyone if they were Juif [Jewish]." Such things weren't done in America. Alper replied "my parents were." The superintendent "immediately wanted to come over and change seats with me," so that they could talk. Later Alper learned his story of escape from a German prison camp. A communist, Alper didn't think of himself as a Jew, as his response indicated. Benedict S. Alper, *Love and Politics in Wartime: Letters to My Wife, 1943–45*, selected and edited by Joan Wallach Scott (Urbana: University of Illinois Press, 1992), p. 21. Letter of December 12, 1943. The superintendent's escape is described on p. 34, letter of January 5, 1944.

50. Letter, Kieve Skidell to Ettie Skidell, January 28, 1945.

51. Letter, Kieve Skidell to Ettie Skidell, January 31, 1945.

52. Ibid.

53. Emphasis in the original.

54. Letters of David Macarov, excerpted in Ben Zion, "My Experiences

and Observations as a Jew in World War II," pp. 18–23. YIVO Essay contest, no. 11. YIVO Institute for Jewish Research.

55. Etta Cherna [Jessard A. Wisch], "Call Me Mister," p. 12. "My Experiences and Observations as a Jew in World War II." YIVO Essay contest, no. 3. YIVO Institute for Jewish Research.

56. Macarov, "My Experiences and Observations," pp. 18–23. YIVO Essay contest, no. 11.

57. Ibid.

58. Service overseas did not eliminate conflicts between Jewish communists and Zionists. Ben Alper went to a meeting in Naples of the Jewish Brigade. It turned out that "the officers have their own mess, much as anywhere else, except that everyone speaks Hebrew—English is spoken only when outsiders like my friend and I were present." To Alper's surprise they had set aside the dietary laws for the duration, so they all ate Spam. "They said they didn't mind it at all," he reported. After dinner "they started to talk. They began with why proposals for a Jewish army had fallen through." Among other reasons, he explained to his wife, were "because the Arabs wanted to join it, too, and the British wanted the Arabs to join it, but the Jews were against it because they didn't want any part of them in their army—just as you wouldn't want Negroes in yours, says one to me." Alper considered this racism. Alper, *Love and Politics in Wartime*, pp. 47–48. Letter of February 2, 1944.

59. Macarov, "My Experiences and Observations," pp. 18–23. YIVO Essay contest, no. 11.

60. Ibid.

61. Interview with Martin Dash, August 18, 1995.

5. Worshipping Together

1. Epigraph: Karl Shapiro, "Sunday: New Guinea," in *V-Letter and Other Poems* (New York: Reynal and Hitchcock, 1944), p. 13.

2. John Keegan, *The Second World War* (New York: Penguin Books, 1989), p. 115. During 1942, U-boats in the Atlantic sank on average nineteen ships of about 100,000 tons before being sunk (p. 118).

3. There are many accounts of the four chaplains, but the material on line is good and comprehensive. See *www.fourchaplains.org/story.html* (May 3, 2002).

4. "Former Rabbi Listed Missing at Sea: One of Four Chaplain Heroes of Sinking," *New York Times,* March 27, 1943, p. 7.

5. Quoted in Rabbi Alex J. Goldman, *Giants of Faith: Great American Rabbis* (New York: Citadel Press, 1964), p. 319. See also p. 322 and quotation from Goode's article, "Ghettos Will Fail," in *National Jewish Monthly,* 1941.

6. Albert Isaac Slomovitz, *The Fighting Rabbis* (New York: New York University Press, 1999), p. 84.

7. The phrase is Chaplain Abraham Ruderman's. Ruderman watched the ship sink. Quoted in Goldman, *Giants of Faith,* p. 324.

8. Frank L. Weil, "Greetings," in *A Book of Jewish Thoughts* (New York: Jewish Welfare Board, 1943), pp. vii–viii.

9. *The Chaplain Serves,* Office, Chief of Chaplains, Army Service Forces, War Department, March 1, 1944, p. 44.

10. Rabbi Philip S. Bernstein, *Rabbis at War: The CANRA Story* (Waltham, Mass.: American Jewish Historical Society, 1971), p. 36.

11. *New York Times,* March 27, 1943, p. 7. The article features a picture of Chaplain Goode under the heading: "Former Rabbi Listed Missing at Sea: One of Four Chaplain Heroes of Sinking."

12. They were awarded to next-of-kin on December 19, 1944. *New York Times,* December 3, 1944, p. 12. "Dorchester survivors credit the chaplains with the saving of many lives by their success in persuading the confused men to overcome their fear of death and not plunge overboard for possible rescue," the paper reported.

13. *New York Times,* December 3, 1944, p. 12.

14. Ibid.

15. See *www.fourchaplains.org/home/html* (May 2, 2002).

16. Mark Silk, "Notes on the Judeo-Christian Tradition in America," *American Quarterly,* 36:1 (Spring 1984), p. 66.

17. Leonard Dinnerstein, *Anti-Semitism in America* (New York: Oxford University Press, 1994), pp. 120–121.

18. Silk, "Notes on the Judeo-Christian Tradition," p. 66.

19. Roy J. Honeywell, Col. Ret. USAR, *Chaplains of the United States Army* (Washington, D.C.: Office of the Chief of Chaplains, Department of the Army, 1958), pp. 247–248.

20. "Not only were differences taken for granted," reported one rabbi after naval training, "but with the proverbial 57 varieties of religious denominations represented, each group was *expected* to be different." This man discovered that the philosophy was "harmony, not uniformity." Quoted in Randall Jacobs, "Religion in the Navy — Differences are the Norm," *The Jewish Veteran*, 13:12 (August 1944), p. 17. Emphasis in the original.

21. Harold Saperstein, letter, August 7, 1943.

22. The phrase comes from Morris N. Kertzer, *With an H on My Dog Tag* (New York: Behrman House, 1947), p. 45.

23. So did many Jewish chaplains, especially in public. See "War Experiences and Post-War Equality (A Symposium)," in *The Jewish Forum* (January 1943), p. 7.

24. Victor B. Geller, "Take It Like a Soldier," n.d., manuscript in the author's possession, p. 319.

25. This appears to have been a standard way of talking about laying *tefillin* in the armed forces. Conversation with Karen Spiegel Franklin, July 27, 2003.

26. Geller, "Take It Like a Soldier," pp. 319–321.

27. Ibid.

28. Kertzer, *With an H on My Dog Tag*, p. 25.

29. CANRA encouraged each of the rabbinical associations to recruit chaplains. The Reform movement's Central Conference of American Rabbis [CCAR] had the most sophisticated system to secure candidates. Not only did it inform recent graduates of their eligibility, but it also obtained agreements from congregations to rehire rabbis who had left for military service. The CCAR screened rabbis prior to recommending them. It placed unmarried rabbis at the top of its list of potential chaplains. Hebrew Union College accelerated its rabbinical training program. Finally, congregations "were asked to pay the difference between the rabbis' civilian earnings and their military pay." The Conservative movement adopted a voluntary system, relying on individuals to make a personal decision and commit-

ment to serve. The Orthodox Rabbinical Council of America asked one of its most eminent leaders, Rabbi Joseph Soloveitchik, whether Orthodox rabbis could serve as chaplains. Soloveitchik's opinions carried weight within the Orthodox world and influenced individuals' life choices. He affirmed that "it is not only permissible, but it is also the duty of every Orthodox rabbi to enlist in the armed forces for the purpose of rendering spiritual guidance to Jewish soldiers." In short, all three religious movements in American Judaism threw their weight behind chaplaincy service. Quoted in Slomovitz, *Fighting Rabbis*, pp. 81, 78.

30. This impressive rate of response compared favorably with Catholics and major Protestant denominations. See Honeywell, *Chaplains of the United States Army*, p. 215 for statistics and quotas. The figures show that 550 rabbis applied to serve but did not meet military requirements; 495 received interviews; and 422 were endorsed by CANRA. Bernstein, *Rabbis at War*, p. 9.

31. Slomovitz, *Fighting Rabbis*, p. 81.

32. Both the Army and the Navy conducted their own tests for chaplains. The Navy paid attention to a man's politics as well as his faith and used personal interviews to weed out "subversive elements." Bernstein, *Rabbis at War*, p. 9.

33. Honeywell, *Chaplains of the United States Army*, observes that "in 1940, the Chief of Chaplains stated that the education of Catholic priests is sufficently standardized in all countries so that the fact of their ordination would be considered evidence of the educational equivalent of the A.B. and The.B. degrees" (p. 227).

34. Bernstein, *Rabbis at War*, pp. 7–9.

35. Jewish protests in World War I had prompted the Army to adopt a special insignia for Jewish chaplains instead of a Latin cross. Before World War II began, the Navy adopted the same practice. See Slomovitz, *Fighting Rabbis*, p. 59 for a full account of the other options.

36. Edward T. Sandrow, "Jews in the Army — A Short Social Study," *The Reconstructionist*, March 17, 1944, p. 13.

37. Mordecai L. Brill, "My Experiences and Observations as a Jewish

Chaplain in World War II." DHL essay, Jewish Theological Seminary of America, December 1946, pp. 10–11.

38. For a good description of a military chapel from a Jewish perspective, see Harold H. Gordon, *Chaplain on Wings: The Wartime Memoirs of Rabbi Harold H. Gordon,* ed. Zev Zahavy (New York: Shengold, 1981), pp. 15–17.

39. Letter, Arthur Gorenstein to "Dear Folks," August 21, 1944.

40. Letter, Artie Gorenstein to "Folks," Erev Yom Kippur [1944].

41. Letter, Artie Gorenstein to "Folks," Wednesday evening, September 27, 1944.

42. Geller writes his account of the non-com's speech in dialect, suggesting a measure of ignorance. Geller, "Take It Like a Soldier," pp. 319–328.

43. Ibid.

44. Ibid.

45. David J. Jacobs in *The International Jewish Monthly* (December 1991), p. 40.

46. Ibid.

47. Ibid.

48. Sandrow, "Jews in the Army," p. 15.

49. Quoted in Slomovitz, *Fighting Rabbis,* p. 98.

50. Bernstein, *Rabbis at War,* p. 37.

51. Solly Landau, "My Experiences and Observations as a Jew and a Soldier in World War II," YIVO Essay Contest [1946], no. 1, p. 6. YIVO Institute for Jewish Research.

52. Arthur Zirul in *The International Jewish Monthly* (December 1991), p. 14.

53. Ibid.

54. Ibid.

55. Harold U. Ribalow, "The Failure of Jewish Chaplaincy," *Jewish Frontier* (June 1946), p. 12.

56. Kertzer, *With an H on My Dog Tag,* p. 36.

57. For discussion of experiences as chaplains, in addition to previous references see Morton Berman, *For Zion's Sake: A Personal and Family Chronicle* (Prescott, Ariz.: Prescott Graphics, 1980); Eman-

uel Rackman, "What Our Chaplains Learned," [Hebrew] *Talpiot,* 3 (1948), pp. 3-4; "Veteran-Chaplain Conference," *The Reconstructionist,* April 5, 1946, pp. 9–31; Morris Adler, "The Chaplain and the Rabbi," *The Reconstructionist,* May 18, 1945, pp. 10–12; "War Experiences and Post-War Equality (A Symposium)," *The Jewish Forum* (January 1944), pp. 3–4, 18.

58. Harry Gersh, "Chaplains on Land and Sea: A One-Man Survey," *Commentary* (August 1948), pp. 172–173.

59. Albert Eisen wrote to his mother: "I went to Jewish Services tonight. I think I can count on the fingers of one hand the times I have gone before. . . . However, as a minority, it becomes necessary for us to declare ourselves to those who, unfortunately, are imbued with anti-Semitic sentiments." Quoted in *Jewish Youth at War,* ed. Israel E. Rontch (New York: Marstin Press, 1945), p. 43.

60. Melvin Preston [Howard Preston Goodman], "My Experiences and Observations as a Jew in World War II," YIVO Essay Contest [1946], no. 51, pp. 6–7. YIVO Institute for Jewish Research.

61. Quoted in Moses Kligsberg, "American Jewish Soldiers on Jews and Judaism," *YIVO Annual of Jewish Social Science,* 5 (1950), p. 263.

62. Ibid., p. 262.

63. Geller concluded: "As Americans we won, but as Jews we could celebrate no victory, even though 'Pharaoh' perished in his bunker. In that German field, our modern day Passover had come too late." Geller, "Take It Like a Soldier," pp. 425–426.

64. Hollywood preferred to show Jews participating in Christian services. "In twenty economical seconds, *Guadalcanal Diary* preached the ecumenical lesson that became holy writ for wartime cinema." It showed two devout Marines singing "Rock of Ages" at a Protestant service presided over by a Roman Catholic priest in full vestments. Then came the close-up on two Marines. "First Marine: Gee, Sammy, you sing pretty good. Second Marine: I should. My father was a cantor." Thomas Doherty, *Projections of War: Hollywood, American Culture, and World War II* (New York: Columbia University Press, 1993), pp. 140–141.

65. Meyer Cherniak [Harold U. Ribalow], "My Experiences and Obser-

vations as a Jew in World War II," YIVO Essay Contest [1946], no. 7, p. 8. YIVO Institute for Jewish Research.

66. Ibid.

67. Kertzer, *With an H on My Dog Tag*, p. 26.

68. Meyer Cherniak [Harold U. Ribalow], "My Experiences and Observations as a Jew in World War II," YIVO Essay Contest, no. 7, pp. 8–9.

69. Ibid.

70. Letter, Harold Saperstein to Marcia Saperstein, n.d.

71. Letter, Harold Saperstein to Marcia Saperstein, May 30, 1944.

72. Ibid.

73. Williamson Murray and Allan R. Millett, *A War to be Won: Fighting the Second World War* (Cambridge, Mass.: The Belknap Press of Harvard University Press, 2000), p. 513.

74. Donald F. Crosby, *Battlefield Chaplains: Catholic Priests in World War II* (Lawrence: University of Kansas Press, 1994), p. 225.

75. Speech of Roland B. Gittelsohn on Iwo Jima at dedication of 5th Marine Division Cemetery in "Chaplain Gittelsohn on Iwo Jima: Kappa Frater Delivers Memorial Address," *The Deltan of Phi Sigma Delta* (May 1945), p. 3.

76. Roland B. Gittelsohn, "Brothers All?" *The Reconstructionist*, 7 (February 1947), pp. 11–12.

77. Ibid.

78. Slomovitz, *Fighting Rabbis*, pp. 100–101, based on an interview in 1992.

79. Quoted in Crosby, *Battlefield Chaplains*, p. 226.

80. The three rabbis were Solomon B. Freehof, Leo Jung, and Milton Steinberg, representing Reform, Orthodox, and Conservative Jews respectively.

81. Bernstein, *Rabbis at War*, p. 18.

82. Letter, Harold Saperstein to "Friends of Temple Emanu-El," September 14, 1944.

83. Emanuel Rackman, Preface, in Harold I. Saperstein, *Witness from the Pulpit* (Lanham: Lexington Books, 2000), p. xii.

84. Patrick Henry, "'And I Don't Care What It Is': The Tradition-His-

tory of a Civil Religion Proof-Text," *Journal of the American Academy of Religion*, 49:1 (1981), p. 41.

85. Kertzer, *With an H on My Dog Tag*, p. 10.

6. Under Fire

1. Epigraph: Howard Nemerov, "IFF," in *Poets of World War II*, ed. Harvey Shapiro, American Poets Project, Library of America (2003), pp. 142–143.

2. Interview with Paul Steinfeld, June 29, 1999. Steinfeld's reflections about what he would do if he survived and the incident with "Hog Trough Charlie" occurred on different nights outside of Metz; I have combined them for economy.

3. Interview with Paul Steinfeld, June 29, 1999.

4. Victor Gotbaum, "The Spirit of the New York Labor Movement," in *Creators and Disturbers*, ed. Bernard Rosenberg and Ernest Goldstein (New York: Columbia University Press, 1982), p. 249.

5. Interview with Paul Steinfeld, June 29, 1999.

6. Ibid.

7. On antisemitism in the military among officers, see Leonard Dinnerstein, *Antisemitism in America* (New York: Oxford University Press, 1994), pp. 136–142; and Joseph W. Bendersky, *The "Jewish Threat": Anti-Semitic Politics of the U.S. Army* (New York: Basic Books, 2000), pp. 287–348.

8. Interview with Jeremiah Gutman, February 13, 1996.

9. Ibid.

10. As part of General Huebner's V Corps, the 69th advanced eastward through Germany toward the Elbe in March and April of 1945. En route they encountered the best of General Hitzfeld's 11th Army at the town of Hann-Muenden. Then they faced the notorious "flak alley," the nickname given by airmen to the fierce anti-aircraft defenses around Leipzig. Charles B. MacDonald, *The Last Offensive*, United States Army in World War II (Washington, D.C.: U.S. Army, Office of the Chief of Military History, 1973), pp. 389–395.

11. Interview with Jeremiah Gutman, February 13, 1996.

12. Ibid.

13. Quoted in Peter R. Mansoor, *The GI Offensive in Europe* (Lawrence: University Press of Kansas, 1999), p. 201.

14. John Ellis, *The Sharp End: The Fighting Man in World War II* (London: Pimlico, 1980; rev. ed. 1990), p. 352.

15. Albert S. Goldstein, "Faith and the Army," part 2, *The Jewish Layman* (November 1943), p. 22.

16. Letter, Harold Freeman to Bea Freeman, July 1, 1944, Tilshead, England.

17. Letters of Harold Freeman to his wife, Bea, Preface, May 1995.

18. In fact, few soldiers had met Jews before enlisting. However, many carried stereotypical views. And Jews held their own bias toward rural southerners.

19. He knew the officer who read his mail and so censored himself. "Once assigned to the 83rd Infantry division, 329 Infantry Regiment, C Company, 1st Platoon, 1st Squad, I knew the censor was an officer I had close contact with every day. In combat I might be sharing a foxhole with him. . . . He read my letters and apparently enjoyed them. If I skipped a day or two he would tell me he missed my letters," Freeman recalled. "However, the most important, and visible, result of censorship by someone you know and is close to you was not only how it effected [*sic*] *what* you wrote but *how* you wrote it. With someone always looking over my shoulder I'm afraid my style was self-conscious, very much so — and often pretentious and didactic." Letters of Harold Freeman to his wife, Bea, from Europe, June 15, 1944, edited by Harold Freeman, May 1995. Emphasis in the original.

20. Letter, Harold Freeman to Bea Freeman, June 15, 1944.

21. Ibid.

22. N. Jay Jaffee, "The Expendable" (1996), unpublished typescript in the author's possession, p. 53.

23. This statement reflected Paul Fussell's own experience, as described in his book, *Wartime: Understanding and Behavior in the Second World War* (New York: Oxford University Press, 1989), p. 141.

24. Letter, Ben S. Alper to Edith M. Alper, New Year's Day, 1944, in

Benedict S. Alper, *Love and Politics in Wartime: Letters to My Wife, 1943–45*, selected and edited by Joan Wallach Scott (Urbana: University of Illinois Press, 1992), p. 33.

25. Michael D. Doubler, *Closing with the Enemy: How GIs Fought the War in Europe, 1944–45* (Lawrence: University of Kansas Press, 1994), p. 228.

26. Tracy Sugarman, *My War: A Love Story in Letters and Drawings* (New York: Random House, 2000), p. 176.

27. Morris N. Kertzer, *With an H on My Dog Tag* (New York: Behrman House, 1947), p. 44.

28. For a good discussion of American soldiers' attitudes toward the enemy in the Pacific and European Theaters, see Gerald F. Linderman, *The World Within War: America's Combat Experience in World War II* (Cambridge, Mass.: Harvard University Press, 1999), especially chaps. 3 and 4.

29. Letter, Tracy Sugarman to June Sugarman, February 23, 1945, LST 357, in Sugarman, *My War*, pp. 173–175.

30. "Anti-Semitic Literature in Military Establishments," December 29, 1943, in Richard C. Rothschild Collection, AJC Correspondence, American Jewish Committee. There were many versions of the "First American," but all of them ended with an obviously Jewish name for the "First American to get 4 new tires." The memo includes a list of diverse publications across the country that reprinted the ditty.

31. Letter, Tracy Sugarman to June Sugarman, May 17, 1944, in Sugarman, *My War*, p. 62.

32. Sugarman, *My War*, pp. 173–174.

33. Letter, Tracy Sugarman to June Sugarman, February 23, 1945, LST 357, in Sugarman, *My War*, pp. 173–175.

34. Sugarman, *My War*, p. 175.

35. Interview with Jeremiah Gutman, February 13, 1996.

36. Interview with Ralph Jackson, February 28, 1996.

37. Both Germany and Britain had abandoned such daytime flights as being too costly and inefficient. The United States refused to modify its policy. Until the opening of a second front in Europe, strate-

gic bombing provided the only offensive available to the United States to assist the Soviet Union. As a result, "until mid-1944 the life expectancy of a bomber and crew was fifteen missions, and a flyer had only one chance of three of surviving a tour of duty," according to the historian Thomas Childers, *Wings of Morning: The Story of the Last American Bomber Shot Down over Germany in World War II* (Reading, Mass.: Addison-Wesley, 1995), pp. 45, 49–50.

38. The theory behind strategic bombing was that it would destroy the capacity of the enemy to continue fighting and the morale of the home front. The problem was that bombers had to fly at a great height to avoid being shot down and therefore could not drop bombs accurately. Gerhard Weinberg argues that "a major role of the strategic bombing was its aid to the Allies in the race against any renewed turn of the war in Germany's favor with new weapons after 1943, because of the great delays it imposed on their development and production." *A World At Arms: A Global History of World War II* (Cambridge: Cambridge University Press, 1994), p. 580.

39. Interview with Ralph Jackson, February 28, 1996.

40. Ibid.

41. Ibid.

42. Leonard Winograd, a lieutenant with the 512th Squadron of the 376th Bombardment Group who was captured in Yugoslavia after his plane was shot down, wrote about a Hungarian Jew named Einhorn who flew with the crew on the day they bailed out because their own belly gunner was in the hospital with pneumonia. "Einhorn was unknown to me before this mission because at our base in Italy, officer flying personnel rarely got to know the enlisted flying personnel socially except, of course, for members of one's own crew." Leonard Winograd, "Double Jeopardy: What an American Army Officer, a Jew, Remembers of Prison Life in Germany," *American Jewish Archives*, 28:1 (April 1976), pp. 3–4.

43. Interview with Ralph Jackson, February 28, 1996.

44. Ibid.

45. The phrase is from an interview with Samuel Klausner, November 26, 1996. Jackson actually thought he had a dog tag without the "H"

for flying but then discovered that it, too, had the "H." Letter, Ralph Jackson to author, March 3, 1996.

46. Jackson stayed only a couple of months at Addlebowden before being moved to a camp in Davos, Switzerland. He received parole to attend services at Koor. Interview with Ralph Jackson, February 28, 1996.

47. Robert Kotlowitz, *Before Their Time: A Memoir* (New York: Knopf, 1997), pp. 117–118.

48. Interview with Harold Radish, August 22, 1996.

49. Lester Bornstein tells such a story. During the Battle of the Bulge, assigned to a bazooka team, Bornstein and Sgt. Hill occupied a foxhole on the shoulder of the road that led to St. Vith. Toward evening a German tank came up the road and fired two rounds. Commanded to load the bazooka, Bornstein "unsheathed the shell from its container. With shaking hands I separated the soldered wires that were to be coiled around the positive and negative leads to activate the weapon. They broke." He tried again. Again he failed. Finally, on the third attempt, he got it right. His partner "took careful aim and fired at the tank which had now advanced within fifty yards of our position. Its treads came to a grinding halt. An eerie silence ensued. Our war had stopped. Suddenly frantic German voices were heard. My sparse knowledge of Yiddish enabled me to interpret what was being said. One soldier was asking another where he thought the shot had come from." As the Germans approached the foxhole, the two men got grenades ready. Bornstein pulled the pin. "I saw my mother crying over my grave. I visualized holding my hands high in surrender while still gripping the grenade and yelling 'Komerade!' at a futile attempt to save our lives." He knew that throwing the grenade would be ineffective in an open space and would just give away their position. "'Kum tzerick!'" a command echoed in the darkness. Hill whispered, 'What did he say?' 'We're saved! He ordered them to come back.'" Bornstein served in the 168th Combat Engineers Battalion. Lester Bornstein, "Kommerade," typescript in the author's possession, n.d.

50. Interview with Harold Radish, August 22, 1996.

51. Ibid.

52. Ibid.

53. Leonard Winograd writes that "the official questions came in correct order — name, rank, serial number, religion. I answered them all to the best of my ability, and when I told them that I was a Jew, I sensed excitement in the room." Winograd, "Double Jeopardy," p. 5. Actually, religion was not "an official question." Sometimes a German officer would inquire about a prisoner's parents and where they were born in an effort to identify Jews. Interview with Frank Glickman, October 17, 1996.

54. Interview with Harold Radish, August 22, 1996.

55. The 350 POWS included 80 Jews. Mitchell G. Bard, *Forgotten Victims* (Boulder: Westview Press, 1994), pp. 77–79.

56. *The International Jewish Monthly*, December 1991, p. 35.

57. Bard, *Forgotten Victims*, pp. 39–40, 73–75. For an account of imprisonment by the Japanese see Alfred A. Weinstein, *Barbed-Wire Surgeon* (New York: Macmillan, 1948).

58. Bard, *Forgotten Victims*, pp. 39, 35.

59. Interview with Harold Radish, August 22, 1996.

60. William J. Shapiro, "My Awakening," January 1996 to date, typescript in possession of the author, pp. 35–36.

61. All this time Rita did not know he had escaped. Interview with Ralph Jackson, February 28, 1996.

62. Interview with Paul Steinfeld, June 29, 1999.

63. As John Ellis writes, "If combat in general was the sharp end, each soldier felt himself at the sharpest end of all. The ordeal was very personal." Ellis, *The Sharp End*, p. 97.

64. Interview with Paul Steinfeld, June 29, 1999.

65. Bazookas required two men: one to load the cartridges and wind the coil of wire, and the other to aim and fire. Interview with Paul Steinfeld, June 29, 1999.

66. Ellis, *The Sharp End*, p. 90, reports that U.S. soldiers rated the 88-mm gun most frightening (48%) and dangerous (62%), followed by dive bomber (20% and 17%), followed by mortar (13% and 6%). Rifles were not considered either frightening or dangerous.

67. Interview with Paul Steinfeld, June 29, 1999.

68. Ibid.

69. Arthur Cerf Mayer was a member of the 327th glider infantry of the elite 101st Airborne and won a Distinguished Service Cross for his role in the fighting around Bastogne. Mayer, an atheist, had been raised as a Christian Scientist by his mother but identified as a Jew like his father and wore an H on his dog tag. Interview with Arthur Cerf Mayer, June 9, 1999.

70. Letter, Samuel Klausner to "Dear Family," September 21, 1944. In an interview Klausner remembers that by the time he got to England, he was "quite aware of what was going on in Europe." He saw himself "not only as defending America but also as fighting a Jewish war." Interview with Samuel Klausner, November 26, 1996.

71. Interview with Jeremiah Gutman, February 13, 1996.

72. Ibid.

73. "The troops could not contemplate without anger the lack of public knowledge of the Graves Registration form used by the U.S. Army Quartermaster Corps with its space for indicating 'Members Missing,'" writes Paul Fussell. *Wartime*, p. 270.

74. N. Jay Jaffee entitled his wartime memoir "The Expendable."

75. Interview with Jeremiah Gutman, February 13, 1996. Emphasis in the original.

76. Ibid.

77. Ellis, *The Sharp End*, p. 352.

7. Liberation and Revelation

1. Epigraph: Anthony Hecht, "The Room," in *Poets of World War II*, ed. Harvey Shapiro, American Poets Project, Library of America (2003), p. 169.

2. S. Hillel Blondheim, "New Year in France, 5705," *Menorah Journal* (Autumn 1944), p. 217.

3. Letter, Harold Saperstein, September 11, 1944, "somewhere in France."

4. Letter, Harold Saperstein, September 28, 1944, "somewhere in France."

5. Morris Kertzer, *With an H on My Dog Tag* (New York: Behrman House, 1947), p. 57. As he soon came to realize, "every chaplain had the uncomfortable role of a messiah." Kertzer considered it "a painful ordeal." He cringed when Jews crushed each other to approach him; he flushed when they reached out to touch his clothes and leaned forward to kiss his insignia or his hands. Jewish obsequiousness embarrassed him. But he had no choice. His uniform labeled him as an American Jew.

6. Harold Freeman, Letters to his wife, Bea Freeman, May 1995.

7. Letter, Harold Freeman to Bea Freeman, September 11, 1944, France, "nr. Tours."

8. Akiva Skidell, Letters to his wife, Ettie, n.d. "France" in "Letters from a Jewish Soldier in the American Army, Second World War: Europe: September 1944–December 1945." Akiva Skidell Papers, O.75/139 Yad Vashem Central Archives, Jerusalem, Israel.

9. Ibid.

10. Ibid.

11. When Ira Koplow got to visit Paris, in November, he noted with surprise that "from all appearances there didn't seem to be a war going on at all." The large numbers of people in the streets "looked well fed and had plenty of clothes." Koplow thought that "none of the French people we have seen so far seemed to have suffered to any great extent. In fact in several places I think they were more satisfied with the Germans than with us." He had not expected such attitudes. After all, he had come all the way from Sioux Falls to help liberate France. "This is certainly a funny war," he concluded. Letter, Ira Koplow to Goldie Halprin Koplow, November 4, 1944, "Somewhere in France."

12. Letter, Harold Freeman to Bea Freeman, September 9, 1944, France, "nr. Tours."

13. It is impossible to tell from Saperstein's letter whether "Of these, only 5 are still alive" refers to the 26 Jews or to the larger unit of 120 men.

14. "When you do" was the answer. Letter, Harold Saperstein, September 12, 1944, "somewhere in France."

15. Ibid.

16. Peter R. Mansoor, *The GI Offensive in Europe: The Triumph of American Infantry Divisions, 1941–1945* (Lawrence: University Press of Kansas, 1999).

17. Letter, Akiva Skidell to Ettie Skidell, October 23, 1944.

18. Letter, Akiva Skidell to Ettie Skidell, December 21, 1944.

19. Ibid.

20. Letter, Harold Freeman to Bea Freeman, October 15, 1944.

21. Neither Freeman nor Skidell attended Rosh Hashana services that year, but Skidell would go to services for Shemini Atzeret, a minor Jewish holiday. Observing Jewish holidays allowed him to connect with other Jews, something he valued. Skidell was a secular Jew but not antireligious.

22. Quoted in Fred J. Lennetz, *The International Jewish Monthly* (December 1991), p. 22.

23. John Keegan, *The Second World War* (New York: Penguin Books, 1990), p. 414.

24. Fred J. Lennetz, *The International Jewish Monthly* (December 1991), p. 22.

25. Ibid.

26. Letter, Harold Saperstein, September 28, 1944, "somewhere in France."

27. S. Hillel Blondheim, "New Year in France, 5705," *Menorah Journal* (Autumn 1944), p. 216.

28. Ibid., pp. 216–220.

29. Letter, Harold Freeman to Bea Freeman, February 25, 1945, Mariadorf, Germany.

30. Quoted in Alex Grobman, *Rekindling the Flame: American Jewish Chaplains and the Survivors of European Jewry, 1944–1948* (Detroit: Wayne State University Press, 1993), p. 45.

31. Letter, Harold Freeman to Bea Freeman, February 25, 1945, Mariadorf, Germany. Emphasis in the original.

32. "Only one German ever admitted to me that he was a Nazi, one!

Nobody was a Nazi! Amazing country, no Nazis, only one! In one town where there were no Nazis," Ben Berch recalled, "we went into the Nazi headquarters office, there was a stack of *Mein Kampfs,* a new edition, waiting to be distributed, and I got myself a Nazi party button." Quoted in Yaffa Eliach and Brana Gurewitsch, eds., *The Liberators: Eyewitness Accounts of the Liberation of Concentration Camps,* Volume 1: *Liberation Day.* Oral History Testimonies of American Liberators from the Archives of the Center for Holocaust Studies (Brooklyn, N.Y.: Center for Holocaust Studies Documentation and Research, 1981), p. 30.

33. Letter, Harold Freeman to Bea Freeman, February 25, 1945, Mariadorf, Germany.

34. Letter, Harold Freeman to Bea Freeman, March 4, 1945, Neuss, Germany.

35. Ibid.

36. Letter, Harold Freeman to Bea Freeman, March 10, 1945, Neuss, Germany.

37. Ibid.

38. Petra Goedde argues that American soldiers held Germans collectively responsible for the war but absolved the Germans they knew individually from guilt. *GIs and Germans: Culture, Gender, and Foreign Relations, 1945–1949* (New Haven: Yale University Press, 2003), p. 74.

39. Letter, Akiva Skidell to Ettie Skidell, February 26, 1945, Germany.

40. Letter, Akiva Skidell to Ettie Skidell, March 8, 1945, Germany.

41. Letter, Akiva Skidell to Ettie Skidell, March 6, 1945, Germany.

42. Ibid.

43. Letter, Akiva Skidell to Ettie Skidell, March 8, 1945, Germany.

44. Maria Hoëhn, e-mail communication to the author, July 11, 2003. The failure of the fraternization ban was evident almost from the moment that American troops entered Germany, and it quickly unraveled over the summer of 1945. A survey in the fall of 1945 suggested that more than 25 percent of American soldiers were having sexual relations with German women. See John Willoughby, *Remaking the Conquering Heroes: The Social and Geopolitical Impact of the Post-War American Occupation of Germany* (New York:

Palgrave, 2001), pp. 32–34. American soldiers also raped German women. One estimate is 500 rapes per week in April and May of 1945. Perry Biddiscombe, "Dangerous Liaisons: The Anti-Fraternization Movement in the U.S. Occupation Zones of Germany and Austria, 1945–1948," *Journal of Social History*, 34:3 (Spring 2001), p. 614. See also Maria Hoëhn, *GIs and Fräuleins: The German-American Encounter in 1950s West Germany* (Chapel Hill: University of North Carolina Press, 2002).

45. Letter, Ira Koplow to Goldie H. Koplow, April 18, 1945, "west of the Rhine."

46. Letter, Harold Saperstein to Marcia Saperstein, April 11, 1945.

47. See the account in Seymour S. Weisman, "My Experiences and Observations as a Jew in World War II," pp. 18–25, YIVO Essay Contest [1946], no. 2. YIVO Institute for Jewish Research.

48. Interview with Jeremiah Gutman, February 13, 1996.

49. Ibid.

50. There was a fine of $65. Letter, Harold Saperstein, April 11, 1945, "Somewhere in Germany."

51. Letter, Akiva Skidell to Ettie Skidell, April 8, 1945.

52. Eric Leiseroff, who had grown up in Germany, spent only three years in the United States before enlisting in the Army. He returned to Germany as a soldier in the 89th Infantry Division. When Leiseroff met Germans, he "used to get a great kick out of telling them" he was Jewish. "'Ich bin ein Jude.' When you come as a G.I.," he recalled, "you feel protected." This was a profound contrast to his experience as a boy in Germany, when he had been weak and vulnerable. Returning as an America soldier, he felt powerful. Excerpts from interview with Eric Leiseroff, Cor. 42061455, 89th infantry, 353rd infantry regiment, January 24, 1979, in Yaffa Eliach and Brana Gurewitsch, eds., *The Liberators: Eyewitness Accounts of the Liberation of Concentration Camps*. Volume 1: *Liberation Day*. Oral History Testimonies of American Liberators from the Archives of the Center for Holocaust Studies (Brooklyn, N.Y.: Center for Holocaust Studies Documentation and Research, 1981), p. 2.

53. Letter, Akiva Skidell to Ettie Skidell, May 2, 1944.

54. See Robert H. Abzug, *Inside the Vicious Heart: Americans and the*

Liberation of Nazi Concentration Camps (New York: Oxford University Press, 1985).

55. Quoted in Ron Rosenbaum, "The Flight From Fortress Salinger," *New York Times Book Review*, October 8, 2000, p. 16. J. D. Salinger fought with the 12th Infantry Division as a staff sergeant and counterintelligence officer. Noga Tarnopolsky, "Middle East Pundits' Rush to Judgment," *Forward*, May 10, 2002, p. 9, quotes Jorge Semprun, former member of the French resistance, who wrote a memoir about his release from Buchenwald at age twenty-two. In an interview about the camps he said, "Do you know that the most important and the most terrible thing is the only indescribable thing? The scent of burning flesh. What do you do with the memory of the scent of burning flesh? For these circumstances, exactly, literature exists. But how do you talk about it? Do you make a comparison? The obscenity of comparison! Do you say, for instance, that it smells like a burnt chicken? Or do you attempt a meticulous reconstruction of the general circumstances of the memory, turning on the scent, turning and turning, without confronting it? I have inside my head, live, the most important scent of a concentration camp. And I can't describe it."

56. Brad Dressler, *The International Jewish Monthly* (December 1991), p. 43.

57. Ibid.

58. Letter, Ira Koplow to Goldie H. Koplow, April 18, 1945, "west of the Rhine."

59. Abzug, *Inside the Vicious Heart,* p. 17.

60. Ibid., pp. 22–27.

61. David Cohen, in *GIs REMEMBER: Liberating the Concentration Camps.* Exhibit Catalog, National Museum of American Jewish Military History, n.d., p. 11.

62. Ibid.

63. Quoted in Abzug, *Inside the Vicious Heart,* p. 30. Emphasis in the original.

64. Ibid., p. 128.

65. Fred W. Friendly interview with Toby Blum-Dobkin, November 20, 1990, Video History Project, Museum of Jewish Heritage.

66. Ibid.

67. Abzug, *Inside the Vicious Heart,* pp. 106–107.

68. Fred W. Friendly, letter to his mother, May 19, 1945, Museum of Jewish Heritage.

69. See Mitchell G. Bard, *Forgotten Victims: The Abandonment of Americans in Hitler's Camps* (Boulder: Westview Press, 1994), pp. 62–69.

70. Fred W. Friendly, letter to his mother, May 19, 1945, Museum of Jewish Heritage.

71. Fred W. Friendly interview with Toby Blum-Dobkin, November 20, 1990, Video History Project, Museum of Jewish Heritage.

72. Fred W. Friendly, letter to his mother, May 19, 1945, Museum of Jewish Heritage.

73. Ibid.

74. David Zahler, in *GIs REMEMBER: Liberating the Concentration Camps.* Exhibit Catalog, National Museum of American Jewish Military History, n.d., p. 27.

75. Quoted in Allan Bérubé, *Coming Out Under Fire* (New York: Free Press, 1990), p. 200.

76. Maurice Paper, in *GIs REMEMBER: Liberating the Concentration Camps.* Exhibit Catalog, National Museum of American Jewish Military History, n.d., p. 46.

77. Harvey Cohen, in *GIs REMEMBER: Liberating the Concentration Camps.* Exhibit Catalog, National Museum of American Jewish Military History, n.d., p. 49.

78. Abzug, *Inside the Vicious Heart,* p. 118. The 71st Infantry Division published a pamphlet, *The Seventy-First Came . . . to Gunskirchen Lager.*

79. Harvey Cohen, in *GIs REMEMBER,* p. 49.

80. Ibid.

81. Interview with Howard Sachs, February 24, 1996.

82. Capt. J. D. Pletcher, in "The Americans Have Come At Last," in *The Seventy-First Came . . . to Gunskirchen Lager,* quoted in Abzug, *Inside the Vicious Heart,* p. 120.

83. Abzug, *Inside the Vicious Heart,* p. 44.

84. Pfc. Joseph Wright, 103rd Infantry Division, 411th Infantry Regiment, Company L. Wright was with the division that liberated Landsberg concentration camp. Yaffa Eliach and Brana Gurewitsch, eds., *The Liberators: Eyewitness Accounts of the Liberation of Concentration Camps.* Volume 1: *Liberation Day.* Oral History Testimonies of American Liberators from the Archives of the Center for Holocaust Studies (Brooklyn, N.Y.: Center for Holocaust Studies Documentation and Research, 1981), p. 32.

85. Eli Heimberg, in *GIs REMEMBER: Liberating the Concentration Camps.* Exhibit Catalog, National Museum of American Jewish Military History, n.d., p. 41.

86. Rabbi Eli Bohnen to Eleanor Bohnen, in *GIs REMEMBER: Liberating the Concentration Camps.* Exhibit Catalog, National Museum of American Jewish Military History, n.d., p. 60.

87. Grobman, *Rekindling the Flame,* p. 38.

88. See ibid., especially chaps. 2–4.

89. Interview with Howard Sachs, February 24, 1996.

90. Ibid.

91. Gulie Arad considers this story a part of American Jewish folklore. She recounts a story of a physician in Cincinnati who was in the service during World War II. His father told him to take his *tallis* with him because it would be the most useful piece of clothing he could carry: he could use it to hang himself, or he could use it to stop himself from bleeding! Its religious significance was minimal. Comments to the author, October 1996, Philadelphia.

92. Interview with Howard Sachs, February 24, 1996.

93. Sachs gave the brothers one more gift. When his unit was about to be transferred, he offered to help the boys get to Palestine. But they told him they wanted to go to America. They had relatives there. An uncle used to send them matzo and kosher food for Passover in Warsaw. Sachs tried to explain that America is a big country. But the boys didn't know any address except America. That night, Sachs sat down to write to his parents. He told them the story of the brothers, Martin and Joseph Gruënfeld, and their uncle, Avraham. But Sachs translated their names into Greenfield. On a whim, his father picked up the Brooklyn phone book and called Abraham Greenfield. "Mr.

Greenfield?" "Yeah." "Did you have any relatives?" "Yeah, I had, my whole family was wiped out in Europe." "Did any of them have children by the name of Martin and Joseph?" "Martin and Joseph? They're my nephews. They were killed, too. They're gone." "They're not gone. My son knows them." Abraham Greenfield came over to the house, and Sachs's father showed him the letter. When Sachs heard from Greenfield, he put the brothers in touch with him, and their uncle arranged to bring them to the United States.

94. Raymond Groden, "The Dragon's Teeth" (1990), unpublished memoir in the author's possession, p. 76.

95. Victor B. Geller, "Take It Like a Soldier," n.d., unpublished manuscript in the author's possession, pp. 448–50, 442.

96. Nearly 12,000 prisoners were taken during the battle. Mansoor, *The GI Offensive in Europe*, p. 185.

97. Samuel Fuller, *A Third Face: My Tale of Writing, Fighting, and Filmmaking* (New York: Alfred A. Knopf, 2002), pp. 195–196.

98. Letter, Akiva Skidell to Ettie Skidell, May 18, 1945.

99. Sy M. Kahn, *Between Tedium and Terror: A Soldier's World War II Diary 1943–45* (Urbana: University of Illinois Press, 1993), diary entry, August 16, 1945, p. 279.

100. Letter, Ira Koplow to Louie and Gang, August 15, 1945, "Bivouaced near Regensburg."

101. Interview with Howard Sachs, February 24, 1996.

102. It might more accurately be translated as "Know before whom you stand."

103. Interview with Howard Sachs, February 24, 1996.

8. Coming Home

1. Epigraph: Louis Zukovsky, "A Song for the Year's End," in *Poets of World War II*, ed. Harvey Shapiro, American Poets Project, The Library of America (2003), p. 37.

2. Victor B. Geller, "Take It Like a Soldier," n.d., typescript in the author's possession, pp. 460–471.

3. Three close friends had been killed, and Geller made it a point to visit their parents after he returned.

4. Geller, "Take It Like a Soldier," pp. 4, 460–471.

5. See Lucy S. Dawidowicz, *On Equal Terms: Jews in America, 1881–1981* (New York: Holt, Rinehart and Winston, 1982), p. 129.

6. Interview with Jeremiah Gutman, February 13, 1996.

7. Arthur Aryeh Goren, "Epilogue: On Living in Two Cultures," in *Divergent Jewish Cultures: Israel and America,* ed. Deborah Dash Moore and S. Ilan Troen (New Haven: Yale University Press, 2001), pp. 333–344.

8. A rally in Washington, D.C. of four thousand Jewish veterans in July 1946 supported the admission of 100,000 DPs into Palestine. The Jewish War Veterans called the reported British demand for American military aid if DPs were to be admitted a "colossal bluff." The veterans promised to recruit a full division of Jewish volunteers for service in Palestine. "U.S. Palestine Unit Offered by Jews," *New York Times,* July 16, 1946; "Truman Weighs JWV Bid to Defend Zion," *Jewish Examiner,* July 19, 1946, p. 1.

9. Interview with Jeremiah Gutman, February 13, 1996.

10. On the postwar triumph of Zionism among American Jews, see Aaron Berman, *Nazism, the Jews, and American Zionism, 1933–1948* (Detroit: Wayne State University Press, 1990), pp. 151–167.

11. Some veterans went on their own to join the various military units fighting for a Jewish state. Jeffrey Weiss and Craig Weiss, *I Am My Brother's Keeper: American Volunteers in Israel's War for Independence 1947–1949* (Atglen, Pa.: Schiffer Military History, 1998).

12. Interview with Jeremiah Gutman, February 13, 1996.

13. On responses to Morgenthau's plan, see Shlomo Shafir, *Ambiguous Relations: The American Jewish Community and Germany since 1945* (Detroit: Wayne State University Press, 1999), pp. 42–52. Henry Stimson (p. 42) called it "Jewish vengeance."

14. Tom Engelhardt, *The End of Victory Culture: Cold War America and the Disillusioning of a Generation* (New York: Basic Books, 1995), p. 73. It would take the maturation of a generation of baby boomers and the popularity of Volkswagens to break the boycott.

15. Marvin Caplan, *Farther Along: A Civil Rights Memoir* (Baton Rouge: Louisana State University Press, 1999), p. 7.

16. Stuart Svonkin, *Jews Against Prejudice* (New York: Columbia University Press, 2000), pp. 88–112.

17. Alexander H. Pekelis, "Full Equality in a Free Society: A Program for Jewish Action," in *Law and Social Action: Selected Essays of Alexander H. Pekelis,* ed. Milton R. Konvitz (Ithaca: Cornell University Press, 1958), pp. 218–219.

18. On the postwar changes in American Jewish communal defense organizations, see Svonkin, *Jews Against Prejudice.*

19. See Gary Gerstle, *American Crucible: Race and Nation in the Twentieth Century* (Princeton: Princeton University Press, 2001), pp. 262–264.

20. The American Jewish Committee commissioned a series of studies of prejudice. One of the volumes, *The Authoritarian Personality* by Theodore Adorno and Max Horkeimer, influenced American understanding of antisemitism. See Svonkin, *Jews Against Prejudice,* pp. 32–37.

21. See Michael E. Staub, *Torn at the Roots: The Crisis of Liberalism in Postwar America* (New York: Columbia University Press, 2002). In 1951 Jeremiah Gutman, having passed the bar and joined his father's law firm, responded to what he considered the civil rights violations of Senator Joseph McCarthy's anti-communist campaign by joining with like-minded individuals to found the New York Civil Liberties Union. *New York Times,* February 26, 2004, p. B10.

22. Patrick Henry, "'And I Don't Care What It Is': The Tradition-History of a Civil Religion Proof-Text," *Journal of the American Academy of Religion,* 49:1 (1981), p. 41.

23. Will Herberg, *Protestant, Catholic, Jew: An Essay in American Religious Sociology* (Garden City: Doubleday, 1955).

24. "Introduction to the Sabbath Prayer Book," *Sabbath Prayer Book* (New York: Jewish Reconstructionist Foundation, 1945), p. 10. The other beliefs that were rejected include the following: doctrine of revelation, doctrine of a personal messiah, doctrine of the restoration of the sacrificial cult, doctrine of retribution, doctrine of resurrection. This prayerbook led to the excommunication of Rabbi Mor-

decai M. Kaplan, its primary editor. The Union of Orthodox Rabbis of the United States and Canada, who pronounced the ban, also burned the *siddur* and prohibited the prayer book's use in synagogues. *New York Times,* June 15, 1945.

25. For a discussion of postwar Judaism see Jack Wertheimer, *A People Divided: Judaism in Contemporary America* (New York: Basic Books, 1993), pp. 3–17, and Jonathan Sarna, *A History of American Judaism* (New Haven: Yale University Press, 2004), chap. 6.

26. C. Bezalel Sherman, "Israel and the American Jewish Community," quoted in Arthur A. Goren, "The 'Golden Decade': 1945–1955," *The Politics and Public Culture of American Jews* (Bloomington: Indiana University Press, 1999), p. 194.

27. For example, see Ben Halpern's article, "America Is Different," in *The Jews: Social Patterns of an American Group,* ed. Marshall Sklare (New York: Free Press, 1954), pp. 23–29.

28. Dawidowicz, *On Equal Terms,* pp. 129–131.

29. Only a distinct minority worried about charges of dual loyalties. See Marshall Sklare's survey of attitudes in Baltimore carried out for the American Jewish Committee in "Jewish Attitudes toward the State of Israel," *Observing America's Jews,* ed. Jonathan Sarna (Hanover, N.H.: University Press of New England for Brandeis University Press, 1993), pp. 89–106.

30. Goren, "Epilogue: On Living in Two Cultures," p. 333. The quote is from "What We Believe," Habonim, Labor Zionist Youth, 1951.

31. Goren, "The 'Golden Decade,'" p. 203.

32. For example, Howard Hoffman. Alice M. Hoffman and Howard S. Hoffman, *Archives of Memory: A Soldier Recalls World War II* (Lexington: University Press of Kentucky, 1990), p. 8. Harold Freeman went to college and got a B.A. after the war. Interview with Harold Freeman, March 29, 1997.

33. Interview with Arthur Aryeh Goren, February 6, 1996.

34. Gerstle, *American Crucible,* p. 251.

35. Raymond Groden, "The Dragon's Teeth" (1996), unpublished memoir in the author's possession, p. 103.

36. On suburbanization, see Marshall Sklare and Joseph Greenblum, *Jewish Identity on the Suburban Frontier* (New York: Basic Books,

1967), and Benjamin Ringer, *The Edge of Friendliness: A Study of Jewish-Gentile Relations* (New York: Basic Books, 1967).

37. Sy M. Kahn, *Between Tedium and Terror: A Soldier's World War II Diary 1943–45* (Urbana: University of Illinois Press, 1993), pp.xv–xxv. Others even refused to talk about the war. Rebecca Schuman's grandfather, who was stationed in Germany, burned his uniform when he returned. Rebecca Schuman, "Going Back Jewish: Why I'm Going JYA to Germany," *Ra'ashan* (Fall 1996), p. 4.

38. Deborah Dash Moore, *To the Golden Cities: Pursuing the American Jewish Dream in Miami and L.A.* (New York: Free Press, 1994), pp. 21–25.

39. "Thousands of veterans had lived with intolerance in the armed forces and hoped to reform the prejudiced nation that they had left behind." Dinnerstein cites the Army publication, *Yank*, which asked soldiers in August 1945 what changes they would like to see in postwar America. A majority indicated "the need for wiping out racial and religious discrimination." Leonard Dinnerstein, *Anti-Semitism in America* (New York: Oxford University Press, 1994), p. 151.

40. Julius Walter, in *The International Jewish Monthly* (December 1991), p. 54.

41. Groden, "The Dragon's Teeth," pp. 101–102.

BIBLIOGRAPHY

✪ ✪ ✪

Primary Sources

Interviews by the author

Henry Baker, February 17, 1996
Lester Bornstein, July 31, 1999
Arthur Breslauer, August 3, 1999
Eleanor Chernick, August 13, 1999
Martin Dash, August 19, 1995
Dr. Irving Fishman, February 24, 1997
Harold Freeman, March 29, 1997
Arthur Aryeh Goren, February 2, 1996
Frank Glickman, October 17, 1996
Jeremiah S. Gutman, February 13, 1996
Carl Henry, June 25, 1999
Wilton Hill, August 21, 1996
Ralph Jackson, February 28, 1996
Herbert Jawitz, August 13, 1996
Lester Klauber, September 22, 1995
Samuel Klausner, November 26, 1996
Artie Kolin, August 23, 1995
Rita Kolin, August 23, 1995
Ozzie Lax, July 23, 2000
Edward Magrill, June 30, 1997
Arthur Cerf Mayer, June 9, 1999
Jerome Minkow, June 30, 1999
Bernard Miller, March 19, 2001
Rabbi Judah Nadich, July 6, 1999
Matthew Radom, June 1, 2000
Harold Radish, November 22, 1996
Merv Reines, March 4, 1997
Sidney Rosen, March 3, 1997

Howard Sachs, February 24, 1996
Arnold Schwedock, February 20, 1996
Philip Soroka, March 4, 1997
Paul Steinfeld, June 29, 1999
Dr. Paul Steinhorn, February 24, 1997
Herbert Walters, September 1, 1995
Newton Walker, January 25, 1997
Harry Wolfe, March 1, 1996

Interviews by the Video History Project
of the Museum of Jewish Heritage

Fred Friendly, interview by Toby Blum Dobkin, November 20, 1990
Dorothy Nash, interview by Rita Davis, October 16, 2000
Emmanuel Rackman, interview by Louis Bobbrow, August 9, 1999
Hyman Samuelson, interview by Susan Perez, November 18, 2000

Letters

The Dragon Weekly
Harold Freeman
Fred W. Friendly
Joseph Goldstein
Arthur Gorenstein
Garson Gruhin
Louis Gruhin
Samuel Klausner
Ira Koplow
Theodore Lasker
Abraham Odessky
Dr. Sidney Rochelson
Rabbi Harold Saperstein
Akiva Skidell

Published letters and diaries

A Book of Jewish Thoughts. New York: Jewish Welfare Board, 1943.
Alper, Benedict S. *Love and Politics in Wartime: Letters to My Wife,*

1943–45. Selected and edited by Joan Wallach Scott. Urbana: University of Illinois Press, 1992.

Blondheim, S. Hillel. "New Year in France, 5705." *Menorah Journal,* Autumn 1944.

Davis, Henry K. *K-Rations, Kilroy, KP & Kaput: One GI's War.* n.p.: Merrick Litchfield Press, 1995.

Golovensky, David I. "Another Chaplain Discusses Combat Religion." *The Reconstructionist,* March 9, 1945, pp. 18–20.

Heymont, Irving. *Among the Survivors of the Holocaust — 1945: The Landsberg DP Camp Letters of Major Irving Heymont, United States Army.* Monographs of the American Jewish Archives, No. 10. Edited by Jacob Rader Marcus and Abraham J. Peck. Cincinnati: American Jewish Archives, 1982.

Kahn, Sy M. *Between Tedium and Terror: A Soldier's World War II Diary 1943–45.* Urbana: University of Illinois Press, 1993.

Oppen, George. *The Selected Letters of George Oppen.* Edited by Rachel Blau DuPlessis. Durham: Duke University Press, 1990.

Pekelis, Alexander. *Law and Social Action: Selected Essays of Alexander H. Pekelis.* Edited by Milton R. Konvitz. Ithaca: Cornell University Press, 1958.

Rontch, Israel E., ed. *Jewish Youth at War.* New York: Marstin Press, 1945.

Roosevelt, Franklin D. *Selected Speeches, Messages, Press Conferences, and Letters.* Edited by Basil Rauch. New York: Holt, Rinehart and Winston, 1957.

Rosenberg, Leon. "A Chaplain Discusses Combat Religion." *The Reconstructionist,* December 1, 1944, pp. 9–13.

Samuelson, Hyman. *Love, War, and the 96th Engineers (Colored): The World War II New Guinea Diaries of Captain Hyman Samuelson.* Edited by Gwendolyn Midlo Hall. Urbana: University of Illinois Press, 1995.

Saperstein, Harold I. *Witness from the Pulpit: Topical Sermons 1933–1980.* Edited by Marc Saperstein. Lanham, Maryland: Lexington Books, 2000.

Shapiro, Karl. *V-Letter and Other Poems.* New York: Reynal & Hitchcock, 1944.

Sugarman, Tracy. *My War: A Love Story in Letters and Drawings.* New York: Random House, 2000.

"The Veteran-Chaplain Conference." *The Reconstructionist,* April 5, 1946, pp. 9–31.

War Letters: Extraordinary Correspondence from American Wars. Edited by Andrew Carroll. New York: Scribner, 2001.

Unpublished memoirs

Bornstein, Lester. "Kommerade!"

Brill, Rabbi Mordecai. "My Experiences and Observations as a Jewish Chaplain in World War II." DHL essay, Jewish Theological Seminary of America, December 1946.

Ershun, Joseph. "A Personal Transition; The Breakdown."

Geller, Victor B. "Take It Like a Soldier."

Groden, Raymond. "The Dragon's Teeth: Memoirs of Raymond Groden," 1990.

Jaffee, N. Jay. "The Expendable," 1996.

Rosen, Sid.

Seiden, Melvin. "Fellow Traveling at Anzio: A Political Memoir."

Shapiro, William J. "My Awakening."

Siegel, Sid.

Skidell, Akiva. "Akiva's Autobiography and Scrapbook."

YIVO Essay Contest, 1946. "My Experiences and Observations as a Jew in World War II." 52 entries. YIVO Institute for Jewish Research.

Published memoirs

Adler, Morris. "The Chaplain and the Rabbi." *The Reconstructionist,* April 6, 1945, pp. 9–13.

Aptheker, Herbert. "An Autobiographical Note." *The Journal of American History,* 87:1 (June 2000), pp. 147–171.

Auerbach, Jerold S. *Jacob's Voices: Reflections of a Wandering American Jew.* Carbondale: Southern Illinois University Press, 1996.

Berman, Morton Mayer. *For Zion's Sake: A Personal and Family Chronicle.* Prescott, Arizona, 1980. Printed by Prescott Graphics.

Berthoff, Roland. "A Rejoinder on Wartime Antisemitism." "A Round Table: The Living and Reliving of World War II." *Journal of American History,* 77: 2 (September 1990), p. 590.

Buchwald, Art. *Leaving Home: A Memoir.* New York: Fawcett Columbine, 1993.

Caplan, Marvin. *Farther Along: A Civil Rights Memoir.* Baton Rouge: Louisana State University Press, 1999.

Dubner, Stephen J. "Choosing My Religion." *New York Times Magazine,* March 31, 1996, section 6, pp. 36–41, 58, 62, 72–73.

Eliach, Yaffa, and Gurewitsch, Brana, eds. *The Liberators: Eyewitness Accounts of the Liberation of Concentration Camps.* Volume 1: *Liberation Day.* Oral History Testimonies of American Liberators from the Archives of the Center for Holocaust Studies. Brooklyn, N.Y.: Center for Holocaust Studies Documentation and Research, 1981.

Frucht, Karl. "We Were a P.W.I. Team." *Commentary* (January 1946), pp. 69–76.

Fuller, Samuel. *A Third Face: My Tale of Writing, Fighting, and Filmmaking.* New York: Alfred A. Knopf, 2002.

Gay, Ruth. *Unfinished People.* New York: W. W. Norton, 1996.

GIs REMEMBER: Liberating the Concentration Camps. Exhibit Catalog, National Museum of American Jewish Military History. n.d.

Gittelsohn, Roland B. "Brothers All?" *The Reconstructionist,* February 7, 1947, pp. 8–13.

Gersh, Harry. "Chaplains on Land and Sea: A One-Man Survey." *Commentary,* August 1948, pp. 169–174.

Gordon, Harold H. *Chaplain on Wings: The Wartime Memoirs of Rabbi Harold H. Gordon,* edited by Zev Zahavy. New York: Shengold, 1981.

Gotbaum, Victor. "The Spirit of the New York Labor Movement." In *Creators and Disturbers,* edited by Bernard Rosenberg and Ernest Goldstein. New York: Columbia University Press, 1982, pp. 246–263.

Green, Paul S. *From the Streets of Brooklyn to the War in Europe.* Tulsa: Council Oak Books, 1999.

Hellerstein, Herman K. *A Matter of Heart: An Autobiography with Adam Snyder.* Caldwell, Idaho: Griffith Publishing, 1994.

Hoffman, Alice, and Hoffman, Howard. *Archives of Memory: A Soldier Recalls World War II.* Lexington, Kentucky: University Press of Kentucky, 1990.

Hoffman, Daniel. *Zone of the Interior: A Memoir, 1942–1947.* Baton Rouge: Louisiana State University Press, 2000.

Howe, Irving. *A Margin of Hope: An Intellectual Autobiography.* New York: Harcourt Brace Jovanovich, 1982.

The International Jewish Monthly. December 1991.

Jacobs, Paul. *Is Curly Jewish?* New York: Vintage Books, 1973.

Kahn, Lakey. "From Chicago to Accord, Autumn 1939: 'That Night, We Learned to See the World Another Way.'" In *Dreamers and Builders: Habonim Labor Zionist Youth in North America*, edited by J. J. Goldberg and Elliot King. New York: Cornwall Books, 1993.

Kazin, Alfred. *A Walker in the City*. New York: Harcourt, 1951.

Kertzer, Morris N. *With an H on My Dog Tag*. New York: Behrman House, 1947.

Kotlowitz, Robert. *Before Their Time: A Memoir*. New York: Alfred A. Knopf, 1997.

Kraines, Oscar. "Antisemitism in the U.S. Army, 1941–1945: A Memoir." *Midstream*, April 1999, pp. 26–28.

Levin, Meyer. *In Search*. New York: Horizon Press, 1950.

Manuel, Frank E. *Scenes from the End: The Last Days of World War II in Europe*. South Royalton, Vermont: Steerforth Press, 2000.

Nemerov, Howard. *War Stories: Poems about Long Ago and Now*. Chicago: University of Chicago Press, 1987.

Neuburger, Gottfried. "An Orthodox G.I. Fights A War." *Commentary*, March 1949, pp. 265–272.

Ours to Fight For: American Jewish Voices from the Second World War. New York: Museum of Jewish Heritage, 2003.

Rackman, Emanuel. "What Our Chaplains Learned." [Hebrew] *Talpiot*, 3 (1948), pp. 3–4.

Ribalow, Harold U. "The Failure of Jewish Chaplaincy." *Jewish Frontier*, June 1946, pp. 10–12.

"Round Table: Living and Reliving of World War II." *Journal of American History*, 77:2 (September 1990), pp. 553–593.

Rosenthal, Rose. *Not All Soldiers Wore Pants: A Witty World War II Wac Tells All*. Rochelle Park, N.J.: Ryzell Books, 1993.

Schneider, David M., as told to Richard Handler. *Schneider on Schneider: The Conversion of the Jews and Other Anthropological Stories*. Durham: Duke University Press, 1995.

Terkel, Studs. *"The Good War": An Oral History of World War II*. New York: Pantheon Books, 1984.

"War Experiences and Post-War Equality (A Symposium)." *The Jewish Forum*, January 1943, pp. 3–4, 18.

Weinstein, Alfred A. *Barbed-Wire Surgeon*. New York: Macmillan, 1948.

Weinstein, Lewis H. *Masa: Odyssey of an American Jew*. Boston: Quinlan Press, 1989.

Winograd, Leonard. "Double Jeopardy: What an American Army Officer, a Jew, Remembers of Prison Life in Germany." *American Jewish Archives,* 28:1 (April 1976), pp. 3–17.

Zinn, Howard. *You Can't Be Neutral on a Moving Train.* Boston: Beacon Press, 1994.

Selected Secondary Sources

Abzug, Robert. *Inside the Vicious Heart: Americans and the Liberation of Nazi Concentration Camps.* New York: Oxford University Press, 1987.

Adams, Michael C. C. *The Best War Ever: America and World War II.* Baltimore: Johns Hopkins University Press, 1994.

Ambrose, Stephen E. *Band of Brothers: E Company, 506th Regiment, 101st Airborne From Normandy to Hitler's Eagle's Nest.* New York: Touchstone, 1992.

Alexander, Edward. "Irving Howe and the Holocaust: Dilemmas of a Radical Jewish Intellectual." *American Jewish History,* 88:1 (March 2000), pp. 95–114.

Arad, Gulie Ne'eman. *America, Its Jews, and the Rise of Nazism.* Bloomington: Indiana University Press, 2000.

Atlas, James. *Delmore Schwartz: The Life of an American Poet.* New York: Farrar, Straus and Giroux, 1977.

Bard, Mitchell G. *Forgotten Victims: The Abandonment of Americans in Hitler's Camps.* Boulder: Westview Press, 1994.

Barish, Louis, ed. *Rabbis in Uniform: The Story of the American Jewish Military Chaplain.* New York: Jonathan David, 1962.

Bauer, Yehuda. *American Jewry and the Holocaust: The American Jewish Joint Distribution Committee, 1939–1945.* Detroit: Wayne State University Press, 1981.

Bayor, Ronald H. *Neighbors in Conflict: The Irish, Germans, Jews, and Italians of New York City, 1929–1941.* Baltimore: Johns Hopkins University Press, 1978.

Bendersky, Joseph W. *The "Jewish Threat": Anti-Semitic Politics of the U.S. Army.* New York: Basic Books, 2000.

Berger, Bennett M. "The New York Intellectuals." *American Jewish History,* 80:3 (Spring 1991), pp. 382–89.

Berman, Aaron. *Nazism, the Jews and American Zionism, 1933–1948.* Detroit: Wayne State University Press, 1990.

Bernstein, Philip S. *Rabbis at War: The CANRA Story.* Waltham, Mass.: American Jewish Historical Society, 1971.

Bérubé, Allan. *Coming Out Under Fire: The History of Gay Men and Women in World War II.* New York: The Free Press, 1990.

Biddiscombe, Perry. "Dangerous Liaisons: The Anti-Fraternization Movement in the U.S. Occupation Zones of Germany and Austria, 1945–1948." *Journal of Social History,* 34:3 (Spring 2001), pp. 611–647.

Birdwell, Michael E. *Celluloid Soldiers: The Warner Bros. Campaign against Nazism.* New York: New York University Press, 1999.

Boyarin, Daniel. *Unheroic Conduct: The Rise of Heterosexuality and the Invention of the Jewish Man.* Berkeley: University of California Press, 1997.

Brinkley, Alan. "World War II and American Liberalism." In *The War in American Culture: Society and Consciousness during World War II,* edited by Lewis A. Erenberg and Susan E. Hirsch. Chicago: University of Chicago Press, 1996, pp. 313–330.

Brodkin, Karen. *How Jews Became White Folks and What That Says about Race in America.* New Brunswick: Rutgers University Press, 1998.

Burstein, Samuel. *Rabbis with Wings.* New York: Herzl Press, 1965.

Childers, Thomas. *Wings of Morning: The Story of the Last American Bomber Shot Down over Germany in World War II.* New York: Addison-Wesley, 1995.

Crosby, Donald F. *Battlefield Chaplains: Catholic Priests in World War II.* Lawrence: University of Kansas Press, 1994.

Danzig 1939, Treasures of a Destroyed Community. Catalog of an exhibit at The Jewish Museum, New York, edited by Sheila Schwartz. Detroit: Wayne State University Press, 1980.

Dawidowicz, Lucy S. *On Equal Terms: Jews in America, 1881–1981.* New York: Holt, Rinehart and Winston, 1982.

Deák, István. "Jewish Soldiers in Austro-Hungarian Society." Leo Baeck Memorial Lecture, no. 34. New York: Leo Baeck Institute, 1990.

Diner, Hasia R. *Hungering for America.* Cambridge, Mass.: Harvard University Press, 2002.

Dinnerstein, Leonard. *Antisemitism in America.* New York: Oxford University Press, 1994.

Doherty, Thomas. *Projections of War: Hollywood, American Culture, and World War II.* New York: Columbia University Press, 1993.

Doubler, Michael D. *Closing with the Enemy: How GIs Fought the War in Europe, 1944–45.* Lawrence: University of Kansas Press, 1994.

Dublin, Louis I., and Samuel C. Kohs, eds. *American Jews in World War II: The Story of 550,000 Fighters for Freedom,* 2 vols. New York: Dial Press, 1947.

Duker, Abraham G. "Emerging Culture Patterns in American Jewish Life: The Psycho-Cultural Approach to the Study of Jewish Life in America." *Publications of the American Jewish Historical Society,* 39:3 (March 1950), pp. 207–317.

———— "On Religious Trends in American Jewish Life." *YIVO Annual of Jewish Social Research,* 4 (1949), pp. 51–63.

Eisen, Arnold M. *The Chosen People in America: A Study in Jewish Religious Ideology.* Bloomington: Indiana University Press, 1983.

Elbogen, Ismar. *A Century of Jewish Life.* Philadelphia: Jewish Publication Society, 1944.

Ellis, John. *The Sharp End: The Fighting Man in World War II.* London: Pimlico, 1980; rev. ed., 1990.

Engelhardt, Tom. *The End of Victory Culture: Cold War America and the Disillusioning of a Generation.* New York: Basic Books, 1995.

Fass, Paula S. *Outside In: Minorities and the Transformation of American Education.* New York: Oxford University Press, 1989.

Feingold, Henry L. *A Time for Searching: Entering the Mainstream, 1920–1945.* Baltimore: Johns Hopkins University Press, 1992.

———— *Bearing Witness: How America and Its Jews Responded to the Holocaust.* Syracuse: Syracuse University Press, 1995.

Foster, Gaines M. "A Christian Nation: Signs of a Covenant." In *Bonds of Affection: Americans Define Their Patriotism,* edited by John Bodnar. Princeton: Princeton University Press, 1996, pp. 120–138.

Freeze, ChaeRan Y. *Jewish Marriage and Divorce in Imperial Russia.* Hanover: Brandeis University Press, 2002.

Fussell, Paul. *Wartime: Understanding and Behavior in the Second World War.* New York: Oxford University Press, 1989.

Gerstle, Gary. *American Crucible: Race and Nation in the Twentieth Century.* Princeton: Princeton University Press, 2001.

——— "The Working Class Goes to War." In *The War in American Culture: Society and Consciousness during World War II,* edited by Lewis A. Erenberg and Susan E. Hirsch. Chicago: University of Chicago Press, 1996, pp. 105–127.

Gilman, Sander. *The Jew's Body.* New York: Routledge, 1991.

Gleason, Philip. "Americans All: World War II and the Shaping of American Identity." *Review of Politics,* 43 (October 1981), pp. 485–518.

Goedde, Petra. *GIs and Germans: Culture, Gender and Foreign Relations, 1945–1949.* New Haven: Yale University Press, 2003.

Goldberg, J. J. *Jewish Power: Inside the American Jewish Establishment.* Reading, Mass.: Addison-Wesley, 1996.

Goldman, Alex J. *Giants of Faith: Great American Rabbis.* New York: Citadel Press, 1964.

Goldstein, Albert S. "Faith in the Army." *The Jewish Layman,* 18:1 (October 1943), part I, pp. 12–15; (November 1943), part II, pp. 22–26.

Goren, Arthur A. "Celebrating Zion in America." In *Encounters with the "Holy Land:" Place, Past and Future in American Jewish Culture,* edited by Jeffrey Shandler and Beth S. Wenger. Hanover: Brandeis University Press, 1997, pp. 41–59.

——— "Epilogue: On Living in Two Cultures." In *Divergent Jewish Cultures: Israel and America,* edited by Deborah Dash Moore and S. Ilan Troen. New Haven: Yale University Press, 2001.

——— "The 'Golden Decade': 1945–1955." In *The Politics and Public Culture of American Jews.* Bloomington: Indiana University Press, 1999.

Green, Nancy, ed. *Jewish Workers in the Modern Diaspora.* Berkeley: University of California Press, 1998.

Grobman, Alex. *Rekindling the Flame: American Jewish Chaplains and the Survivors of European Jewry, 1944–1948.* Detroit: Wayne State University Press, 1993.

Halpern, Ben. "America Is Different." In *The Jews: Social Patterns of an American Group,* edited by Marshall Sklare. New York: Free Press, 1954, pp. 23–29.

Handlin, Oscar. "Old Immigrants and New." In *Race and Nationality in American Life.* Garden City, N.Y.: Doubleday, 1957, pp. 74–110.

Heinze, Andrew R. *Adapting to Abundance*. New York: Columbia University Press, 1989.

Henry, Patrick. "'And I Don't Care What It Is': The Tradition-History of a Civil Religion Proof-Text." *Journal of the American Academy of Religion*, 49:1 (1981), pp. 35–49.

Herberg, Will. *Protestant, Catholic, Jew: An Essay in American Religious Sociology*. Garden City: Doubleday, 1955.

Hoëhn, Maria. *GIs and Fräuleins: The German-American Encounter in 1950s West Germany*. Chapel Hill: University of North Carolina Press, 2002.

Honeywell, Roy J., Col. Ret. USAR. *Chaplains of the United States Army*. Washington, D.C.: Office of the Chief of Chaplains, Department of the Army, 1958.

Horowitz, Roger. "It Is 'the Working Class Who Fight All the Battles': Militarism, Patriotism, and the Study of American Workers." In *American Exceptionalism? US Working-Class Formation in an International Context*, edited by Rick Halpern and Jonathan Morris. New York: St. Martin's Press, 1997, pp. 76–100.

——— "Oral History and the Story of World War II." *The Journal of American History*, 82:2 (September 1995), pp. 617–624.

Howe, Irving, and Kenneth Libo. *World of Our Fathers*. New York: Harcourt Brace Jovanovich, 1976.

Jacobson, Mathew Frye. *Whiteness of a Different Color: European Immigrants and the Alchemy of Race*. Cambridge, Mass.: Harvard University Press, 1998.

Joselit, Jenna Weissman. *The Wonders of America: Reinventing Jewish Culture 1880–1950*. New York: Hill and Wang, 1994.

Katznelson, Ira. "Strangers No Longer: Jews and Postwar American Political Culture." In *Divergent Jewish Cultures: Israel and America,* edited by Deborah Dash Moore and S. Ilan Troen. New Haven: Yale University Press, 2001, pp. 304–318.

Kaufman, Isidore. "The Story the Figures Tell." In *American Jews in World War II*. New York: Dial Press, 1947, vol. I, pp. 348–356.

Keegan, John. *The Second World War*. New York: Penguin Books, 1990.

Kennett, Lee. *G.I.: The American Soldier in World War II*. New York: Charles Scribner's Sons, 1987.

Kirshenblatt-Gimblett, Barbara. "A Place in the World: Jews and the

Holy Land at World's Fairs." In *Encounters with the "Holy Land": Place, Past and Future in American Jewish Culture*, edited by Jeffrey Shandler and Beth S. Wenger. Philadelphia: National Museum of American Jewish History, 1997, pp. 60–82.

Klier, John. *Imperial Russia's Jewish Question, 1855–1881*. New York: Cambridge University Press, 1995.

Kligsberg, Moses. "American Jewish Soldiers on Jews and Judaism." *YIVO Annual of Jewish Social Science*, 5 (1950), pp. 256–265.

Kolsky, Thomas. *Jews Against Zionism: The American Council for Judaism 1942–48*. Philadelphia: Temple University Press, 1990.

Kozloff, Max. *New York: Capital of Photography*. New York: The Jewish Museum; New Haven: Yale University Press, 2002.

Kraut, Benny. "A Wary Collaboration: Jews, Catholics, and the Protestant Goodwill Movement." In *Between the Times: The Travail of the Protestant Establishment in America, 1900–1960*, edited by William R. Hutchison. Cambridge: Cambridge University Press, 1989.

Landes, R. "The Jewish Soldier." In "A Report on National Character." Columbia University Research in Contemporary Cultures, February 1951, pp. 135–155. Prepared for Working Group on Human Behavior under Conditions of Military Service. Capt. P. E. McDonall, Research and Development Board, Chairman.

Levine, Peter. *Ellis Island to Ebbets Field: Sport and the American Jewish Experience*. New York: Oxford University Press, 1992.

Levitt, Laura. *Jews and Feminism: The Ambivalent Search for Home*. New York: Routledge, 1997.

Linderman, Gerald F. *The World Within War: America's Combat Experience in World War II*. Cambridge, Mass.: Harvard University Press, 1997.

Lipstadt, Deborah. *Beyond Belief: The American Press and the Coming of the Holocaust*. New York: Free Press, 1986.

Lookstein, Haskel. *Were We Our Brothers' Keepers? The Public Response of American Jews to the Holocaust, 1938–1944*. New York: Hartmore, 1986.

MacDonald, Charles B. *The Ardennes: The Battle of the Bulge*. United States Army in World War II. Washington, D.C.: U.S. Army, Office of the Chief of Military History, 1965.

———— *The Last Offensive.* United States Army in World War II. Washington, D.C.: U.S. Army, Office of the Chief of Military History, 1973.

Mansoor, Peter R. *The GI Offensive in Europe: The Triumph of American Infantry Divisions, 1941–1945.* Lawrence: University Press of Kansas, 1999.

McGill, Nettie Pauline, and Ellen Nathalie Matthews. *The Youth of New York City.* New York: Macmillan, 1940.

McGreevy, John. *Parish Boundaries: The Catholic Encounter with Race in the Twentieth-Century Urban North.* Chicago: University of Chicago Press, 1996.

Meyer, Michael A. *Jewish Identity in the Modern World.* Seattle: University of Washington Press, 1990.

———— *Response to Modernity: A History of the Reform Movement in Judaism.* New York: Oxford University Press, 1988.

Mintz, Alan. *The Holocaust in the American Imagination.* University of Washington Press, 2001.

Moore, Deborah Dash. *At Home in America: Second Generation New York Jews.* New York: Columbia University Press, 1981.

———— *B'nai B'rith and the Challenge of Ethnic Leadership.* Albany, N.Y.: State University of New York Press, 1981.

———— "Jewish GIs and the Creation of the Judeo-Christian Tradition." *Religion and American Culture: A Journal of Interpretation,* 8:1 (Winter 1998), pp. 31–53.

———— *To the Golden Cities: Pursuing the American Jewish Dream in Miami and L.A.* New York: Free Press, 1994.

Morse, Arthur D. *While Six Million Died: A Chronicle of American Apathy.* New York: Random House, 1968.

Mosesson, Gloria R. *The Jewish War Veterans Story.* Washington, D.C: The Jewish War Veterans of the United States of America, 1971.

Murray, Williamson, and Allan R. Millett. *A War to be Won: Fighting the Second World War.* Cambridge, Mass.: The Belknap Press of Harvard University Press, 2000.

Nathans, Benjamin. *Beyond the Pale: The Jewish Encounter with Late Imperial Russia.* Berkeley: University of California Press, 2002.

Novick, Peter. *The Holocaust in American Life.* Boston: Houghton Mifflin, 1999.

O'Neill, William L. *A Democracy at War: America's Fight at Home and Abroad in World War II.* New York: The Free Press, 1993.

Oren, Dan. *Joining the Club: A History of Jews and Yale.* New Haven: Yale University Press, 1985.

Panitz, Esther. "In Defense of the Jewish Immigrant (1891–1924)." *American Jewish Historical Quarterly,* 55:1 (September 1965), pp. 57–97.

Portelli, Alessandro. *The Battle of Valle Giulia.* Madison: University of Wisconsin Press, 1997.

Ringer, Benjamin. *The Edge of Friendliness: A Study of Jewish-Gentile Relations.* New York: Basic Books, 1967.

Rosenstone, Robert A. *Crusade of the Left: The Lincoln Battalion in the Spanish Civil War.* New York: Pegasus, 1969.

Rozenblit, Marsha L. *Reconstructing a National Identity: The Jews of Hapsburg Austria during World War I.* New York: Oxford University Press, 2001.

Sandrow, Edward T. "Jews in the Army — A Short Social Study." *The Reconstructionist,* March 17, 1944, pp. 10–17.

Sanua, Marianne. "From the Pages of the *Victory Bulletin:* The Syrian Jews of Brooklyn during World War II." *YIVO Annual,* 19 (1990), pp. 283–330.

Sarna, Jonathan D. *A History of American Judaism.* New Haven: Yale University Press, 2004.

Schultz, Debra L. *Going South: Jewish Women in the Civil Rights Movement.* New York: New York University Press, 2001.

Shafir, Shlomo. *Ambiguous Relations: The American Jewish Community and Germany since 1945.* Detroit: Wayne State University Press, 1999.

Shapiro, Edward S. *A Time for Healing: American Jewry since World War II.* Baltimore: Johns Hopkins University Press, 1992.

——— "World War II and American Jewish Identity." *Modern Judaism,* 10:1 (February 1990), pp. 65–84.

Silberman, Charles E. *A Certain People: American Jews and Their Lives Today.* New York: Summit Books, 1985.

Silk, Mark. "Notes on the Judeo-Christian Tradition in America." *American Quarterly,* 36:1 (Spring 1984), pp. 65–86.

Sittser, Gerald L. *A Cautious Patriotism: The American Churches and the*

Second World War. Chapel Hill: University of North Carolina Press, 1997.

Sklare, Marshall. *Observing America's Jews.* Edited by Jonathan Sarna. Hanover: University Press of New England for Brandeis University Press, 1993.

Sklare, Marshall, and Joseph Greenblum. *Jewish Identity on the Suburban Frontier.* New York: Basic Books, 1967.

Slomovitz, Albert Isaac. *The Fighting Rabbis: Jewish Military Chaplains and American History.* New York: New York University Press, 1999.

Sorin, Gerald. *The Nurturing Neighborhood: The Brownsville Boys Club and Jewish Community in Urban America, 1940–1990.* New York: New York University Press, 1990.

Stanislawski, Michael. *Tsar Nicholas I and the Jews: The Transformation of Jewish Society in Russia, 1825–1855.* Philadelphia: Jewish Publication Society, 1983.

Staub, Michael E. *Torn at the Roots: The Crisis of Liberalism in Postwar America.* New York: Columbia University Press, 2002.

Steinbaum, I. "A Study of the Jewishness of Twenty New York Families." *YIVO Annual of Jewish Social Sciences,* 5 (1950): 232–255.

Stember, Charles Herbert, et al. *Jews in the Mind of America.* New York: Basic Books, 1966.

Stern, Guy. "In the Service of American Intelligence: German-Jewish Exiles in the War against Hitler." *Leo Baeck Year Book,* 37 (1992), pp. 461–477.

——— "The Jewish Exiles in the Service of US Intelligence: The Post-War Years." *Leo Baeck Year Book,* 40 *(1995), pp. 51–62.*

Stouffer, Samuel A., Edward A. Suchman, Leland C. DeVinney, Shirley A. Star, and Robin M. Williams, Jr. *The American Soldier: Adjustment During Army Life,* vol. 1. New York: John Wiley and Sons, 1949.

Svonkin, Stuart. *Jews Against Prejudice.* New York: Columbia University Press, 2000.

Tynan, Kenneth. "Profile of Mel Brooks." *The New Yorker,* October 30, 1978, pp. 46–130.

Voss, Frederick C. *Reporting the War: Journalistic Coverage of World War II.* Washington, D.C.: Smithsonian Institution Press for the National Portrait Gallery, 1994.

Weiss, Jeffrey, and Craig Weiss. *I Am My Brother's Keeper: American*

Volunteers in Israel's War for Independence 1947–49. Atglen, Pa.: Schiffer Military History, 1998.

Wenger, Beth S. *New York Jews and the Great Depression: Uncertain Promise.* New Haven: Yale University Press, 1995.

Wertheimer, Jack. *A People Divided: Judaism in Contemporary America.* New York: Basic Books, 1993.

Westbrook, Robert B. "'I Want a Girl, Just Like the Girl That Married Harry James': American Women and the Problem of Political Obligation in World War II." *American Quarterly,* 42:4 (December 1990), pp. 587–614.

Willoughby, John. *Remaking the Conquering Heroes: The Social and Geopolitical Impact of the Post-War American Occupation of Germany.* New York: Palgrave, 2001.

Wyman, David S. *The Abandonment of the Jews: America and the Holocaust 1941–1945.* New York: Pantheon Books, 1984.

ACKNOWLEDGMENTS
✪ ✪ ✪

I have piled up a heavy indebtedness in the course of researching and writing this book. First and foremost, I want to thank the men and women who invited me into their homes and told me their stories. In particular, my father and the Dragons — Artie, Herbie, Henry, Wilty, Lester, Ralph, Bernie — have waited patiently to see what those interviews would yield, and I apologize to them for not being able to include all of their stories in the end. What they told me shaped my understanding of that time and place. It was a privilege to meet and listen to individuals who served their country more than half a century ago.

Not all of those who entered the armed forces enjoyed long lives, and I depended upon the next generation to share their father's or uncle's letters and memoirs. Susan Gross, Jeffrey Gurock, Cyrisse Jaffee, Eileen Kreeger, Bobby Kushner, and Peter Schweitzer all gave me access to valuable letters and memoirs. I am grateful to Marc Saperstein, professor of Jewish Studies at George Washington University, and to Rabbi David Saperstein of the Religious Action Center of Reform Judaism, who generously shared with me the letters of Rabbi Harold Saperstein. Breakfast with the historian Joshua Freeman led not only to the discovery of compelling letters but also to the opportunity to interview the man who wrote them, his father, Harold Freeman. Comparing letters with memories enhanced my understanding of the constraints of both sources of historical knowledge.

As I was researching this book, the Museum of Jewish Heritage in New York started a project to conduct four hundred oral history interviews for a major exhibit, "Ours to Fight For: American Jews and the Second World War." As a guest curator for this project I benefited from collaboration with talented professionals working on the exhibit, including Louis D. Levine, Director of Collections, Ivy L. Barsky, Deputy Director for Programs, and Jay Eidelman, Historian. I appreciate, too, access to the museum's oral histories.

Audiences have provided me with critical and insightful comments. I began talking about my preliminary findings in 1994 when I gave the David W. Belin Lecture in American Jewish Affairs at the University of Michigan. It seems that I have not stopped talking about the war since then, and after each talk I hurriedly jotted down relevant remarks. I am grateful to all, especially colleagues who responded with suggestions.

I have been fortunate to have the help of several Vassar College students in my research, especially in transcribing oral history interviews. Several students at the University of Pennsylvania wrote useful papers for a seminar I taught. I want to thank Beth Wenger for sharing David Frankel's senior thesis with me. One Vassar student deserves particular thanks: Rachel Weinstein, who worked with me as a Ford Scholar during the summer of 1999. She mastered the skills of interviewing as well as conducting research at the U.S. Army Archives in Carlisle, Pennsylvania. She also wrote a conference paper whose insights on the military experience of American Jews can be found in this book. After graduation she took her expertise to the Museum of Jewish Heritage, working on their exhibit. Finally, she has helped me get many of the vital details correct in her capacity as editorial assistant at Harvard University Press. I could not have finished this book without her.

Even a book that depends heavily on oral histories, letters, and unpublished memoirs requires archives and libraries. I began my work at the New York Public Library, using their unmatched collections. Marek Web at the YIVO Institute for Jewish Research very early urged me to consult the YIVO Essay Contest on "My Experiences and Observations as a Jew in World War II." His recommendation led to a treasure trove of memoirs written by veterans shortly after they returned home. I am grateful for his assistance and that of Frume Mohrer. Charlotte Bonelli at the American Jewish Committee Archives generously alerted me to important documents in the Richard C. Rothschild Collection. Aviva Astrinsky at the Center for Judaic Studies graciously obtained many volumes of military history for me. I benefited as well from the libraries and archives of the American Jewish Historical Society, the American Jewish Archives, and the Jewish Theological Seminary of America and from illuminating exhibits at the National Museum of American Jewish Military History and the National Museum of American Jewish History.

I was fortunate to receive fellowships at different stages of my research and writing that complemented Vassar College's sabbatical leave policy. In 1996 I spent five months on a Skirball Visiting Fellowship at the

Oxford Centre for Hebrew and Jewish Studies at Yarnton, England, followed by another five months at the Center for Judaic Studies of the University of Pennsylvania. That year allowed me to develop the book's conceptual basis. Then as I contemplated another sabbatical, I learned that Yale University had awarded me a Pew Fellowship at the Institute for Advanced Study of Religion for 2001–2002. Writing about the attack on Pearl Harbor as I sat in an office in the Whitney Humanities Center in New Haven on September 11, 2001, cast an eerie light on the creation of historical consciousness. Finally, Florida International University appointed me to a term in 2003 to the Gene and Jordan Davidson Chair for a Visiting Eminent Scholar, which allowed time to revise the book. I am grateful to Jon Butler and Harry Stout at Yale, David Ruderman at the Center for Judaic Studies, Howard Rock and Nathan Katz at Florida International University, and Bernard Wasserstein at the Oxford Centre for providing ideal conditions in which to pursue scholarship.

Earlier versions of material in this book appeared previously in *Religion and American Culture: A Journal of Interpretation* and were included in lectures at the University of San Francisco, Swig Judaic Studies Program, and at the Jean and Samuel Frankel Center for Judaic Studies at the University of Michigan.

Vassar College supported my work in ways both material and spiritual. It provided grants-in-aid at the early stages, as well as a final grant to complete the manuscript. And my colleagues have consistently encouraged me. In the Religion Department, these include current members Marc Epstein, E. H. Rick Jarow, Tova Weitzman, Lynn LiDonnici, Lawrence Mamiya, Michael Walsh, and Judith Weisenfeld, as well as retired members Betsy Halpern Amaru and Robert Fortna. I found engaging discussion partners in Peter Antelyes of the Jewish Studies Program and Maria Hoëhn and David Schalk of the History Department.

Then there were those who stayed around for the long haul that this book involved, starting with my dedicated editor at Harvard University Press, Joyce Seltzer, who served as touchstone and outspoken critic during the process of writing and revision. I am very grateful for her guidance. My other patient critic, MacDonald, has lived with the war now for close to a decade. He taught me how to set up video interviews, helped me purchase portable equipment, and explained the intricacies of editing tapes on the computer. He also read and critiqued every version of the book and encouraged me not to lose sight of my goal when other responsibilities intervened. He put up with my extended absences and my self-absorbed presence. He helped me to think, gave me time to write, and listened as I summarized yet another moving interview. He surely knows the depths of my gratitude and love.

Several dear friends read the manuscript. Pamela Brumberg read the book, chapter by chapter, during her chemotherapy treatments. I have saved her handwritten comments because they constitute a final link for me to an extraordinary woman. When I left for Yarnton, Pamela initiated a correspondence that helped to assuage some of the loneliness of doing research abroad. When I returned she supported a grant from the Lucius N. Littauer Foundation, where she worked with William Frost, himself a veteran of the war. Pamela possessed an exceptional vision and enthusiasm for Jewish studies scholarship coupled with a pragmatic realism in matters of everyday life. She believed in this book, and I am profoundly sad that she did not live to see it published. Her imprint remains on its pages. Other friends made important contributions as well: Paula Hyman, friend and colleague for more than three decades, made useful suggestions throughout. Judith Goldstein, Mark Cladis, and Gerald Sorin also read and commented on the manuscript. Andrew Bush read and commented on numerous drafts. His marvelous marginal notes could make me laugh and cry; his criticism never stung and his enthusiasm was irresistible. I am lucky to have such a good friend in my corner.

When I thought I was done, Leonard Dinnerstein did his best to keep me honest. Riv-Ellen Prell graciously guided me through the intricacies of the narrator's craft and pushed me to rethink as well as rewrite. Despite the help of all of these friends and Mary Ellen Geer, who improved my style and corrected errors, I alone am responsible for what remains between these covers.

Since I began this book my family has changed. I am fortunate to be able once more to thank my parents, Irene and Martin Dash, for their unfailing support. My father's willingness to talk about his experiences before I was born provided an initial impetus for this book. My son, Mordecai Moore, a teacher of social studies, loves to discuss history. In writing about World War II, I feel that I am returning to one of his early interests. His brother, Mikhael Moore, together with Deborah Axt and their son Elijah Mateo Axt, have taught me how personal choices cannot anticipate history. They have repositioned me in the chain of generations, for which I am most grateful.

This book is dedicated to the man who famously "fought the battle of Appalachicola." Arthur Aryeh Goren would surely protest the dedication, for reasons both personal and political. A veteran and a historian, he saw only a small slice of the war, was never posted overseas, and expressed his doubts about this book and my interpretation of past events. Yet he generously shared his letters written to his folks, submitted to an oral history interview, alerted me to rich materials, suggested useful leads, and critiqued the book. He has been a model and guide in and to the past, as well as a friend and mentor, colleague and teacher, adept at effortlessly bridging worlds and generations. I hope that this book, too, can connect generations separated by history.

ILLUSTRATION CREDITS

✪ ✪ ✪

Page 5: Photograph by Wendell S. MacRae, reprinted by permission of Scotia Wendell MacRae and the Witkin Gallery. Courtesy of the Metropolitan Museum of Art, Purchase, Lila Acheson Wallace Gift, 1983 (1983.1189.8).

Page 24: Photograph by William Engels, courtesy of the *New York Daily News* (n1669694).

Page 29: Courtesy of the American Jewish Historical Society, Newton Centre, Mass., and New York, N.Y..

Page 34: Courtesy of Martin Dash.

Page 38: Photograph by J. Baylor Roberts, National Geographic Image Collection. Courtesy of the National Geographic Society.

Page 55: Courtesy of Arthur A. Goren.

Page 61: Courtesy of Jerome Minkow.

Page 65: Courtesy of Herbert Walters.

Page 75: Reprinted with permission of Temple Beth El. Courtesy of "Lives of Quiet Affirmation: An Alabama Jewish Community," and Sherry Blanton; the Museum of Jewish Heritage (2003.F.65).

Page 82: Courtesy of Arthur Kolin.

Page 95: Courtesy of Hyman Samuelson.

Page 99: Courtesy of National Archives and Records Administration (ARC 513213).

Page 102: Courtesy of Sy Kahn.

Page 112: Courtesy of David Macarov.

Page 120: Courtesy of the Chapel of the Four Chaplains.

Page 127: Courtesy of Victor B. Geller.

Page 135: Courtesy of the Museum of Jewish Heritage.

Page 142: Courtesy of the United States Military History Institute (Signal Corps 184440).

Page 146: Courtesy of Marc and David Saperstein.

Page 158: Courtesy of Paul Steinfeld.

Page 162: Courtesy of Jeremiah S. Gutman and Marilyn Gates Gutman.

Page 164: Courtesy of the National Archives and Records Administration (111-SC-189099).

Page 166: Courtesy of Harold Freeman.

Page 173: Courtesy of Ralph Jackson.

Page 180: Courtesy of Harold Radish.

Page 194: Courtesy of Samuel Klausner.

Page 214: Courtesy of Harold Freeman.

Page 225: Courtesy of the United States Holocaust Memorial Museum (00641A).

Page 238: Courtesy of the United States Holocaust Memorial Museum (26278).

Page 243: Courtesy of Yad Vashem Archives (1537/1). Reprinted with permission of Yad Vashem and Sima Cohen and Sara Ben-Ari.

Page 250: Courtesy of Victor B. Geller.

Page 255: Photograph by Charles Hoff, courtesy of the *New York Daily News* (n1985342).

INDEX

✪ ✪ ✪